ITALY: Society in crisis/ Society in transformation

JOHN FRASER

ROUTLEDGE & KEGAN PAUL
London, Boston and Henley

First published in 1981
by Routledge & Kegan Paul Ltd
39 Store Street,
London WC1E 7DD,
9 Park Street,
Boston, Mass. 02108, USA, and
Broadway House,
Newtown Road,
Henley-on-Thames,
Oxon RG9 1EN
Printed in Great Britain by
Thetford Press Ltd,
Thetford, Norfolk.

British Library Cataloguing in Publication Data

Fraser, John Duncan
Italy.
1. Italy - Social conditions
2. Italy - Politics and government
I. Title
945.092168 HN471 80-42297
ISBN 0-7100-0771-X

CONTENTS

ACKNOWLEDGMENTS

I should like to thank the Istituto Gramsci, Cespe (the research centre for economic and social questions of the Italian Communist Party, responsible for the periodicals 'Politica ed economia' and 'Congiuntura sociale'), and the library of the Fondazione Basso, all in Rome, for their assistance in facilitating the research for this book. All opinions expressed are, of course, my own.

INTRODUCTION

The 'Italian case' might appear an ideal empirical referent for the 'crisis' theories of James O'Connor (fiscal), Jürgen Habermas (rationality) and Klaus Offe (legitimacy). (1) The coexistence of cyclical and structural economic crises and an apparently permanent governmental crisis also stimulates interest in classical Marxist theories of the 'general crisis', and the logical-structural tendency to collapse, of the capitalist mode of production, theories which achieved their most rigorous formulation in the work of Henryk Grossmann.

For the most part classical 'crisis theory' has been based on optimism regarding the possibility of transition, or of transformation, to a qualitatively higher state. Even when theories of capitalist crisis have been most 'catastrophic', or most cautiously stressed the tendential aspect of the laws of capitalist morbidity, such analysis was situated within the political and ideological tradition of socialism as a real or realizable higher condition of production. By biological analogy, every crisis is one of growth/recovery or decay/death. This analogy is too simple, however, when the assumption is added that subjective, political, mediation can deliver a healthy infant from the womb of its dying parent. Suggestive though classical 'crisis theory' is, it generally does not confront the problems of decline in transitional phases and does not examine the limits of the morphology of a given social system. 'Crisis' becomes a term descriptive of a chronic pathological state if the notion of transition/transformation be removed.

The current more realistic and sceptical attitude towards 'real socialism' is certainly healthy. A crisis of decline, however, involves in that decline precisely the forces traditionally intended to resolve the contradictions, and eliminate the problematic, of bourgeois society. So long as Italy seemed to combine the optimism of a society 'catching up' with her neighbours, with a high degree of politicization, the question of how powerful and how innovative the Left really was scarcely needed to be put. The power of the historical, and the 'new', Left was seen as expressed in contestation and confrontation. The goals of 'rational productivism' and 'rational administration' were until recently not considered in the light of a crisis of material production and productivist ideology, while the paradoxical conclusion of Weberian total bureaucratization - that a totally administered system has no goals, no future beyond the rules of office management - was overlooked by the advocates of efficiency. In short, optimism is now more difficult. The conflicting and contradictory components of socialist theory as a basis for a practical transition are far from resolving the classical bourgeois problems of 'democracy and the state'. One should, perhaps, accept the permanence of aggravated crisis as the threshold not of transformation/transition, but rather of modification. In Italy the development of a 'modern state', with all its weaknesses (low consensus, high level of repression), is accompanied by the continued presence, even growth, of interstices of autonomy and of the 'social' (corporations and movements). These areas of autonomy are potentially reabsorbable by the state, but they are also areas of high conflictuality. Although the marginality and subordinate condition of these areas tend to exhaust their champions, permitting re-entry and recomposition into institutionalized, legitimated, forms of social relations, it is also true that from time to time a potentially explosive conjuncture of social forces does appear. Thus, though the 'Italian case' is nationally specific, it provides a series of lessons for the Left, generally of a cautionary kind.

The weaknesses of theories of structural (economic) crisis are well known: the political and social factors which re-establish the capitalist mode, and not merely effect repairs from 'cyclical' damage but also restructure social relations, are of course beyond their scope. So too is a concrete discussion of political organization, and the transformation of the state. They also underestimate the significance of the 'image of modernity' as a model for development, a major theme for Lenin, and one of the basic elements of Gramsci's thought. In other words, Marxist politics have tended to rely not only on the well-known and notorious positivist conception of progress and progressivism but more understandably on that of modernity - as against both 'backwardness' and 'traditionalism'. It was Gramsci's success in separating the latter concepts, and confronting the question of modernity (Americanism and Fordism), which introduced a new and difficult element to the notion of hegemony as 'alternation' of class for class. Classical crisis theories, too scarcely dealt with the problem of bureaucracy and elitism, with the latter as the solution to the Weber paradox, that of the relation of rationality to power. Nor did it face the question of the nature of traditionalism and consensus, that of routinized power.

In short, classical crisis theory provides basic but limited insights. Italian theorists have added little to it, especially since the Communist Party in the early 1970s, under the influence of its predominantly marginalist economists, ceased to regard (state) monopoly capitalism as the key target for a strategy of transition. Later 'crisis theories', from that of the 'second slump' (Mandel) (2) to those of the crisis of the Keynesian-interventionist, or consensual-repressive, state (the crisis of crisis-management) also lack not only predictive capacity but a logical derivation of political strategy. They fail, in other words, to carry analysis of generic crisis to the specific complexity of political and social forces conventionally or theoretically concerned with the 'management', 'overcoming' or transformation of the crisis. At this point it is useful to turn to work on the mode of production, carried out - among many others - by Meillassoux, Hirst, Hindess and Rey. (3)

In that context, Italy is dominated by a relatively strong, relatively socialized, finance capital, but has a relatively weak industrial and agrarian capital. The historical weakness of the materially productive sector in turn produces distortions in the operations of finance capital, which become privatized, corporatist. The weakness appears as a form of borrowing to support industry and unproductive employment. In classical terms, this not only precipitates a transformation-realization crisis, but further dis-articulates the historical levels of the mode of production. That is, state finance capital vainly tries to rationalize and administers 'its own' industrial sector - public employment, the tertiary sector, 'semi-public' and nationalized industry - a sector of low profitability, low productivity, subsidy and 'capitalist welfare'. However, despite its hybrid public-private character, this is state capital, and also international capital through the state, especially the policies of the Bank of Italy.

The problem of maintaining the dominance of finance capital (that is, of state finance capital) is made difficult by the so-called parasitic and non-productive nature of the state sector and the current difficulties of big private/semi-private (corporate) industry. This difficulty highlights one of the basic peculiarities of the Italian case - the uneven and partial development of the historical levels of the mode of production. This, of course, is not an absolute disarticulation, nor is it a wholly negative feature. Advanced industry, requiring a degree of provision of security, social services and planning which, at least expressed as a need, spills over to other sectors, co-exists with varieties of paleocapitalism, artisan and family industry, the 'black economy', parasitic and pensioned state sectors. This creates sectoral, compartmentalized, strength as well as creating the 'inefficiency' notorious in Italian society. The strength lies in the fact that Italy may in some respects be the 'last of the nine in the EEC', but also aspires to retain a competitive position in the Community and beyond.

The Italian mode of production contains many levels of technology, many wage levels, many types of labour market. It includes quasi-autonomous, 'separate', economies - the 'open' and the 'black', the modern industrial triangle of the centre North, the new middle and small industry in the Centre and the Centre East and a potential area of Southern development. (4) These sectoral divisions represent historical-cultural discontinuities which, since the Resistance, the parties of the Left have attempted to connect by political means. It is simplistic to talk of economic crisis as affecting only certain sectors, or of being contained by the sectorialization of the economy. However, the historical levels of the mode of production do provide a cushioning effect for the crisis. 'Things go on' in small industry and commerce, though areas of the public sector and big industry may appear paralysed. Discontinuity also provides an intense, focused, but also contained and limited, conflictuality in specific sectors. In this sense, then, politics - the 'massified consensus' of the Left, the traditional 'clientelismo' of Christian Democracy - have had a 'bridging' and articulating function not supplied by the social relations of capitalism as the 'system in dominance'. Italian capitalism has not clearly established which historical level is 'in dominance', and this has provided an unusual potential initiative for the political apparatus.

The separation of the political class from the class (or class fractions) that are productively dominant becomes a problem to some extent resolved by the growth of a state bourgeoisie, concerned with the reproduction of the dominance of capital through the dominance of state capital. (5) However, this implies conflict not only with entrepreneurial capital but with the conditions of material production themselves. This brings us to the second peculiarity of the 'Italian case'. There is a relative disarticulation of the mode of production and inadequate domination by a state bourgeoisie because this does not have the policy backing and authority of a political class, and, given the weakness of its own attempts to organize production efficiently when the private sector cannot, it has instituted a type of speculative-welfare capitalism. The problem is compounded at the state and ideological levels by the failure to universalize, ideologically and institutionally, the social function of capitalist production.

In other words, the disarticulation of the mode of production is reflected in the disarticulation of state functions: the state articulates interests but does not aggregate them, and thus loses itself in the discontinuities of the historical mode of production. It achieves a partial dominance because the mode of production is open only to partial dominance, even by finance capital, not to the formation of a 'general interest'. However, the penetration of the social by the state and the creation of particularistic fiefs or public-private interest groups explain the strength of the command, if not the legitimacy, of the system and the containment of high levels of conflictuality. It also explains the ease with which the Left is confined to sectoral or administrative issues, or, in the past at least, to utopian schemes for radical reform or total planning.

In the perspective of the modern state, the Italian state is certainly 'in crisis'. Though there is no viable 'alternative of the Left', the presence of the historic Left accentuates the low level of consensus and legitimacy of the state as party-regime. In administration and the economy, the state rejected Weberian and Keynesian 'rationality'. Given the degree of uneven development in the mode of production, elements of the Bourbon, rather than the modern, state persist. In view of the partial development of sectors of the economy (for example, the regionalized developments of large-scale industry), great faith in the efficacy of political commitment has tried till now to supply the necessary social cohesion which a more uniform and integrated system of social relations would supply elsewhere. This situation is potentially explosive since it is based on representation of divisions in society. It is also the ground for the recomposition and reintegration of social forces, given the separation of the ideological-ideal-rhetorical political level from the pragmatic, economic sphere. Thus, the relative autonomy of political (party) and economic levels also to some extent cushions the political mediators from the intense, but sectoral, confrontations at the economic level.

At this point we may cite an example of how disarticulation of the state apparatus is a cause of 'crisis', but also provides its own palliative. Crisis occurs as a result of a lack of adaptability. An obvious case in Italy is provided by the university system. Challenged to modify the elitist university adapted to the labour market of the professional strata, the government 'democratized' the university. This 'democracy' meant, in practice, opening up admission without appropriate funding, restructuring the teaching profession, or providing means for 'valuing' university qualifications in the labour market. What had apparently been a significant state apparatus, in terms of personnel as well as ideology, and a vast area of socialization and politicization of the young was - to generalize - left to discover its own means of survival, to fend for itself. It became a 'subversive space' - or briefly so. On the other hand, it effectively ceased to be an organic responsibility of the state. From the state's point of view, the 'space' is now an interest group in a corporatist framework, a dependent structure.

Any explanation of why the Italian state attained a high degree of bureaucratization and economic intervention without passing through either Keynesian or Weberian orthodoxy should take into account the fact that the archaic features of the state were a response to economic and social development which had produced pathological forms. Economic development was rapid, spontaneous and socially corrosive. It was often precarious, and historically reliant on salvage operations from the state. The 'economic miracle' of the 1950s and the early years of the 1960s was based on economic, but not social, neo-capitalism. That is, it gave employment but without guarantees of the social planning and amenities, still less the cultural continuity, which other entrepreneurs and governments had attempted to secure from each other before or during boom conditions. This dislocation and disarticulation between economic and political systems has taken many forms. In general, the pathological extremes of Italian society, the contrast between periods of intense technical and political activity and the 'long fuses' of 'traditional' society combine, paradoxically, to provide space and opportunities for mediation for the political class. As a strategy of self-defence, botched or piecemeal reform and neglect, with the state constructing or promoting corporate interest groups, symbiotic but fragmentary structures may be more effective than a centralized, policy-centred, consensus-seeking apparatus. It is not, though, a recipe for 'modern' growth.

The Italian case, then, does demonstrate features of the 'general crisis', but certain elements are more significant than specific historical variations on the theme of declining 'advanced capitalism'. The fragmentation mentioned above, which virtually eliminated post-war Keynesian or Weberian influence, generates centrifugal forces which help to account for high levels of political confrontation, social autonomy and corporativism. Though confrontation tends to be based on class hostility, it has also been largely recomposable, institutionalized by the dominant culture and the reproducibility of social relations as regular recognized procedures, mutually acknowledged though not necessarily non-conflictual or 'equal'. Hence we have the peculiarity of a rapid absorption by, or insertion of intense militancy into, convention-bound systems of social relations. The rapidity and the violence of passage from extra- to intra-systemic activity accentuate the contrast between the 'margins' (6) and the 'institutions' of Italian society. The latter express a historical class militancy, and so do not easily lend themselves to reformism. On the other hand, the 'margins', or the 'movement', have historically been part of a process of assimilation as well as of radical disruption. The signs are, therefore, that with the productive system in decline, the reproducibility of the pattern in social relations of 'rupture-assimilation' is drawing to a close.

This book is an account of some of the theoretical foundations of the Left's response to the Italian crisis. The crisis, while only a province of a vaster whole, is still capable of producing both explosive and re-integrating phenomena. This presents the Left, institutional and extra-institutional, with an immediate and contradictory choice of strategies. One is to concentrate on the process of social disintegration and collapse by strengthening the institutions of authority (and, incidentally, of command) in order to continue reproducing a system of social integration, but one in which the subaltern classes, through their political representatives, would appear as active powers, not passive functions. The other is to consider social disintegration as a logical-structural necessity of the system of dominance, as itself an objective of the subaltern classes. (7) The inability to reproduce on a universal scale the social relations of dominance and subordination leads to the collapse of authority in the state, but leaves 'command' (authoritarianism) intact or reinforced. How, then, is command to be attacked from the margins, especially when the insertion of the subaltern classes into the state is presumed to recreate its authority?

Part one starts with an examination of the classical Marxist analysis of capitalist crisis. This analysis does not restrict itself to specific countries, nor does it predict the length of transition, the possibility of political and social recomposition during the crisis, or, in general, the part played by crises of values and institutions accompanying the structural and cyclical economic crises. In this sense, the classical case for crisis as experienced through social relations of production tends to be excessively limited to the mechanism of the mode of production rather than speculating on the political and social behaviour of proletarians faced with intensifying exploitation or elimination from the productive (and hence the socio-political) system, or of capitalists reacting to a falling rate of profit. In chapter 2 one aspect of the political reaction to crisis and transition is examined, that of the recomposition, or formation, of a 'composite' ruling class. This is a technically qualified group of politicians, not a social class in the proper sense. This implies a capacity of 'traditional' culture to absorb the 'modern' and to integrate its political agents. This theme is central to Pareto, Michels and Mosca: its corollary is that 'political behaviour' tends to regress to 'traditional behaviour'. Machiavelli made the point in a more sophisticated way when he constantly crossed the barrier between myth (or mystique) and history, the non-rational imagination (tradition) and the pragmatic historical necessity of absolutism (modernity). In both Gramsci and Togliatti the problem of the reassertion and transcendance of the traditional is central. Gramsci's analysis of popular culture and Togliatti's strategy regarding the popular masses demonstrate the need for alliance between traditional culture and modernity 'from below'. For both, the link between popular tradition and the political tradition of Bonapartism, demagoguery and - as the reverse of that coin - bureaucracy, was expressed in a consensual, if not reactionary, pre-capitalist ideology of pragmatic conciliation. Now, when neither factory nor 'mass' politics seem viable vehicles for modernity, a return to the 'traditional', the personal, mystified and private, is a possibility.

However, the analysis of 'traditionalism', especially for Gramsci, was not simply made from the standpoint of a polar opposite such as 'proletarian democracy'. For

Gramsci, the problematic of Italian 'backwardness' was central. Italy had existed as a culture when politically 'backward'. Under fascism, this culture itself, for reasons which antedated, as well as helping to explain, the victory of fascism, had shared the condition of crisis of the dominant socio-political bloc. To a fading traditionalism Gramsci counterposed modernity, or Americanism. Adoption of this model of modernity was, of course, not uncritical, nor was traditionalism the dark enemy it had been for many Russian revolutionaries. However, the problem remained that revolutionary transition required a 'telos', historically delimited, but more than a mere reshuffling of a formerly subordinate 'traditional' element.

The contemporary crisis of 'Americanism' as progressive modernity, as well as that of the socialist 'realized' alternative, challenges the basis of the hypothesis of Italy's economic backwardness, and hence the possibility of its economic 'modernization'. 'Catching up' may be impossible, and self defeating even if possible. It also challenges the thesis of her political 'super-advancement'. In the Communist Pietro Ingrao's view, for example, Italy is experiencing a crisis of the future of capitalism because mass political sensitivity, and political instruments capable of reshaping institutions and initiating a transition to socialism, provide a pre-vision, a prototype, of the decline and replacemnt of bourgeois society. The category of 'modernity' is thus elusive, but central to the Marxism of a country which classifies itself as 'backward'. Indeed, one of the (largely unspoken) issues dividing the Italian Left is the complex question of whether Italy is trying to catch up with a modern world already in existence, or instead is breaking through to an 'invented modernity' such as 'realized communism', or to a society of non- or post-labour.

Part two starts with a composite account of the main social, political and economic aspects of the 'Italian crisis'. These are general categories of a crisis in the reproduction of social relations. Thus the fact that the general economic crisis affects different sectors in different ways does not mean that the crisis is not structural. On the other hand, strategies for resistance to crisis and for 'crisis management' necessarily stress the relative autonomy of sub-systems, and especially that of the autonomy of political initiative. It is clearly a difficult but essential matter to differentiate between what is 'pathological' and what is 'normal' in phases of capitalist development, and in those of decline. To determine what is a pathological feature with structural causes and what is a distortion produced by, say, political miscalculation becomes a crucial question. In this context, marginalist economists (dominant in the Communist Party) use quantitative criteria based on other advanced industrial societies. Sociologists tend to relapse into moralistic notions of 'civil society and civil behaviour', while the ideal-type of the political theorists is generally that of organic-rational self-administration. In short, the basic assumptions by which social scientists assess the gravity of crisis are not necessarily more historically relevant than those of the philosophers of catastrophe. Nor, indeed, do they establish a connection between crisis and transition. Carlo Donolo, for instance, is one of the few to state clearly the problem of distinguishing between change and transition, or defining social 'disintegration' or disaggregation ('disgregazione'). The political scientists for the most part are concerned with questions of how to strengthen institutions in order to deal with social and economic crises, despite the evidence that a major problem lies in the weakening of institutions based on procedurized, consensual power (authority) and the strengthening of those directed towards repressing conflict (command).

The final chapter is concerned with some of the main political strategies suggested for transforming the 'crisis' into a form of transition to socialism. Such strategies range from the politics of dissent of Gianni Scalia to the social liberalism of Norberto Bobbio, and the libertarian socialism of Federico Stame. These are all to some extent interlocutors of the Communist Party (PCI), in which we can distinguish various currents of opinion: Pietro Ingrao's somewhat vague search for the 'third way' to socialism, the 'workers' centrality' of Mario Tronti (with Alberto Asor Rosa, Massimo Cacciari and Aris Accornero), the liberal statism of a Giorgio Amendola, the consensual statism of Luigi Berlinguer, the organicism of Franco Rodano and the would-be emergency populism of Enrico Berlinguer.

In practice, the weight of the institutional Left, especially that of the PCI, is likely to be lent to the strengthening of administration and institutions (i.e., of legitimacy) albeit from a subordinate position. The PCI, for instance, already provides practical evidence of its administrative capacity and priorities in lower levels of government. Therefore, while describing schemes for practical reform as well as overall political analyses, the present work takes as a basic assumption that an administrative solution to the crisis will be selected, and that competition for legitimation and influence will also render possible a resurgence of consensual backing for the Christian Democrat state bourgeoisie. This means that the contending forces on the Left are, for different reasons, all committed to long-term strategies. As for the 'area of autonomy', though Negri implies the possibility of rapid transition to an effectively post-socialist society, this transition lies in the unspecified future. The 'armed party' has not rapidly destabilized the political system, nor indeed has 'diffused violence'. The 'operaisti' and 'ingraiani' in the PCI do not have a major influence. Indeed, the problem for the PCI is how to increase its share of political power without simply reinforcing its subordinate position as a procedurally correct party of 'efficient administration'.

It seems, in short, as though the divisions on the Left themselves are sufficient to contribute substantially to a situation where, in the long term, the crisis is neither resolved, nor becomes transition, but rather is 'administered'. A state of permanent, managed, conflictuality rather than a struggle between power and counter-power, or autonomy versus organization, would seem indicated. Both consociational unity and an alternative model of socialism seem realizable only on paper. The reasons for this should be sought not only in the objective difficulty of devising a strategy which takes account of both the reciprocity of social relations in bourgeois (and representative) society, and the potential autonomy (or hegemony) of the subordinate classes. Nor should they be related only to the unpredictability of crisis (and hence of response to it), and the advantages of a governing class with long experience in letting 'nature' take its course. They must also be sought in the fragmentation, corporatism and autonomies of an imperfectly modernized and rationalized capitalist mode of production. Despite the viability to extend and reproduce a dominant, universal, system of social relations in the whole society, the weakness of the system, from the standpoint of Weber or Keynes, becomes its strength. A state which has never been fully legitimated, a ruling fraction whose hegemony has been fading for decades and a public administration never rationalized have traditions of survival, of continuity, that more responsive, more 'artificial', ones lack. In addition, the imperfect dominance of the 'advanced' sectors of the economy and of society involves a constant search for the ad hoc, the private, the improvised, the unofficial solution. The lack of a model of modernity and of its centrality (that is, of consensus regarding the future, based on the legitimacy of present arrangements) may be untidy, but it dissipates conflict and divides purpose. The 'inefficiency' of the state is also both a grievance and a reassurance to its individual and corporate pensioners. The chronic lack of active consensus reduces the impact of a so-called acute crisis of consensus. This weakness of centrality means that crises of the dominant bloc are also transmitted as a myriad of mini-crises throughout the subaltern classes, strengthening what is optimistically termed 'pluralism', but is really corporate conflictuality.

We see, then, a crisis of the dominant form of the mode of production which calls in question modernity as a value, and economic modernization as a means of rational social renovation. In order to restore this confidence (confidence shaken by the failure of Keynesian economics and the paradox of Weberian rationality), the state structure would need to reform itself to find a way out of its own fiscal and legitimacy crises. Yet it is precisely the indulgence of the state, like a lazy uncle funding his favourite nephews, which keeps the truculent relatively quiet and the family business running without too close attention from the accountants.

It would be rash to underestimate the possibilities of a reactionary backlash (the 'Chilean' scenario of Enrico Berlinguer), or of a radical breakthrough. Italian society and politics, however, are not organized on a single axis, are not like the Maginot Line. It is hard to believe in the 'war of movement', in overall reform, or indeed in effective self-criticism by the restructured political class of the 1970s, with its professional Communist administrators caught in their own local fiscal crises, trying to deal with the corporatist demands of their own public employees. The emergence of the political administrator is a mark of the modernization, that is, the professionalization and secularization, of intellectual functions. Instead of a dialogue between philosophers and Party ideologues and politicians, the specialized technician has become an organic element in the Party's functioning - an ironic comment on Gramsci's 'organic intellectual', whose intelligence provided him with privileged access to the masses. Competition with Christian Democrat technicians and administrators is thus in the sphere of 'problem-solving'. The formalization and professionalization of government functions in the institutional Left tends to cement the difference between it and the small parties of the former 'extra-parliamentary Left' and of the volatile, even anomic, 'movement' beyond them. There, the prestige of the traditional literary intellectual, the revolutionary with the typewriter, combining philosophy with ideological and mobilizing skills persists, albeit much reduced.

Modern capitalist society produces an increasing social marginality of the educated poor, economically 'useless', feared and despised. The 'crisis of decline' has also reduced or destroyed expectations. The message of liberation of the late 1960s led many of its prophets politically to the Communist Party, and socially to the professions and technical expertise, their horizons now confined by their material absorption into the tertiary sector. However, the hope of liberation, linked (consciously or not) with productivism, has become soured in the period of decline. This is a disappointment of intellectual values and perspectives, as well as a material one. For instance, when women and the young find themselves excluded from the labour market and financial independence, forced back willy-nilly onto the family and dependence on it as economic unit, or as authority structure, it is easy to see how hollow the 'liberation' of middle-class radicalism, and also that of the mini-parties of the 1970s, sounds.

These distinct but short-lived cultures of the extreme Left have, of course, their 'superstructures', their leaders or quasi-leaders, organizational forms or forums for discussing organization. The modern state can both divide dissent into institutional and non-institutional ('subversive') forms, and further profit from the discontinuities and cultural particularities of its critics. The state is strengthened by its victories in a way in which the Left, it seems, is not educated by its defeats. De-legitimation reinforces the repressive machinery of the modern state. So, in a different way, does efficient administration. The compartmentalization of institutions, economies and political cultures tends to localize conflict, to focus it intensely but away from the strategic points. In that sense, the supposedly inefficient Italian state is perhaps pretty well equipped to survive high and permanent levels of conflictuality without aspiring to 'Germanization'.

One school of thought argues that Italy is indeed still capable of 'modernization'. Thus, it is argued, terrorism ran virtually the whole gamut of tactics in 1977-8 without destroying the political system. The PCI is committed to moderation, compromise, integration in the political system and the insertion of the working class into the bargaining cycles of industrial society. In contrast, however, we see new, volatile subjects created, subjects which share, in heightened forms, the disappointment of many 'in the system' with the traditional parties. Such 'disappointment' is less likely to be concerned with an epistemological crisis in Marxism than to see Marxist analysis as justified by evidence of the collapse of liberal capitalist structures. 'Modernization' has ceased to be a guarantee of stability and purpose. The political augurs' belief in party competition and alternation of government on a post-ideological terrain presents only a formal solution to this difficulty. It takes note neither of the professionalization of politics nor, indeed, of the decline of the liberal notion that politics is a social activity outside the state.

How convincing are Marxism's claims to be a philosophy of modernity, in distinction to the liberal model of inter- and intra-party competition? One problem is that we borrow the modern, and add to it our own contradictions. The modern is imitation, always second-hand. Marxism, as we have seen, is the reverse of backwardness, but not of tradition, the philosophy of those who live for the present. Traditionalism is not properly conservatism, as it does not value or idealize the past but rather recognizes it as the living centre of the present. The illogic of modernity as the cure for backwardness (not tradition) is the assumption that those furthest behind have furthest to go. Once history loses the 'ratio' of progress, the modern is demystified. It is no longer utopia but a problematic version of another society's past. Tradition, the third term between modernity and backwardness, becomes the normal, universal condition. From the laws of growth-transformation we return to those of decay-extinction. Dialectics is not the transformation of caterpillar to moth which conserves the 'caterpillar-potential' in the new form: it becomes a process of reproduction for survival. It prefigures a return to the primal condition, not a search for the third term. It is, perhaps, akin to what Scalia terms the dissociation between value ('techne', reason, power) and life.

Marxism is absorbed by the struggle for survival of the modern state, a struggle it recognizes because of the latter's Hegelian features: the centrality of the state form, and the equation of order with reason. We may be sceptical, in this context, regarding the frenetic, millenarian modernism of Negri's vision of imminent communism. (8) Yet Marxism now confronts itself in the forms of institutionalized party and non-institutionalized movement, as state-ideology and anomic dissent. The PCI has helped to insert the traditional working class and the 'new' workers of the 1960s (9) into the state as organizer of production and the reproduction of social relations, at the moment when the productive system itself is tendentially eliminating living labour and dissolving social ties, obligations and expectations.

Though there is a general tendency for institutions to be overtaken by the development of productive forces and transformed by 'charismatic movements', the reasons for such a process meeting strong counter-tendencies in Italy should be noted. This is in part because she has been so closely and dependently linked to the international capitalist system. However, if instead of 'transition' or 'transformation', there may be modification or adjustment and disarticulated, sectoral administrative and organizational reform, this is determined in part by the historical condition of institutional disarticulation and polycentrism in the formal, as well as the informal, power system. It is also due to the division of the Left into a majoritarian, institutional force (internally diversified) and a minoritarian, anti-institutional and extra-institutional one. This is also cemented in the differences between reformism, social democracy and revisionism as against revolutionary socialism. It contains levels of differential powers: for instance, the subordinate, administrative type of power of the PCI as against the moralistic, submerged, 'witnessing' of autonomy ('autonomia'). Furthermore, the end-state of movement and institution, socialist society or socialist state, is qualitatively different.

The 'unlearned' lesson of 1968 was well learned by the defenders of the status quo. In modern society a 'movement' could indeed shake institutions which were archaic and designed for emergencies of a different order. The tendency to insertion and institutionalization of the historic Left in Italy is to be seen in the context of a generalized anti-movement strategy, a resistance to transformation - and to transcendance - which, for different reasons, is increasingly shared by political Right and Left. This does not exclude further working-class influence in the state. Probably, however, the choice will be made to mediate such class influence by channelling it through institutions representing partial, non-totalizing, interests. A limit is thus set to that restructuring of totality which is the first message of the charismatic movement.

Part one

Chapter 1

CRISIS THEORY: structure and conjuncture

Marx conceived of the transition to socialism as a relatively brief process, in which a socialist movement, rationale and theory had already been constructed. The limit of capitalism was capital itself, rather than a natural limit to production and the breakdown of the connection between progress and production. Capitalism tendentially failed to maintain its dynamic, to sustain the rate of profit and employ living labour on an increasing scale so as to guarantee rising production and consumption, the reproduction of social relations of dominance by abstract labour (surplus value), and the cyclical crises ultimately, tendentially, reached a structural limit. Capitalist crisis, tendentially eliminating living labour from the productive process (and hence from consumption), was not analogous to the crisis of feudalism whose lengthy decline witnessed the assisted rise of capitalism as, at first, a weaker productive force. The case for capitalist crisis is inextricably connected with the philosophical necessity and potentiality of an advanced socialist socio-economic formation as an immediate alternative to capitalist statis.

Classical theories of capitalist crisis based on Marxist premisses generally adopt Marx's own productivist and political optimism. 'Decline' is primarily a decline of the rate of profit, accompanied by crises of overproduction and underconsumption. Exploitation is intensified, and living labour replaced by machines - labour now destined for a political 'reserve army', no longer as reservoir of productive capacity and a competitive threat to the employed. Hyperproductivism 'emancipates' labour by radically devaluing it, and excluding it from even its subordinate position in capitalist social relations of production. Class unity, however, remains, morale is high despite the decline in consumption and weakening social authority. The proletariat retains its skills, and seeks to master production. In Italy, Antonio Negri's 'Marx oltre Marx' typified such millenarian modernity, casting the communist emancipation of man from the necessity of labour in Marx's most optimistic terms.

In reality, though there is a tendency towards homogeneity in the condition of the proletariat, in the figure of the diffused 'societal worker' ('operaio sociale'), there is a simultaneous movement towards its differentiation and loss of unity. In Italy, the new working class of the 1960s, of the 'mass worker', politically ebullient and inventive, status- and culturally deprived, composed of first-generation immigrants from the South, has been overlaid by the 'diffuse' worker of the submerged economy, the worker-student, and the un- or non-employed worker. Superexploited but aspiring to a post-industrial society (post-human labour), where it is not merely apolitical or anomic, this third wave expresses a subversive dissent, a maximalism which appears as a centrifugal force in the subjective unity needed to turn capitalist crisis into transition to socialism. Where crisis marks the limit of capitalist growth, political unity is imperative. However, it is fragmented by decline itself, both of production and in the reproduction of social relations of production.

Where the political will does not find clear expression, and where the decline of the mode of production is associated with the decline of the commodity form itself as a 'natural object' of societies founded on exchange, the connection of socialism with productive growth is broken. Also significant is the absence of critical stimulus from other legitimated, 'real', socialist societies. In the Italian Communist Party, these problems are summed up in the contrasts between a strategy to 'reform and develop the economy' and Ingrao's inconclusive quest for a 'third way' to socialism and a 'model of development' which recognizes the new economic parameters circumscribing growth. In this pessimistic or uncertain perspective, the classical Marxist theory of crisis needs modification. For Marx, crisis implied both increasing repression and a collapse of the profit system, that is, of the price system, thence jeopardizing the value system itself. Each revision of crisis theory has tried to rectify mistaken forecasts on this basis in the past. The economism of the theory of crisis before 1917 was replaced by the hyperpoliticism of the Third International. The third crisis has produced analyses predominantly in the classic optimistic mode, both excessively political (Offe), and excessively economical (for example, Amin's overoptimism regarding the possibilities of economic development in poor countries).

Italy does not fit unequivocally into the economic 'weak link' pattern. Her existence as a highly industrialized capitalist country is not crucial to the international capitalist mode of production. She has a highly differentiated, segmented economy, parts of which are typical of advanced, and advanced-declining, capitalism, others typical of pre- or early capitalism. In a sense the country is positioned midway between the vulnerable extremes of poverty and (profligate) wealth. This diversity is to be seen in the ideological 'spread' between 'permanent insurrection' and 'consociational responsibility': extremes which also reflect a wide range of social interests from the marginal 'new poor' and 'working poor' to the integrated intelligentsia of the tertiary sector.

Historically, the economic, structural account of crisis produced during the Second International (for example, the Bauer-Hilferding-Kautsky notion of capitalist collapse) was not so much opposed as complementary to the ethical notions of Bernstein and Tugan-Baronovsky. Both positions assumed that an active mass would be ready to assume control after a 'passive crisis'. In practice, of course, the crisis managers have been far from 'passive', and the strategy has turned out to be one not of hegemony but of the patient insertion of the working class as a subordinate bloc into capitalist society. Gramsci fleshed out the thesis of hegemony so that emphasis lay not on the economic limits of capitalism (which had not in any case been reached) but with the political limits of the ruling class. He was representative of the Third International's emphasis on the crucial significance of ideologies, of intermediate strata and of political generalship.

In the current crisis, however, no such coherent analysis has emerged. The complicated process, for instance, whereby Italy simultaneously 'modernizes' (accepts the notions of rationality, of 'Gesellschaft', a functional, stratified and mobile productive society) and maintains an ideological commitment to 'socialism', when both concrete images of modernity and 'real socialism' are blurred if not erased, clearly requires a critical re-examination. We might argue, for instance, that the real debate in the Communist Party is concerned with the switch from a commitment to modernity in the grand manner (overall social and economic planning) to a reformism which stresses the fragility of state institutions and the possibility of developing social relations in the private economy. The latter approach tends to weaken the ideological solution though it does not eliminate the function of ideology as mobilizing agent and as a determinant of goals.

Grossmann and Rozdolski (1) expressed Marx's theory of capitalist crisis as one of logico-structural necessity. They did not accept the possibility that during the lifetime of capitalism the natural potential of material production would be exhausted. The change in the organic composition of capital (replacement of living labour by constant capital) produces the symptom of the falling rate of profit to which the answer is 'more machines and/or more exploitation'. One strategy for expansion would be the export of capital. Superexploitation and/or technological innovation accelerate monopoly concentration and also differential sectoral development. Increasing impoverishment intensifies class struggle: to repress and mediate this, the state becomes both a major employer and spender. This 'unproductive' sector produces pathological economic effects ('welfare capitalism' and the 'state bourgeoisie'), and increasingly substitutes its employees as a quasi-autonomous political class administering the varied interests of entrepreneurial-managerial capitalism. The crisis of overproduction-underconsumption is expressed in the logical-structural problems of transformation (the relation of value to price), and of realization (of relative surplus value). Conjunctural difficulties will establish the cyclical recurrence of these symptoms, but not the organic pathology of the structure itself.

Subsequent crisis theory has often attempted to add a statement of the tendential laws of social recomposition. Potentially at least, this was Gramsci's concern in his characterization of Italy as 'backward' - that is, a country where capitalism, despite its crises, was a decisive and potent force for modernization. He could not, naturally, foresee the formation of a new political or state class, in which communist (and socialist) administrators operated the machinery of lower levels of state power and state capitalism. In abandoning the catastrophic interpretation of crisis, Gramsci introduced the notion of a stage of 'preparation for transition'. He also avoided the Jacobin notion of the manipulative aspect of class alliances and that of the division of society into two opposed blocs, given the element of ideologically consensual reciprocity of social relations. If we accept his implicit criticism of 'crisis as catastrophe', it is still important to notice that the conception of crisis as process of transition has its weaknesses. Where Jacobinism is incurious regarding the nature and function of the state, and the relation between democracy and pluralism, theories of transitional crises are apparently founded on the tension between revolution and passivity, of restoration-revolution. They are complex and contradictory. Their duality raises the problem of legitimacy: must not a dual state, the state of transition, far from being a mass democracy, be one of deep conflictuality and of fragility of legitimacy? Will the fragmentation involved in mediating contradictory interests not divide and weaken the state with regard to both production and protecting of the various (and conflicting) class interests it is intended to maintain? Will the state not increasingly look to, and recruit its personnel from, precisely the strata expert in mediation, but whose own interests cannot be expressed in the inter-class mediations it undertakes?

For instance, we have already observed the disjuncture between political and economic dominant class. This reflects different, if complementary, techniques of social hierarchization in the capitalist as against the client/welfare structures. There is disjuncture between the politically dominant 'popular-restoration' mode, and the economically determinant one of productivist neo-capitalism. Rather than the simple 'couple' of revolution-restoration, there are in the present crisis three elements of recomposition, each existing in both economic and political spheres: restoration, transformation and neo-capitalism. We might characterize these as the client/welfare, rational/efficient and productivist systems. It is clear that such a characterization breaks radically with Gramsci's schema of transition-from-and-in-crisis. It cuts across traditional party ideology and organization. These are 'tendential laws of social recomposition' which, in a declining mode of production, assert themselves after the failure of revolution on the 'upward curve'.

Italy, in short, is not unequivocally in a catastrophic, bipolar, situation. Nor does she correspond to Amin's Third World notion that an elite will choose a strategy of autonomy/modernization and thus in turn ensure that a socialist path, not a hierarchical-welfare one, is chosen. (2) Many elements help to resist transformation: for example, modification in the structure and political consciousness of the proletariat leaves its parties increasingly preoccupied with their own continuing organization and survival. The universal mediation of interests within, as well as by, the governing party (presenting the disarticulation and arbitrariness thus produced as pluralism) may also be a form of hegemony. The tendency of the Communists to reduce political to administrative questions makes the politician separate and technical, rather than autonomous and connecting. Crisis, instead of being cyclical, becomes a relatively stabilized condition in which the variety and disagreeableness of therapies proposed leaves doctors and patient alike bewildered and exhausted. Christian Democracy is a more skilfully constructed bloc than was fascism. It has also refused to modernize and thus aid reformism. Unlike the Christian Democractic state, a modern bureaucratic-rational state would have stifled just those energies which in reality opposed the ideology of reformism. Again, contradictions in the goals and strategies of the powerless, or the holders of subordinate power, not only allow the Christian Democrats to perpetuate crisis, but tend to centre the debate on an ambiguous conflict between traditionalists and modernizers, protectors of property and upholders of planning, and between varieties of popular democracy and centralized democracy. This does not mean that Marx was wrong about the inescapability of capitalist crisis, but simply that the particular socio-political terms in which it seemed likely to be fought out, and the probability of a revolutionary and emancipatory outcome, have now to be revised.

We must question the notion that 'general crisis' theory is linked to the theory of a general collapse. Marx, in the 1859 Preface, formulates a theory of collision between productive forces and social relations - a form of institutionalized conflictuality which does not, however, preclude the insertion of elements of the proletariat into institutionalized consensus. Lenin's conception of the 'general crisis' of capitalism requires the political collapse of the dominant coalition, a failure of its project and ability to conciliate. In an era of 'post-catastrophic Marxism', a principle of dialectical conciliation survives, though its Hegelian paternity is denied: this is the metaphysical power of knowledge. Dialectical conciliation becomes the central element of the view of the state as relatively autonomous, and thus open to a 'political project' of recomposing the (autonomous) political class as representative also of the class interest of the subordinate classes. Dialectics as conciliation through technical knowledge is at its height in the representative, mediating, state.

This is a kind of secularized Hegelian version of the 'people as sovereign through their representative sovereign'. To the PCI, whether this political project starts in the state (as for Amendola), or from the concentric circles of elected assemblies (which still concentrates on the centrality of representation and the supremacy of parliament) as for Ingrao, the principle of representation is central. Even the 'operaisti' in the Party, who consider the apparently consensual and uniform transformation of conflictuality into centralized and distanced institutions to be a betrayal of the centrality of class politics and institutions, may be accused of underestimating the relation between economic weakness, or fragmentation, and political fragmentation and conflictuality. We might say that class politics is not autonomous or uniform; workers' 'centrality' tends to become bureaucratic, administrative centralization. The various currents of opinion in the PCI are also vulnerable to the charge that their concentration on the Italian case, and on the co-existence of weak institutions and strong parties, perpetuates the parochial concerns of Italian politicians (the 'strapaese' fixation), as against a realistic consideration of the general nature of the crisis and the political implications of various European efforts to 'manage' it.

The relative autonomy provided by representation is in fact limited by conflictual factors organic to the crisis. At the same time, these also break up and fragment the conflictual potential of class politics. These factors include the tendency of technological innovation and redeployment to 'sectorialize' the crisis, and the strengthening of institutions to introduce representatives of the working class to 'bureaucratic rationality', which in turn may mean 'rationalizing' the organized working class to accept high levels of unemployment in exchange for its own greater security. The absorption of part of the working class into administered channels tends to reduce the imaginative response of its leadership, producing a weak and subaltern compromise between 'red administrators' and 'spontaneity'. Finally, Marx's tendential laws imply negative entropy and exhaustion as well as greater conflictuality: indeed, the two may not be polar opposites.

Gramsci's own ambiguous remarks (ambiguous, as their historical context is not specific) on the natural path of the party to the state, the bureaucratization of intellectuals, the technicization of politics and the identification of politics with rational administration have much relevance in the pragmatic Hegelianism of the PCI. In practice, if this 'entry to the state' is possible because of the declining hegemony of the dominant class, not by its removal from the apparatus of power (and the maintenance, however precarious, of its dominant position in social relations), the absorption is that of a subordinate class. The proletariat enters the state not so much identifying its class interest with the state interest, as the interests of the state's administration with those of its own intelligentsia.

This reflects the paradoxical element of the Marxist

project, of making the subordinate dominant, the powerless powerful. Traditionally, the heightening of crisis has in fact led to an exponential weakening and confusion of the Left: so much so that Poulantzas abandons even the 'weak link' theory of revolutionary breakthrough and sees the latter as produced by the accumulation of 'mistakes' by a ruling class. (3) This analysis underestimates not only the social and economical conditions which makes miscalculation crucial but also the objectively complicating factor of the diversity of political 'autonomies' in the under-classes. True, crisis is a general crisis of ideology and of the rationality of the present. However, it is also a crisis of the future power-order. This may be seen in the questioning of the rationality of the administrative core of the state and its 'universal legitimacy'. In other words, calling into question the specific raison d'état introduces the question of raison d'état in general. The parasitism of the centre is mirrored in the condition of the excluded periphery, but the centre retains political power and initiative.

To what extent does the crisis of economic rationality (in classical terms, the transformation and realization problems) produce a general crisis in the discourse concerning political rationality? Italy, as a society which has missed two of the main experiences of modern rationality - the Keynesian and the Weberian - and whose traditional culture situates reason either as a tool or enemy of metaphysics, has a distant relation to rationality and its crisis. Passing from a prospect of managing development to that of managing crisis, the historic, institutionalized Left is often attracted by the suggestion that the crisis is primarily social and political, and resolvable politically, a question of power rather than reason. Economic questions become technical, not rational - enlarging the productive base, encouraging small and medium industry, confronting the problem of the South as the key to the 'Italian case' and making the labour market more permeable. Clearly the crisis of reason, of rationale, is not resolved by the socialists' 'counter-power', nor the Communists' 'long march through the institutions', since neither responds to the logico-structural arguments of Marx on the crisis of the mode of production (and of reproduction of social relations).

Against this background, the idea of crisis as one of backwardness, and as a general crisis in which Italy is caught as an organic dependent part of the whole, leads to a strategy of modification, not of transition. True, this does not contradict Marx's view that political conclusions, and catastrophic theories, should not be drawn directly from the analysis of the limited logic of capitalist production. By the same token, it does not provide the armed party, or 'autonomia', with a strategic significance derived from connecting subversive dissent with a new rationale.

In the 1950s Christian Democracy tried to continue intensive capitalist exploitation while acting as spokesman for traditional values. This was an unconvinced flirtation with the 'modern', seeing it as a potential rival, and with little understanding of the necessary mediations required to contain social conflict during the period of recruitment of the working class of the 'miracle'. The Left organized to 'catch up' in the 1960s, mostly outside, and hostile or indifferent to, the rapidly falling fortunes of reformism. As the PCI 'de-ideologized' itself after Togliatti's death, the unions assumed the economic power the Party once wielded. By the mid-1970s, though the PCI had made political gains commensurate with the unions' success in protecting their members' wages from inflation, it was clear that this 'catching up' had many deficiencies. Both the PCI and the unions, for instance, were involved in potentially conflicting strategies of self-defence: both were forced to attach themselves - under protest - to situations and situational logics of their opponents' making. The PCI was becoming committed if not exclusively to compromise with the dominant power, then to austerity and to thankless, subordinate, administration. The unions were paying the price for their lack of political programmes, and a wage policy which at best pursued inflation levels. There was relative failure to articulate a new rationality and a new rationale which would transfer the share of power to be expected as a result of contestation cemented by electoral success. In short, one feature of the crisis in the 1970s was the integration of part of the working class as an interest group, with a responsibility for crisis management which it had neither the power nor, arguably, the ideology, to discharge. The so-called crisis of governability is really a search for new bargaining rules and parameters superficially incompatible with the old state philosophy and system of industrial relations. However, as we shall see, these novelties are not fundamentally incompatible with a mixed economy dominated by capitalism. If resistance to modernization is a sign of the weakness of the dominant class, it is none the less a remarkably effective pursuit of a mistaken strategy. Resistance by Christian Democracy in the 1960s to Americanization as a threat to its own power structures has been complemented in the 1970s by a relatively successful attempt to protect and expand those power structures, despite steeper economic and social costs. In this context, not only the revolutionary subject but the revolutionary goal has been profoundly modified, despite Togliatti's original insistence that the PCI should be a party of government, not of a rhetorical, ideological 'revolution'.

The problem of organic and artificial limits to capital is well expressed by Rozdolski. Taking the position that capital pushes labour beyond the limits of its natural needs, he also points out that this creates a richer personality, and is thus a relation vital to the development of productive forces. When this ceases to be so, it is because the productive forces find a barrier in 'capital itself'. Labour then examines scientifically the process of its production. There can be no transition, however, if adequate material conditions are not present, and they appear when needs so develop that surplus labour in excess of what is necessary becomes a general need, and past accumulated labour becomes the general possession of the new generation. (4) Rozdolski (and Grossmann) dispose of Hilferding's equilibrium theory - that of the potential of capitalism to extend commodity production indefinitely. (5) Capitalism is greedy for goods which are also values: the realization problem concerns values as commodities with 'something added' (Sismondi). Its expansion, despite theoretical 'stable states' and empirical periods of actual quantitative increase, leads to an expansion of the terrain of crisis, until a limit is reached. Tendentially, then, capital tends to overcome its limits and also to find them again at a higher level. (6)

In a concrete case, there is no symptom of this final 'level' save in the scientific examination of the relation between the limiting nature of crisis and the productive potential and needs of labour. (7) Labour time becomes shorter through mechanization, but this very devaluation of living labour itself accelerates the problem of the growing element of constant capital in the organic composition of capital. The rate of profit falls, and crises of underconsumption and overproduction represent the crisis in the value relation between use value and exchange value. The crisis of valorization of labour power thus clearly jeopardizes the mechanism of production and power of capital over living labour.

What is needed, then, for agreement that a 'final' stage has been reached? May not sections of labour themselves aid the postponement of crisis for their own short-term interests, and may not capital indirectly profit from restrictions imposed by state policy and working-class action? The failure of capital rapidly and spontaneously to enter its terminal crisis may prolong its life. Mandel supplies a missing element: supporting Rozdolski's critique of the thesis of absolute immiseration, he says: 'two elements - physiological and moral or historical - determine the value of the commodity of labour power.' (8) The struggle over surplus value refers not to a question of the absolute mass of goods produced and available but to a fall in the value of labour power. Science and technology cannot wholly overcome this contradiction. Thus the 'intensified struggle over the rate of surplus-value' leads to 'qualitatively sharpened class conflicts, which will bring the endemic crisis of capitalist relations of production to explosion point.' (9)

This conflict, however, is seen as inherent in that between the capitalist commodity form and technology: (10)

> the objective opposition between partial rationality and overall irrationality, which is rooted in the growing contradiction between the growing socialization of labour and private appropriation and is a hallmark of the capitalist mode of production, acquires such explosive potential that the overall irrationality of late capitalism threatens in the medium term not only the existing form of society, but human civilization altogether.

In this scenario, in short, conflictuality leads to a situation where labour fights to diminish surplus value, with the long-term goal of increasing productive rationality. This is threatened, however, by the prospect of a political victory (the end of civilization) on the part of capital. A proletarian strategy of continuing high conflictuality and encouragement to introduce technological rationality would seem justified.

Samir Amin sees not technology so much as repression as the technical innovation of a capitalism in search of a social pact with the proletariat. He conceives of an authoritarian neo-social democracy which postpones discussion of the basis of capitalism. (11) His notion that this non-revolutionary path leads to the recomposition of a class society is significant. Both Mandel and Amin are inclined to argue that the classical statement of crisis theory not only precludes drawing precise political conclusions but, as in Mandel's case, that the end of accumulation and the beginning of decline encourages political pessimism. In other words, if socialism is at best an even chance, despite the presence of a classical crisis of overproduction, even conflict without such an ideological commitment may produce catastrophe. Thus, while retaining much of the traditional Marxist analysis of tendential crisis, the conclusions become increasingly sombre, the time scale increasingly longer, more elastic. Clearly, beneath this lies the feeling that the limit of capitalism has been reached in such a form as to preclude its export to the periphery in an advanced form while the dangers of 'breaking the chain' at the centre increase with the difficulty of the operation.

Michio Moroshima provides one of the more 'optimistic' versions of crisis as an element of growth theory, that of the 'reproduction and circulation of the aggregate social capital'. (12) The 'aim of Marx was not to establish the proportionality of prices and values in a capitalist economy, but, on the contrary, to explain why they may differ from each other when the workers cease to possess the means of production, so that they have to sell their labour-power in the market.' (13) Moroshima conceives of a capitalist strategy which largely escapes the association of technology with repressive technique mentioned previously: (14)

> In a centralized economy where labour is the sole scarce factor of production, techniques of production would be chosen so as to minimize the employment of labour. On the other hand in an economy where the capitalist mode of production prevails individual entrepreneurs are not interested in minimizing total employment, but adopt those techniques which maximize the rate of profit, calculated in terms of equilibrium prices.

In fact, a theory of growth which attaches qualitative importance to the strategy of capital but not to that of labour must be cautiously received. Amin and Mandel do emphasize the latter, though in terms of a counterposition between barbarism and socialism. Tendentially, different economic theories of crisis point to different strategies in the political sphere. They do so, however, with little clarity regarding the existing variety of conceptions of socialism, and in general by continuing to postulate that socialism is a term open to reduction to a vague 'socialism', a moralism which generally does not belong in the classical theories.

Crisis theory suggests that there is an intrinsic limit to capitalism as a mode of production based on growth. We must distinguish, on the other hand, between the expression of this limit as structural crisis (with 'conjunctural' causes which may themselves be 'natural' limits), and the socio-political limit of the impossibility of 'continuing in the old way'. The re-importation of the ideological certainties of the Internationals, even expressed as pious hopes, does not assist as regards two problems: first, that specific expressions of the general crisis show different configurations. For instance, different societies may export capital rather than importing technology, or reward one section of the working class while 'super-exploiting' another, or simple exclude the reserve army of labour from the calculation of the value of labour. Second, the effect of such strategies helps to determine the counter-strategy, alliances, and 'ideologization' of the working class, and this reciprocal effect cannot be excluded from the apparatus of crisis theory itself.

The tendency to deepening structural crisis, and hence the need to 'manage' it (especially in the face of aggravating conjunctural effects, which may be no less than the exhaustion of sectors of nature as satisfier of needs), seems confirmed in reality. Marxist theory has provided a basis for equilibrium theorists (for example, Bauer and Hilferding) as well as a case for 'collapse' enunciated by Luxemburg (and, for example, Sternberg). The position of Grossmann, however, was basic to theories of monopoly accumulation - a view widely held in the PCI until the movement in the 1970s to a marginalist orthodoxy. Grossmann supplied an explanation of boom as well as of tendential crisis. In order to maintain a growing rate of surplus value an enormous mass of commodities is required - an overproduction in relation to the amount of living labour employed, and one which requires for its realization a further process of capital accumulation and still less quantitative use of living labour. The increasing difficulty of equilibrating value and productive technique leads to a 'splitting' of the two sides of capitalist production - the value of commodities tends to fall, while the mass of material goods increases. At this point, classical political economy breaks down into continued disequilibrium.

Elsewhere, (15) Grossmann explains that whilst the search for a theory of collapse is properly Bernstein's, there are 'tendential laws' of both crisis and collapse in Marx. However, to Grossmann, a planned system, far from extending capitalism, rests on the overaccumulation of capital. Once social needs can be anticipated, capitalist value is no longer required as an a posteriori reconstruction of social equilibrium. To what extent, then, would a labour strategy of restricting the labour force, lowering productivity and maintaining the highest price of labour actually accelerate collapse? Would it not accentuate the counter-tendency of capital to abandon these sectors of the economy - to seek managed conflictuality rather than the static 'equilibrated conflictuality' of industries where capital had technically overaccumulated, where the rate of profit constantly falls towards zero? What is the effect of the ending of a competitive reserve army, and its incorporation into public service/public welfare? The problem for the PCI is clear: the crisis of big industry is not decisive; the growth of parasitism diminishes the potential mass of commodities; the movement to profitable industry is a strategy which prolongs the life of capitalism. On the other hand, without such development there would seem to be a hiatus in the very development of contradiction in social relations of production and the socialization of production. In other words, the Party is now in the position of denying that monopoly is the highest and most productive form of capitalist production, and thus is the threshold to transition. The state too cannot be exclusively that of monopoly capitalism if the Party is to be a 'party of government'.

Racinaro approaches the problem from an instructive angle - that of the concentration in the 'culture of crisis' from Heidegger to Karl Schmidt on the 'essence of technique. The problem is to penetrate the politics of technique.' (16) The politics of technique (in short, the technique of politics) concerns the avoidance of a merely catastrophic end to a capitalism whose own subjectivity destroys the productive forces it cannot articulate within its own mode. In this scenario, capitalism has reached its limit in one sector, that of monopolistic manufacture, but it has yet to reach its limit in other sectors and is thus able to satisfy material needs as well as continue to establish surplus value as dominant.

Sweezy (17) described some counter-tendencies for slowing down and prolonging development, such as the growth of new industry, erroneous investment (both leading to increased rates of consumption), increasing population, unproductive consumption and state expenditures (limiting excessive development of the means of production). These, however, seem merely quantitatively delaying factors. Thus, in connection with the Italian strategy, the submerged economy does not effectively reflect socialized production: intervention by the Left in this area relates to satisfaction of basic needs and concern for national competitiveness rather than socialization. The trend till recently has been for state expenditure to rise and indeed to limit the growth of production. Extending the life of capitalism becomes in practice equivalent to prolonging the crisis of its decline. The politics of decline are not clear and unequivocal. Kalecki's (18) comparative figures, for instance, shed little light on the sociopolitical outlet and outcome for the 'last phase'. For, in Italy, crises of overaccumulation exist simultaneously with counter-tendencies - as of rising public expenditure. Does this then point to a 'welfare decline', a social transformation of capitalism akin to Tugan-Baranovsky's ethical revisionism?

The key question would seem to be whether a positive attitude towards growth, and the view that capitalist development in certain sectors had not reached the point of crisis (the public sector being at least partly parasitic-welfare, not a safety brake on the overaccumulation of capital in the productive sectors), is compatible with the theory of transition rather than being a theory of equilibrium. In one sense this is an ideological question. Revisionists may also believe in transition and crisis theory. Instead, we have to ask whether the Italian crisis is properly one of a pathological development of an earlier stage of capitalism rather than the advanced one the political preparedness of the proletariat suggests. Either the proletariat does not yet see its future coherently as socialism, or the structural weakness evident in monopoly manufacture has yet to manifest itself in a modern form. In either case, the strategy of the PCI would justify itself on the grounds that one can simultaneously accept marginalist approaches for capitalist development while accelerating the process of socialization of the means of production and increasing the mass of commodities as a prelude to transition. Sweezy too suggests that Keynesianism does not involve the Marxist problematic - and that possibly class society will remain such. (19) The institutional Left may argue both that the crisis is structural and that it can be managed, or modified, by state intervention.

In fact, this double argument is not convincingly made, nor is there a convincing discussion of the 'Italian case' as simply a local variant of the classical 'disproportion' theory (sectorially uneven development). In short, the process of de-ideologizing within the PCI since the mid-1960s has retained optimism in productivism, while accentuating the trend to a revised ideology, reconciling class and national, or national-popular, interests. Yet classical Marxist crisis theory, despite its lack of ideological and political guidance for action, still demands attention. As Giacomo Marramao's important books (20) show, the classical debate raised the questions affecting the Italian Left today: the role of class struggle when parties and unions become absorbed in the state, and Lenin's examination in the 1890s of 'backwardness' as a revolutionary accelerator. Of course, Italy is not a relatively autonomous national unit, in the peculiar circumstances of Russia in 1917, and is clearly not 'at the frontiers of modernity'. At this point, it can only be emphasized that a new version of the nature and goals of transition - even granted that 'situations absolutely devoid of a way out never exist' - needs to be formulated by the institutional Left. Capitalism has already demonstrated a capacity to operate the strategies outlined in Gillman's 'The Falling Rate of Profit', such as a diversification from capital export to home, or government, consumption. The falling rate of profit in some circumstances is compatible with rising real wages (and unemployment). (21)

One counter-tendency to the falling rate of profit is an attack on its very mechanism. That is, technique may raise profit when capital realizes the need to concentrate its efforts only on profitability (not productivity), and correctly to translate values into prices of production. In other words, a conflictual class society might continue in prolonged 'transition' under the political domination of capital. This is akin to Bettelheim's notion of transition as 'a specific form of coexistence, or simultaneous presence and interaction of several modes of production', (22) dominance maintained by the specific political subject with the power to establish a hierarchy of modes, and stages of modes, from varieties of state capitalism to 'proletarian capitalism', or Amin's notion of transition from dependent capitalist development to self-centred national development (i.e., relative national autonomy). (23)

Again, having established that transition is not mental, a void or a no-man's-land between modes of production, we are again faced with the question of the logic and characteristics of the PCI's choice of specific strategy for a specific transition, based on an overall view of the crisis. Partly because of problems and deficiencies in Marx's theory, and of the specificity of subsequent interpretation and debate, the development of crisis theory and strategy seems at present to have lost touch with its origins. Michele Salvati, for instance, relates this disjuncture to the fact that over- and underproduction are symptomatic of periodic crises, while the squeeze on profits is a sign not of capitalist structural collapse but of working-class power. (24) The latter, however, does not mean the end of capitalism, which still creates the labour force it requires. There is, in short, no scientific justification for believing in tendential fall in the rate of profit leading to a new mode - though there is a clear social and political case.

According to the PCI, only by strengthening the (pluralist) party system and institutions can the needs of the subordinate classes be registered and their interests protected - for Enrico Berlinguer, even from a Chilean coup. For the socialists - to generalize - the danger of simply strengthening institutions is that these become the (corporate-pluralist) preserve of the governing party (or parties). The problem is not so much the weakness of institutions, but the lack of effective centres which can compel the institutions to use their strength in the public interest. Neither case, as we shall see, is trivial. We must, however, continue to emphasize that the tendential fall in the rate of profit still involves the need to propose alternatives to capitalism. The need is pressing if capitalism has indeed reached its historical limit: even if it has not, and need not, it is still important to analyse the basis and tendencies of class struggle.

One interpretation on the Left prefers instead to stress the international and monetary factors in the crisis. Guelfi and Olmeda, (25) for instance, relate the crisis to such indicators and causes as oil prices, German-US hegemony, low productivity, currency problems, inflation and unemployment. Officially, says Guelfi, the answer is agreement to regulate trade, balance of payments and currency fluctuations. Unofficially, the slight recovery after 1976 was financed by the worsening US balance of payments resulting from international conflictuality. The solution would be a new, effective system of international collaboration. (26) Despite the market conditions which underlie this crisis, in other words, and which are reflected in the Italian case at the domestic level, the assumption of a general interest to 'manage' the crisis is increasingly made. Such views are commonplace among PCI economists, and the political project suggested by this is at once radical and naive. This agreement assumed and the collaboration proposed could be achieved domestically by repression of conflictuality, or the insertion of the conflicting interests as corporate 'interests' within the public sphere ('pluralism').

This view is too rigid as regards the structural causes and permanent conflictuality of a competitive system. It is no mystery that the oft-lauded 'moderation' of the PCI allows it to consider an accommodation with capitalism, as capitalism did with feudalism. What is surprising is that the theoretical and practical implications for its members, its electors and its political future, have been seemingly accepted so decisively and conclusively since the pace of strategic realignment quickened in the early 1970s.

Thus, on the one hand, class struggle is imported into the heart of the state, in forms such as the question of the share of the social product destined for the workers or the distribution of social capital. On the other hand, not only is the logic of 'the worse it is, the better' (for the Left) rejected, but a new, implicit formulation enters. That is, that transformation takes place in, through and despite the projected recovery of the capitalist system. One finds a similarity between this and the situation in France, as analysed by Poulantzas, who argues that the national bourgeoisie may be won over to a conception of 'advanced democracy' since its interests lie with non-monopoly capital in opposition to American monopoly capital; with the nation, not the state. In the Italian case, however, national capital is dominated by the banks, and both state and nation by the influence of German hegemony, the balance of payment crisis, foreign loans and competitiveness in the foreign market. It is true that internal contradictions between finance and capital monopoly and manufacturing industry exist. However, the concrete question for politicians is: how is social capital to be allotted to the various sectors of non-monopoly capital and to state monopoly, semi-public and private monopoly capital?

In short, there is a difference between using these internal contradictions to try to organize resistance outside the state in the case of the French Communist Party (PCF), and using the state to mediate between their differential successes and claims, as does the PCI. It is not that every administrator permanently becomes a servant or member of the state bourgeoisie, and thence of capital, so much that class alliances formed by instrumentalizing the investment of social capital, tacit encouragement to the 'black economy', and the promise of sympathetic treatment by the state put relations on a pragmatic material basis, as against the mainly ideological one advocated by the PCF. It is more secure, but imports the contradiction of social relations of all these forms of capitalism into the party-state-as-mediator. Again, this is not simply a dogmatic denial that at times pursuit of the 'national interest' may indeed be in the interest of the proletariat. Rather, the observation to be made is that cementing class alliances via the state tends to erase the class specificity of a party and thus its capacity to act on behalf of the subordinate classes. The PCI, it should be remembered, increased its distance from national government not because its economic project failed, but because it was not permitted by the Christian Democrats to win the power to make that alliance.

Poulantzas is correct to point to the complexity of economic, political and ideological levels of class identification, the inseparability of power from struggle (power is not simply state power), and to make a distinction between authoritarian democracy or 'étatisme' (or the 'new' democratic 'form of the bourgeois republic', of an administrative democracy) - as distinct from simple fascistic authoritarianism. Poulantzas is describing, however, a rapidly stabilizing state capitalist system, with the PCF regarded as unequivocally 'outside' the system. This stabilization can now no longer be assumed, and in Italy the PCI must be seen as equivocally 'inside' the system of state power. (27) Yet the latter development does not simply represent a tendency to social homogenization, to employee, dependent, status and to tertiarization. The bourgeoisie is fragmented into a state and state-petty bourgeoisie, finance, manufacturing and 'black' bourgeoisie, the professional, technical and experts dependent on the bourgeoisie proper, as well as the artisans. The working class itself, organized and unorganized, pursues corporatist, competitive, strategies which accentuate the volatility of the class and the diversity of its leadership.

To Poulantzas, state ideology reflects the state of political relations between classes, and the exclusion of the working class from state power. In Italy, the situation is more complex, as to some extent class struggle is transported onto the terrain of the state, even though the presence of the working class in the state is tendential and fleeting. Yet there is a sense in which the end of the struggle to penetrate the state is representation: and that is why the autonomy of the politician may involve the absorption of the (legitimated) political into the state sphere as 'representation of interest'. This is not a situation of permanent harmony: it is a stage in the recomposition of the leading classes in conflict, which sets the limits of conflictuality arising from the crisis. It is an agreement to avoid a sudden and engineered collapse of capitalism, without raising the question of the implications of tendential crisis. It is a policy for survival, and against catastrophe. It involves the simultaneous possibility of a new capitalist alliance, and that of 'transformation' of the working class from a subordinate position, within the parameters noted above. The autonomy of the politician lies in the conviction that the passage from one mode of production to another, their combination, and their feasibility involve essentially political judgments.

What, then, is the rationale for undertaking transition

from within 'state politics'? Massimo Cacciari speaks of the subject outside the universal (state) form as not 'radically free', but conceived of as an element of family, tradition or occupation. The state is the location where the subject enjoys radical freedom. (28) Crisis is not negation, but the terrain of negative thought. For Cacciari crisis is compatible with the development and positivity of knowledge: crisis is a context, a conditioner of thought, not negativity itself. Implicitly, the Hegelian dialectic - the philosophical core of the central Marxist tradition in Italy - triumphs over Nietzsche's pessimism, and does so in the state, but only if the subject realizes himself as universal. (29) Two important conclusions follow: Cacciari, as one of the theorists for the 'autonomy of the political' in the PCI, does not see crisis as a state of thought, but rather thought as reconciling, transcending in crisis and through the state. Second, the notion of crisis is transposed from political economy - which is both dignified and diluted by being the theory of the formation and distribution of general wealth - to politics. This transposition, as we have seen, has been made with the approval of marginalist economists who avoid discussing either the finality of economic crisis or transition. Yet it is hard to see how there can be a Marxist theory of the state which divorces class struggle from economic crisis and development. Politics, in Cacciari's view, becomes the representation of a unitary subject in the state. This wholly rejects Lefebvre's suggestion that 'the working class should therefore only become politicized in order to supply itself with the means to bypass politics and cause it to wither away.' (30)

Politics in the state is traditionally the technique of constructing a dominant ideology in order to present the general interest of a class as a universal interest. The working class as a political subject in the state with other classes can formulate a general interest compatible with universality only if it abandons an understanding of crisis in economic growth as one of human needs and class conflict. In other words, abandoning the theses of Grossmann and Rozdolski means also that crisis ceases to be an acute one of rationality and of legitimation (Habermas). (31) That is, access to state power is no longer sought because of the finality of the crisis, but because the economic crisis can be transformed or managed by political means. The transformation of the political system required to accomplish this immediately resolves the political crisis - by identifying politics and state. Gianni Scalia's cry of 'enough of politics!' (32) is understandable at this point, as politics has come to equal state power, not a force of change or alternative to it.

In part, the discourse of the autonomous politicians (or states-men) is permitted by the political vagueness of the economists. Polanyi (33) spoke of socialism as the conscious subordination of the self-regulated market to a democratic society. However, a democratic society - in one of its aspects - is a self-regulated market. Suppression of the capitalist law of value is after all to be accomplished by the state, rather than by society. Economic crisis threatens the rationale of industrial society. But it does not establish a 'rationality' for the marginal, those who 'do politics' outside the state. Beyond the limited rationality of capitalist society, and that part of the working class which accepts it, there still stands the broader, alternative rationality of an alternative organization of production. Institutional politics must, though, recognize the damaging and destabilizing effects on both forms of rationality of the collapse of capitalist productivist rationale. (34)

It is often said that the similarities in the strategies of state capitalism and state socialism reduce the question of transition to one of administrative choice or technical adjustment. It is also arguable that Lenin's definition of communist labour as 'performed without the condition of reward' (35) is as utopian as 'realized socialism' is unattractive to the 'society of producers' in advanced capitalist states. Politically, this conclusion would make the primary problem for the Italian parties that of 'group access to the decision-making process versus administrative planning'. The question of rationale and rationality would become secondary to the form of political process. Yet, if the 'real barrier of capitalist production is capital itself', (36) this must remain the primary political argument. Either this crisis is not terminal, or it is undesirable that capitalist development should stop, or again public intervention and austerity can limit its effects - in any case, the argument must be made on these issues. Instead, the PCI has argued that its power is sufficient to propel it into the state, but not enough to compel a transformation of the state from outside. The question of rationality will thus be posed within the state.

The Left has been transformed by the crisis of capitalism-as-modernity. The theory of the autonomy of the political within the state not only tends to de-legitimate the autonomy of those outside, let alone opposed to, the state but concentrates on the dialectical transformation of the state by the principle of representation. Marx is replaced by Hegel, the search for a new rationality by unity in representation. In the crisis of values, the Left, under the banners of liberalism and of Leninism, has chosen to use the values of bourgeois society against those of capitalist society.

This distinction is implicit in Negri's critique (37) of capitalist values. He stresses the inherent contradiction and the dangers of proclaiming consumerism and productivism as values, and the impossibility of demonstrating that, properly maintained, such values promote social harmony. Yet, as Cacciari points out, it is another matter when we try to apply the category of 'crisis' to thought itself and 'bourgeois thought' in particular. Ideologies or values, destined to be realized in practice, raise a question of moral responsibility for their consequences which refers back to their philosophical origin (for example, Marx's responsibility for the 'gulags'). (38) This observation can be reduced to two elements. On the one hand, this reaction to a 'value-crisis' becomes a simplistic critique of all ideologies and hence proposes the need for intellectuals to oppose any formulation which may be connected with power. On the other hand, it surreptitiously makes the intellectual a commanding figure - whether in his 'positive' form, as founder of regimes, or the 'negative' one, using his typewriter against Power.

Koselleck's view, that the bourgeois state is founded on absolutism and enlightenment, the latter leading to utopianism, points to historical and structural reasons for a tendential legitimation or value crisis. However, utopianism in crisis may easily, as he admits, be reduced to a simple optimism - that 'the end of the critical condition is imminent'. (39) The rise of 'democratic authoritarianism' is the product and continuation of low levels of legitimation. But it differs from other authoritarianisms in that its proclaimed value is the value of survival, not the universalization of the values of a dominant class. The argument is partly circular, since the interest of a dominant class in time of crisis is survival. The point is that this survival should have the 'democratic' consensus to excuse low levels of success and high levels of repression against the resulting conflictuality. In this situation, critical intellectuals have no philosophical space. Scalia expresses this by pointing to both the dangers of 'realized thought' and the steady decline in its plausibility. Bourgeois values are restored as power, consensus not rationality.

This position reflects not only the disappointment of the critical literary intellectual with the institutional

Left, but this type of intellectual's marginality with respect to the new administrative intellectuals - the technicians of the crisis - those who, rather than the 'committed' literary intellectual, have actually emerged as the political intellectuals. (40) One must distinguish, therefore, between a crisis of the intellectuals and a crisis of values. The latter is primarily embodied in a crisis of the structures transmitting dominant values. The family, the educational and religious apparatuses and the parties have all suffered in varying degrees from neglect or from exceptionally rapid and precarious modernization in the past ten years. Economic pressures, such as shortage of housing and youth unemployment, have reversed much of the trend to 'liberalize' family structures. The women's movement - because of the weak market for female labour - has reached a crucial material barrier, and for economic motives many women have been forced back to, or to continue in, traditional family roles without traditional family values. Demoralization, underfunding, and disconnectedness with the labour market are notorious in most branches of secondary and higher education. If young people have been returning to the youth sections of the parties of the Left, this is partly due to the disorganization of the non-institutional Left and the attempts to 'criminalize' militancy outside the parties, but perhaps more especially because of disillusion with a non-institutional politics which promises neither power, patronage nor responsibility. The old relation between intellectual activity and political militancy is perhaps being replaced by a more prosaic and less discursive attachment to organized political structures in the area of government.

To say that the economic crisis suddenly threw into reverse the 'modernization' of values and structures - some by erosion, some by frontal assault - does not mean that alternative values were strengthened. The opposite is probably true. As we shall see, it is precisely because of the setback of the 'modernizing' trend that the search for, and faith in, the 'modern alternative' has become so problematic.

In North America, as Lasch and Bledstein (41) have recently pointed out, the collapse of traditional values and their transmitting structures was followed by the dominance of experts, of professionals, who had assisted in the process. This involved a 'professionalization' of broad sections of the middle strata which both supply, and are dependent on, professional expertise. Thus the transition from traditional (private and individual, family and community (or class)) values was made relatively smoothly. The 'modern' values of deference to objective, general expertise, conformity to public role expectation (based on occupation and respect for qualification), belief in secular rationality and efficiency as alternatives to personal bargaining served as social cement as well as the bases for new privilege. In Italy, the modern values largely remained problematic at the level of rhetoric, and so could be disputed, or ignored, at that level. These 'modern' values were not those of a socialist industrial society. Many felt, however, that an unequivocal attack on traditionalism might have isolated the dominant political class. Instead, these modern bourgeois values, promoted by the Left, went into crisis themselves.

An attack on traditionalism, in any case, is seldom unequivocal. For successful modernization, expertise needs people who can afford to consume its services, and its first task is to organize these on a mass-consumption basis. This requires a productive base which has a reciprocal, organic, relation with the tertiary sector. Lacking this, 'modernization' will be a pathological overproduction of qualified experts who are unusable, and to that extent parasitic. Thus, while Italy meets to some extent two of Giddens's criteria of neocapitalist development, the insertion of the working class into the political system, and the access of the intelligentsia 'to professional or managerial occupations', (42) it is significant that it does so only partially. The 'choice' of a model of development (to neo-capitalism or state socialism) has yet to be definitively made, and also produces attempts to recast traditionalism in a radical mould. This case could be made partially in terms of the area of 'autonomia', where advanced communism is reached by leaping over the intermediate, state-directed stages by means of mass insurrectionary subversion or where indeed subversion and destabilization are valued in themselves. It is unequivocally present in 'Comunione e liberazione', a radically anticapitalist, communitarian, Catholic movement.

However, returning to the case for 'value crisis', the general crisis of 'capitalist values' produces a frustrated modernization of bourgeois values. This has important implications for the construction of political and class alliances. Since the crisis of the 1930s, political intervention in and aid to modernization have deprived economic development of its spontaneous appearance. (43) The choice of different combinations of traditional and modern values lets the 'traditionalists' back into the game. Partial modernization is 'managed' by traditionalists. This means that potential discourse now concerns control of value-transmitting structures, not the values themselves and their relation to the development of the productive forces.

As Cardechi points out, every activity which 'recomposes' a class then requires the composition of political alliances within that extended class, (44) an extension of class culture. The institutional Left has always been culturally subordinate in Italy. Symptomatic was Togliatti's acceptance of the autonomy of 'high culture' as the product and preserve of intellectuals, while trying to establish the political predominance of the PCI. (45) The administrative culture associated with Emilia-Romagna put primary emphasis on honesty and efficiency. It is thus not axiomatic that as old values wither an alternative system replaces them. The fragmentation of value systems and a pragmatic process of devising local value schemes for transitory phenomena are a probable response.

In fact, the classical case for economic crisis providing the basis for transition to socialism has two major forms of weakness. First, the more historically complex and extensively interdependent the capitalist mode of production becomes, so the various counter-tendencies, and the structures these counter-tendencies have inserted into the mechanisms of the mode, become stronger and more complex. Second, crisis does not wait upon analysis, but on the political intervention of the contesting classes. Healthy though it may be to reject a 'realized' model of an alternative transitional form, this reflects a weakening of the values of proletarian rationality. True, the silence of the institutions under the control of the dominant fractions of the ruling class, their moral and practical emptiness vis-à-vis the crisis, are significant. So too, however, is the loss on the institutional Left of a notion of the finality of the crisis, or of the limit of the mode of production being reached. It is as though a notion of neo-capitalism as 'an example without historical precedent - a hierarchical society in constant mutation' had cancelled out that of the collision of productive forces and relations of production, as well as the basic problem of translating labour value into (decreasing) price and rising surplus value. (46)

The loss of a notion of 'finality' has been related primarily to the 'insertion' of intellectuals into the power state. Foucault has said: (47)

> The intellectuals themselves are a part of the system of power, and the idea that they are the agents of 'knowledge' and discussion is a part of this system. The role of the intellectual is no longer to put himself 'a little in front or a little on one side', to speak everyone's silent truth, but it is rather to

struggle against the forms of power where he is at once its object and its instrument - in the ordering of 'knowledge', 'truth', 'understanding', 'argument'.

But, as Baudrillard replies, Foucault's theory is but a reflection of the power he describes, and power for him is the equivalent of desire - the genetic key to modern society. There remains, however, the possibility of challenge or dissent as a permanent riposte to power. (48) This does not suggest there is a crisis in the system of power - something like Scalia's 'war crisis' - where resistance, inseparable from dissidence, challenges the combination of power with terror. (49) An attempt to relocate the critical intellectual outside institutional politics (though not within violent resistance) is still at the point of generic statements. Thus Scalia says rebellion emerges from the crisis (of Marxism, of realized socialism) as the independence of philosophy from politics. (50) The enemy, as for André Glucksmann, is totalitarianism, as against the autonomy of thought, of freedom, of refusal to be 'systematized'. This is a kind of measured pessimism. Behind all these formulations is the belief, first, that the crisis will be surmounted or managed repressively, and second, that this project already shows that there is no 'crisis of power'. Realized socialism and authoritarian democracy appear as different strategies for, in both cases, the difficulties of economies where the classical law of value - and hence the classical revolutionary recipes - no longer obtains.

The Italian institutional Left has modified its view of capitalism, and while insisting that there is economic, social and political crisis, it no longer connects this with arrival at the limit of the mode of production. Better, if limit there be, either it has not been reached, or it is a permeable, transformable barrier, a long complex transition to a 'difficult socialism'. A second modification to crisis theory proposes withdrawal from political involvement in institutional politics because of its authoritarianism - whether of Right or Left. The first version, naturally, is the only one to suggest a positive view of transition. Three points may be made here: first, the radical rejection of politics-as-power-as-terror-as-philosophy-of-death expresses a disillusion with the passage of intellectuals into the parties, from reason to power. Where, as in Italy, this mood also affects a mass of intellectual labour power, it contributes both to militant 'de-legitimation' and to political apathy. Second, there is little evidence that shifting the crucial level of analysis from economics to politics has enabled politicians to respond to economic or social crisis, and to strengthen sociality in social decline. In Italy, the mood of the Left has gradually returned to the defensive. Third, the process of recomposition of the social structure has thrown into relief the problem of a strategy for modernizing the backward, when the modern itself is in crisis. The crisis is producing a 'new backwardness'.

For example, the exclusion of living labour from the production process, realization and transformation problems and that of over-production/underconsumption are all foreseen in classical crisis theory. Concretely, this involves divisions in the reserve army between the unemployed and the precariously employed. Those 'inside' the system are forced to rely on traditional structures. New entrepreneurial ventures develop that rely heavily on cheap technology and a larger organic component of living labour. Organized labour is tempted by a strategy of corporate defence of interests. Deprived of the safety-valve of migration and emigration, Southern families combine sub-subsistence agriculture with precarious urban employment. Public administration becomes a vast system of indoor relief for its personnel, administering a still vaster system of outdoor relief for its clients.

Now these may indeed be symptoms of late capitalism: but they are a mixture of late-industrial and pre-industrial phenomena, with the latter predominating. Late industrial the most advanced sectors may be, where profitability and productivity is low and the potential for destructive production great. A society which produces cars and dangerous chemicals but not housing is an advanced capitalist industrial society from the point of view of human needs. In addition, it is the growth of earlier forms of production, the artisan's workshop, the cottage industry, precarious and illegal employment of all kinds, which, though they flourish, require caution when one speaks of homogenization of the condition of dependent labour.

The regression to primitive forms does not contradict classical crisis theory, but it certainly changes the political climate of 'transition'. In Italy, when the Censis reports speak of these developments as marks of irrepressible vitality and inventiveness (of the little man as entrepreneur, or improviser), they do not explain that the class and political consciousness acquired in the 1960s is being, if not lost and anomic, modified. Fragmentation, regression and improvization have an effect in the 1970s as much as the experience of the confluence of apparently disparate groups in 1967-9. Marx underestimated the inventiveness of the capitalists and the nonlinearity of progressive development: the fact that History might be radically concerned with power, not reason, and attached to repressively stratified society. In the decline of the dominant mode, sociality in general declines, and alienation assumes tangible forms for the subordinate classes of exclusion from, and the weakening of, social processes.

Chapter 2

MODERNISM, TRADITIONALISM AND REFORMISM

This chapter examines how the Italian Marxist Left attempted to counterpose 'modernity' to the 'traditional' hegemony of the political class. For Gramsci, modernity is expressed as Americanism, for Togliatti as reformism. The descriptive analysis of traditionalism has a venerable history, and is a key element of the elitist theories of Michels and Pareto. As we shall see, tradition and modernity are not polar opposites: 'tradition' provides pragmatic political management, 'modernity' destroys tradition but is re-absorbed by the traditional ruling class. Traditional ruling classes survive the failure of capitalist modernization, and the Marxist modernizers are left with no proposals save to penetrate the traditional elite.

The opposite of traditionalism is not secularization but the formation of a modern world system, a modern state and a composite political class. This 'world order' is characterized by extremes of uneven development, and by a process of decline reviving 'traditional' forms of privatization. The political class tends to lose authority and legitimacy, and adopts a defensive attitude, rather than ideological optimism. In such a situation, where the strategy of capitalism is to cut back production and productive employment, the real choice is perhaps between productivism-with-inequality, rather than non-production-with-inequality. However, the philosophical superstructure of Marxism as emancipation from necessity seems definitively dismantled. For Italy, as for other less developed countries, the crisis is a pre-vision of the future, but not of a superior alternative. It is the decline of a world system in which capitalism remains the mode in dominance, and in which national strategies have decreasing influence.

In crisis theory there remains an unresolved question as to whether higher, or state monopoly, forms of capitalism have the capacity to perpetuate themselves indefinitely and, if they do not, how the 'decline' or 'collapse' will affect the class structure and political organization of its opponents. A further difficulty in the Italian case arises from the already discussed non-Weberian and non-Keynesian development of a rapidly and fragmentarily assembled, unevenly modern, capitalism. Apparently arriving at its 'limit', Italian capitalism seems to have 'regressed' to earlier productive forms, leaving unsettled the role of state monopoly and total planning. There is, in effect, a tendential return to traditional practices, albeit in a narrower, more sombre, context.

The theme of traditionality and modernity runs deep in Italian thought, as can be seen in the contrast between Guicciardini's optimistic localism and Machiavelli's uncompromising modern absolutism, with consensual mass mobilization. The analysis of these contrasting images of society involves questions of social perception beyond class origin or ideological commitment. Thus both the socialist Michels and the liberal Pareto provide an account of traditional structures and behaviour, and their persistence. On the other hand, Gramsci's 'Americanism' and Togliatti's reformism are essentially transitional strategies for a 'traditional' society in the process of modernization. In other words, in Italian social thought, 'traditional' and 'modern' conflict and co-exist as accounts of both structures and behaviour. They supply polarities which underlie and influence the debate on transition, and which illuminate many of the perplexities which arise from pursuing a strategy of transition to modernity. These include, for instance, the tension between administrative rationality and participation: between the formation of a new political class and the powerlessness of those it represents: between the parasitic nature of 'reformed' (i.e., state patronized) structures and the vigour of improvised enterprise.

It is not suggested that traditionalism and modernity, or elitism and Americanism, need form a central part of the sociological vocabulary. They do, however, represent terms in which, historically, contrasting attitudes regarding the limits and direction of a strategy of 'transition' have been expressed. An elite is clearly not closely definable, but 'elitist theory' does express a belief in the recomposition of a professional political class, or caste, after mass mobilization. It refers to the power of the reassertion of tradition, and of traditional political behaviour associated with a pre-modern or 'non-scientific' (non-Weberian) political leadership. Pareto indeed adopts Machiavellian imagery - without, of course, justifying this in terms of a 'modern absolutism' - in order to show how alien the conservative psyche was to scientific innovation and rules. Michels (1) was less interested in the relation between the party elite and other elites than in the institutionalization of the leadership of the mass party and its crystallization into the traditional form of social control, the oligarchy. As the core of a theory of politics, elite theory is ahistorical, and its definitions approximate. As an oblique comment on the Italian political class, though it appears to cast its net wider, it is pertinent. It is relevant, albeit in a limited sense, for all societies in which the paradox of the modern enters the arena of political choice. The paradox is that the modern, which is presented as innovation, is really only the adoption and adaptation of that which already exists elsewhere, introduced into a context where traditional behaviour and cuture retain a capacity for survival and for absorption of the novel which is as yet unexhausted. The 'modern' is imitation, 'tradition' is the political management of the present.

Both Gramsci and Togliatti faced this problem. Gramsci dealt with it in terms of the introduction of Americanism from a country 'without a culture' to one where political class and subordinate classes shared traditional culture. The new technical culture required a political leadership which could be provided only by detaching intellectuals responsible for the 'high culture' of the bourgeoisie. Togliatti saw the necessity for modernization as preliminary to, and precondition for, transition, and as connected essentially with reformism. In their work, we may speak of the formation of 'images' of society - imaginative constructs based on the present (tradition) and travelling to the future (the modern). We must thus distinguish between the actual (tradition-in-dominance), and the future (modern-in-dominance).

A paradox of capitalism as representing the future-as-reason, from the point of view of tradition, lies in its being not reason but rather a self-sufficient and limited rationality. When this self-sufficiency itself breaks down, the typical response is to make the 'non-rational' adjustments which may help it to survive. Survival in a modified form may enable another evolutionary escape-route to be located, and the extinction of the species thus avoided. A traditional society modernizing is thus pragmatic, and dominated by political managers. Gramsci's notion of Italy was of a country divided by more factors than simply capitalist entrepreneurial relations of production. If the existing hegemony failed, capable though it was of surviving social fragmentation and uneven development, more than economic factors were involved, and a key element was the breaking of the precapitalist relation between notables and the 'simple masses'. The mass party enables a contact between leaders and led based on the cement of intellectuals, not the divided relation of benevolence-patronage and deference-service.

However, as Gramsci himself saw, the danger of adopting Leninist centralization in the party tended to perpetuate the division between leaders and the simple. The problem was that of detaching people from dependence on traditional structures which are not open to rational self-modification but are capable of maintaining reciprocally functioning relations. He stressed the radical nature of the connection between technological knowledge through industrial development, and the diffusion of political knowledge. He correctly saw both kinds of knowledge as a technique - at times seeming to argue that both kinds of knowledge entered the state through the mediation of the intellectual-as-politician-technician. The end of the mass party, too, is to enter the state.

Togliatti, however, faced a different situation: first, he may have overestimated the necessity of the relation between economic growth and reformism. Historically, growth was a necessary but not a sufficient condition of reformism. Second, Togliatti's strategy left the PCI in its present quandary: the mass party in its function as a party of mobilization remains outside the institutions it is trying to reform. It 'transforms' from without, while its own institutional forms remain those of the mass party. Yet the logic of the representational system is such that it is impossible to remain outside institutions: the mass party becomes a 'party of government' but is itself transformed. Mass institutions attach themselves to bureaucratic ones: the party provides administrators who mediate between organizations. Individuals are called on to participate, but as demobilized inputs to administrative rationality.

This is an oversimplified picture, since the Party is still stronger than the sum of the institutions its representatives control. However, the Party becomes an apparatus concerned in the selection of potential administrators and the recruitment of those who are at present technicians. Irrespective of any ideological development, it tends to develop away from the Togliattian strategy of demonstrations by massive numbers towards intra-systemic activity and intra-systemic recruitment. The question of what form of transformation this implied depends on two factors: whether the penetration of the administration can go beyond the assertion (or eventually, perhaps, the practice) of bureaucratic rationality, and, second, whether contact with the now demobilizing mass can be re-established through new institutions. Administrative decentralization was intended to be one means for this. However, participation in the formulation of administrative decisions is notoriously a haphazard as well as a subordinate (or co-opted) form of influence. Such 'participation', even if indefinitely forthcoming, socially homogeneous and politically coherent, inevitably requires mediation and formulation by the administrative apparatus itself. Modernity becomes synonymous with administrative rationality, but as an administration without the raison d'état of a dominant social formation.

Enrico Berlinguer's remarks on the relation between growth and reformism, and decline and compromise, are instructive. Resistance to crisis was strong, but the latter's effects on developed and marginal areas alike was leading 'towards a decline'. That is, the crisis affects the developed and the backward areas: it is not a crisis of overdevelopment, or backwardness, but both. It even raises the question of 'why produce', to which the PCI answer is, in fact, no answer, but 'austerity'. Politically, the solution is to appeal to the non-conservative forces in the Christian Democrats. As Leonardo Paggi, in the same review, is at pains to point out, this follows Togliatti's revision of Gramsci's views on the incompatibility of reformism and communism. Reformism failed in the 1960s because political leaders were more interested in coalescing than in reform. Interest in reform even existed in tradition, among the Christian Democrats, though with its frustration in the 1960s the initiative passed from bourgeois to a more radical reformism. (2)

The emphasis here, it would seem, is less on the tactical question of parliamentary alliance than on the implications for social image (3) of the loss of the imaginative possibility of sustained growth. The loss of the image of a modern society, of 'modern' development, implies also the loss of that of a transitional society, of modernization achieved by raising performance. Gramsci regarded Italy's political and economic backwardness as reasons for accepting a transitional 'popular democratic' period. Togliatti took this faith in the prospect of growth as the basis for reformism. Now, however, the prospect of growth leads to a different conclusion: alliance with 'progressive traditionalism' in a period of decline is different from the same alliance with a prospect of unlimited growth. It is linked to an image of regression, of a hollow anti-capitalism when capitalism is in decline, and of austerity as resignation to reduced capacities.

The Left's social image of Italy has been built through the ideological advocacy of socialist and communist reformisms, the first in a period of relative equilibrium, the second of subordinate administrative management in a period of decline and crisis, without formal governing responsibility. The chances of building a 'modern' ruling class and ruling institutions seem slight, even in Ingrao's 'third way'. Italy now seems trapped in its history: as a culture (or a language) before being a nation, as victim of the collapse of industrialization in the South, of the lack of a solid national bourgeoisie, and the persistence of a particularistic, pre-industrial urban life. In this context, modernization may seem to have mainly negative connotations. It has eroded much of traditional popular culture, threatened traditional urban life and destroyed traditional rural life, while maintaining the power of notables and extending the patronage functions of state and parties. There is, historically, a sense in which religion, liberalism and Marxism have all tried to come to terms with the destructive, anomic, character of 'rational modernity' in Italy, and failed. The values of modernity - simplicity, centralization and standardization, meritocracy and technique - could as well be those professed by Agnelli and Olivetti as by the PCI. Neither neo-capitalism nor the Communist Party, however, has established a vigorous modernity.

This creates specific problems in the political sphere. We must first distinguish between 'elitism' as the congealing of a centralized hierarchy, and the 'pre-modern' behaviour of politicians - that is, the non-routinized, non-technical politician. This is an area full of paradox. Modernity offers rationality, but, as Weber said, in democracy it offers greater power, hence greater military capacity. Rationality becomes bureaucratic. Pareto, on the other hand, stresses the perpetual subversion of reason by faith and self-interest, Mosca and Michels the circularity of the history of organizations from movement to institution. Pareto stands on the side of reason, but argues that the forces which defeat it themselves stand for social cohesion and stability. To Michels, the historic mission of the working class was frustrated not so much by its opponents, but by its own bureaucratic centralism which demobilized the class and prevented its remobilization. Mosca saw the political leadership of any organization or society as monopolizing power, with or without consensus. These are partial insights, but they illuminate some aspects of the current competition to occupy the state in Italy, the tendency to make compromises between modernity and traditionalism (or between convention and tradition), and view concentration of power as a historical accumulation of power. Politics is generally the preserve of traditional, legitimated, elites, not 'masses'

The institutional Left, however, has long pursued the 'modern' alternative of mass democracy. So, to Gramsci, Americanism would create an enlarged working class, a progressive, productivist culture and the basis for transition. Traditional society was well adapted for excluding the mass of the population from the political process. Power was privatized, personalized or became corporatist, whereas links between corporations were based on personality. Technique is of relatively little consequence in this situation. The weakness of civil society as against the state was to some extent deceptive, as the strength of the state lay in its ability to co-ordinate, and indeed create, manageable corporate interests based on the dominant corporatist ideology.

In practice, since the war it has been the parties which attempted to fulfil this state function. The varieties of anti-capitalism in the Christian Democrats, Socialist Party and the PCI, while helping to maintain a distance between policy-formation and productive system, encouraged the notion that the state was the organizer of social capital. Sub-state capitalism, alongside more typical forms of state capitalism, has developed without criteria of economic viability or social utility. The lack of a rational unilinear conception of the purpose of economic development is not unusual, but it was distinctive in a country effectively under one party government for a generation. This is one reason why the Left argues that the Christian Democrats never conquered the state, but preferred to use it as a channel for public funds to a variety of projects which satisfied neither the laws of the market nor those of social need. Thus, from the PCI's standpoint, the immediate principle behind Italian 'state' capitalism was party principle, the principle of Christian Democratic oligarchs.

In every advanced capitalist society, of course, development was both 'personalized' and based on party concerns, to a greater or lesser extent. The difference between Italy and other European countries would seem to be one of degree, and of tendentially sharp conflict between the monetary conservatives (the Bank of Italy), entrepreneurs and the dispensers of patronage. Such a regime has reinforced the image of Italy as backward and patronage-ridden. In other words, rather than seeing Italian state capitalism as a local variant of a general development, the local specificity obscures the lines of general development. Therefore the harder problem of establishing criteria of efficiency in a society in crisis - or transition - are secondary to the problems of personalized patronage and a parasitic (i.e., a welfare) public service. The 'modern' solution thus seems to lie in replacing a corrupt elite by technical-rational principles of expanding the productive base.

However, the traditionalists also have their theorists. Mosca's theory that every organized society implies, or presupposes, the existence of a ruling minority rests on a more interesting assumption: that of the certainty that substantial changes in society are impossible. Like capitalism for Catholicism, for the liberal-conservative Mosca fascism was a 'necessary evil'. (4) It was, in short, a demonstration of the limits and assertion of the natural order. Pareto too rooted social articulation in individual psychology, rather than in history or social laws, thereby confusing the logico-experimental and the historico-comparative methods. The struggle for life itself produced hierarchy as a natural phenomenon. In his own political attitudes, Pareto was reconciled to Italy only through nationalism (i.e., through fascism); that is, not by what fascism was, but by what Italy was. In the cases of Mosca and Pareto, the fatalism of the identification of nature with social tradition is paralleled in life by the acceptance of social irrationality as the natural condition for social cohesion.

To Pareto, elitism is a psychological condition as much as a sociological one (for Mosca too, the elite is composed of the clever, courageous and able). In Pareto's case, fatalism formed part of a rationalization for a lack of political involvement: in 1903 he wrote 'the first freedom is that of enjoying one's own possessions in peace.' (5) This private pleasure is vulnerable to the kinds of disturbance which fascism appeared to remove - resentment, marginality and impotence, pessimism, and a feeling for the precariousness of order. In short, fascism is the answer to insecure individualism, to the need for political participation, demanding no direct involvement. Politics is always dangerous territory where only foxes, lions and wolves feel at home.

Michels concentrates on a more 'modern' structure than Pareto - the mass party. His message, however, is equally fatalistic. Though parties become hierarchical, they alone are the products of mobilization. Certainly, there is a contradiction between the party - as opposed to the movement - form and the promise of Rousseauan democracy. However, Michels brings to organization (rather than elite) theory the assumptions of an anarcho-syndicalist. His message implies that parties reinforce only the qualitative difference between the mass and the minority: thus there seems no advantage for the mass to belong to the parties, or to mobilize at the outset.

Another current of elitism accepts the idea of the parties as qualitatively superior leaders, but regards this as their advantage. Gobetti, for instance, believed the PCI to be useful because it was a minority party which offered guidance and discipline to the proletariat. Where fascism rejected seriousness, personal sacrifice and autonomy, the PCI fulfilled the important ethical role of the politician - that of disinterested activity. (6) This view also lacks Gramsci's historical perspectives, as does Banfield's attack on traditional, or backward, society.

Banfield saw the cause (rather than the agent) of poverty and backwardness as the incapacity to act together for the common good, or indeed to give ethical significance to anything outside the interests of the nuclear family. His critics correctly argued that this was effect, not cause, and that the real cause of poverty was the general subjection of the peasants. They substantially agreed, however, that the attitude of 'there is nothing to be done' is objectively justified. In short, a 'traditional' response to traditional neglect and repression throws people back on primary supportive structures, (7) and even frustrates the emergence of corporate ideology.

The point is not that Italy is uniquely clientelistic, but rather that there has been an influential intellectual current which argues that these 'pre-modern' attitudes are natural and/or inevitable. The struggle against the traditional, the irrational and the backward produces strange political alliances. Traditionality, after all, is a commonplace of the political class. Mosca's interest, for instance, was to identify the 'constant psychological tendencies which determine the action of the masses'. (8) Social evolution was 'basically an organic process, and though more complicated, similar to that taking place in all animal and vegetable nature.' (9) The political class is both accomplished and inert: its function and aim is solely the exercise of political power. It 'fulfills all political functions, monopolizes power and enjoys the advantages connected with it; whilst the second, more numerous, [class] is led and controlled by the first, more or less legally, or more or less arbitrarily and violently.' (10) The political class is maintained 'by traditions and customs of the environment'. (11) Replacing itself by molecular modifications, the political class attains the summit of conservative power by the exploitation of 'habit, by which many consign themselves to remaining lowly'. (12) This describes the behaviour and psychology of the pre-modern, pre-industrial politician, whose absolutism is limited by the weakness of the structures he works within. It describes the pursuit of politics as an end in itself, as the terrain for dominance and recognition of the 'superior qualities', not ideologies, or performance. In a society in which a 'modern' solution no longer seems an alternative, perhaps because 'democracy' becomes a much more complex and less satisfying concept when linked to the reality of representative and administrative power than when ideologically associated with justice and equality, the unitary political class, or at least a recomposed stratum of politicians 'administering the permanent crisis', becomes a possibility.

Faced with the 'mechanical and technical impossibility' of mass sovereignty, and also its cultural-psychological impossibility, (13) an elite of the working class develops. This is based on specialism, and on the incompetence of the masses. Then the 'intellectuals who have entered the party under the spur of idealism soon feel humiliated and disillusioned', (14) as the pursuit of power points to the fact that power is always conservative. The working-class party, based on authority and discipline, 'becomes a governmental party, that is to say, a party which, organized like a government on a small scale itself, hopes one day to assume the reins of government upon the large scale.' (15) It would be an exaggeration to say that, in a situation where the advanced sectors are in decline, austerity is increasingly the future of the subordinate classes and growth elements a regression to unregulated market economics, the institutional Left must necessarily finish up on Animal Farm. However, the defeat of traditionalism, and the need to expand the working class and democratic consciousness to accomplish this, in the past required both an image of the modern and a reality of economic growth. Now, though 'modern' absorption in the party-state or bureaucratic state is equivocal for the subaltern classes, it is much more so in a period of decline.

Pareto seems to be describing the present situation when he wrote: 'Whoever best understands the art of weakening the adversaries of corruption, to recover by fraud or trickery what it seemed to have given up to force, is the best of the rulers.' (16) A ruling class divided into idealists, the (honest) power-enjoyers, and (dishonest) money-seekers, the speculators 'who are pressured by the present and worry little about the future, sacrificing their defenders without the slightest scruple to their adversaries', is familiar enough. (17) Pareto's is a psychological account of resistance to modern thought (and indeed of the irrational basis of thought itself). 'Men let themselves be persuaded for the most part by sentiments (residues), and we can thus foretell, as is later confirmed by experience, that derivatives will draw strength not from logico-experimental considerations, or at least not exclusively from these, but rather from sentiments.' (18)

In his work there is a rough, street shrewdness which sounds incongruous in so ambitious an academic: Napoleon 'wasn't an idiot, nor a man of little account, as are so many millions'. (19) The aphorisms, flat though they are, condense myth and history in Machiavelli's fashion, but for a conservative purpose. Politically, he identifies the recurrent theme of corporatism: 'We now have, in different forms, a new feudality which, in part, reproduces the essence of the old.' (20) He was convinced that the source of humanitarianism, democracy or any altruism was hypocrisy: power might as well be naked. Contemporary society, in short, was not 'modern', logical and purposive society, not the society of ethical liberalism and moral socialism, but one of pagans, the beasts of the psyche - lion, fox, client, speculator. Logic was not a matter of self-evident truth, but self-interest, point of view. When it comes to finding someone who really wishes to give his possessions to others, the task is possible, but 'not easy'. Saint-Simon, for instance, enjoyed giving away his possessions because he was proud of being the Messiah of a new religion. (21)

Mosca, Michels and Pareto give a fine picture of the 'simple', intuitive, politician whose power and prestige distinguish him from the powerless 'semplici', his constituents. Not, of course, that these are psychologically or intellectually his inferiors: indeed, they understand and pursue non-logical interests as eagerly as the political class. What they lack is power (and here, knowledge is not power). There is no structure to give them power. If they try to take it, they will suffer, or, if successful, they recommence the cycle.

Now, these are not only attitudes to which the leaders of the PCI, for instance, counterposed modernity. They presuppose a consensus which legitimates, and the conditions and structures which perpetuate, them. Decline, immobilism or restoration strengthen this visceral, exploitative, traditionalism and the complicity-understanding-resignation, or simple resentment, with which it is perceived by the subordinate classes. Without the potential for changing the material conditions and the day-to-day consciousness of the subordinate classes, traditionalism in some form becomes the only prospect for their parties.

This conservatism is a commonplace in the sociology of (social) perception, but has attracted less comment in Marxist circles. Halbwachs, for example, said, 'social thought is essentially a memory, and all its content is made up only of collective recollections.' (22) Social image is constantly reconstructed, but, as common sense, is rooted in past experience, transmitted through concretely present social structures. Caramella, to whose work Gramsci referred, expressed the contrast between traditional and scientific (and utopian) thought, or between common sense and philosophy, as follows. (23)

> Common sense, on the other hand, appears both to theoretical reflection and to moral knowledge as their opposite, something these must criticize and dissolve to assert themselves. It manifests itself, in other words, in the form of a conglomerate of opinions, beliefs and customs, insurmountable for men in general and assimilated by their common minds, which the philosopher and the reformer propose to transcend and replace in the name of a regenerated, new mind. Thus it seems one cannot expound a speculative truth, or propose any practical principle without going first through this essential crisis and solution. In particular, since modern philosophy is mainly idealist and at all events is always post-critical, it maintains that its first task is the refutation of the anti-idealistic, or at any rate acritical, attitude on which common sense is normally rooted. Philosophy is presented as a critique of common sense, of ingenuous knowledge, or vulgar realism and utilitarianism. Yet, in that, it shows the desire to affirm that common sense is a mental form, certainly pre-critical and pre-philosophical, but in some way particular to human nature.

In due course the attack on idealism itself as 'critical' theory was joined by della Volpe, whose 'scientific' Marxism was to prove an embarrassment to the Hegelo-Marxists of the post-war PCI. Della Volpe argued that idealism in fact exalted practice (common sense as 'good sense'), and suppressed theory at a time of crisis. It isolated culture, describing it as a moment of lyrical purity. This exaltation and isolation represented a clear abdication of responsibility by those intellectuals who thus removed philosophy from crisis and idealized it as technique.

The link between the crisis of bourgeois customs which della Volpe considered to be revealed in the non-technical insights of Nietzsche, and the ability of intellectuals to transfer their critical activity and their personal allegiances to the objective of survival, had particular force in Italy during the war. (24) This is also a central theme in Gramsci, where the intellectuals form first the hinge which articulates the leaders and the led in the party, and later enter the state. There they act as the technical-political organizers both of the proletariat and of the traditional intellectuals who are converted to serve the new dominant class. But Gramsci remained philosophically an idealist, and his notion of scientific and economic development remained strictly at the level of technique. Americanism meant introducing new processes rather than new modes of thought: American workers had no culture, and so were vulnerable to unrestricted manipulation. The Italian workers, however, had 'culture' on their side, despite a crisis of the bourgeoisie reflected in the defection of its intellectuals.

The danger of this combination in the PCI of idealism and a view of modernity as technique is that it encourages the pragmatic absorption of 'science' into the all-embracing dialectic of reconciliation. (25) The notion of bureaucratic rationality as essentially neutral, or even as class technique, enters the strategy of the Party. There still remains the problem of the intellectual and political content of the composition of social images, and the method of overcoming traditional thought, which clearly includes not only common sense, but philosophy transformed into common sense: 'Reality is socially constructed ... and the sociology of knowledge must analyse the processes in which this occurs.' (26) Primarily, common sense, the 'realissimum', accepts the web of social relations. It embraces contradictions in social relations because they exist, until they become intolerable or until, by modification, they present themselves differently. In other words, the formation of social images (and the sociology of knowledge) tends to conservatism (co-existence of contradiction), or to pluralism (autonomous provinces of meaning). The thesis that intellectuals play a magician's role in presenting social images (which are indeed imagined) in order to gain followers or the advantage of being 'cosmically ordained designers' or experts refers to a small, active minority. These intellectuals are seen as at odds with reality and existing symbolic universes. Certainly, this critical and potentially crucial minority exists. Gramsci, however, is surely correct in postulating that at least the immediate future lay with the organic intellectual, the bureaucratized, technical intellectual.

The problem of creating a social image which is not utopian in the future, and conservative in the present, is a theoretical problem also because of the problem of theory-construction itself. Stark puts the problem thus: 'If and in so far, then, as a man entertains an idea or system of ideas in the psychological origin of which some selfish or sectional interest or desire has played a part and which would have been different if that interest or desire had not entered in, his thought is to be characterized as problematic, or, to use the technical term now universally applied for the description of such states of mind, ideological.' (27) Stark thus effectively conflates traditional and modern, experience and innovation, into ideology, and leaves the sociology of knowledge with a new subject matter, fact-determination. Stark did not resolve the problem that fact-determination is impossible in a human context, and (quoting Marx) the same as 'the abstraction of movement - mors immortalis' (28) - another variety of Berger and Luckmann's 'idea-ism'. The difficulty is twofold: to criticize a reality which, by existing, is 'traditional', and thus ideology ('that part of culture which is actively concerned with the establishment and defense of patterns of belief and value'), and to do so in the paradoxical terms of a modernity which exists really or potentially 'somewhere else', as becoming, not being (i.e., as theory of transition or sociology of knowledge).

It seems that the distinction between 'ideology'-commitment and 'science'-disinterestedness (29) does not hold when it comes to the production of a theory of transition. Since the take-off point for such a theory is existing social perception, traditional thought and behaviour, the contrast is still between the traditional and a modernity which is paradoxically both innovative and imitative, qualitative transcendance and rule-bound. Gurvitch confronted this problem by presenting a schema of traditional peasant thought as against (among others) that of the techno-bureaucrat. The peasants' cognitive class knowledge is ordered thus: perceptual knowledge of the external world, common sense, political knowledge, knowledge of the other and, finally, technical knowledge. The techno-bureaucrat had as his knowledge-hierarchy, technical, scientific and political knowledge, perceptual and, finally, philosophical knowledge. (30) These categories, as they stand, can exist in any society, though their hierarchies may be distributed differently. Our problem is that of accounting for a change not only in distribution but in the quality of knowledge - from a society characterized by 'normal' perceptual knowledge and common sense in preference to one which expresses modernity's experimental, or hypothetical, element (though modern thought is also 'normal' where it is realized).

The dynamism of the interaction between traditionalism and modernity here starts to fade. For modernity must either be imitation, or transposition, translation, or else it is a social image not formed from traditional perceptions, or indeed from classifications of types of knowledge. The notion of modernity which persists in Italian Marxist discussion is not the movement in consciousness Sartre described as the rising class becoming aware of itself. (31) Perhaps because of the historical distance between Italian intellectual consciousness, and the social repository of traditionalism which is basically the peasants and those classes concerned with their management, 'ideas' are generally seen by the institutional Left as moving uni-directionally from intellectuals. However, this same tradition has tended to see modern thought, in so far as this is associated with scientific and bureaucratic-administrative logic, as essentially technical. However, technical knowledge is immediately absorbable by traditional knowledge. The alternative is a condition such as Marx's 'reign of liberty' which begins outside that of labour imposed by necessity and external finality, and beyond material production. Otherwise, Gramsci's discussion of Americanism would be no more than an appeal, easily recognizable in its ambiguity, to expand the productive base.

If crisis involves automatic collapse without automatic socialism, then a strategy of transition is required to avoid this kind of collapse. If crisis can be modified into what may be called 'transitional equilibrium', a combination of modes of production susceptible to political determination and control, then a strategy of transition based on the significance of modernization is required. This needs analytical understanding and imaginative prevision. Farber says: 'As for dealing with "attitudes towards existence", and in particular one's own existence, that may be done in different ways: (a) with the "natural attitude", on the ground of the natural world and on the given cultural level; (b) with the attitude of "pure" or completely "critical" reflection, with "inner" description; or (c) with the balanced complete method of reflection, which makes use of (b) and all other procedures, including causal analysis.' (32) But such procedures 'leave everything as it was'. When we criticize the deficiencies of Gramsci's and Togliatti's notions of modernity in relation to transition, and to the contemporary eclipse of the concrete models of modernity, it should be clear that theirs was a project to be elaborated, not shelved. In the idealist tradition, reflection on the dominant social image could not make modernity radically and qualitatively diverse by explaining how the Marxist trick of squaring the circle (apparently) could be undertaken: that of avoiding reabsorption by the concrete (Schutz's 'growing older together'), (33) or reducing the modern to technique, for instance, stressing the technical development of the productive forces as against the logical inflexibility of the valuation process. Schutz indicates an approach to rethinking modernity when this no longer 'works' as a real and imaginative social magnet, in that of the '"epoche", the suspension of our belief in the reality of the world as a device to overcome the natural attitude by radicalizing the Cartesian method of philosophical doubt.' (34) However, to stop at this point merely means abstracting the observer. Schutz suggests logical fallacies in modernity-as-expectation, which also relate to our own problem: 'in common-sense thinking our knowledge of future events consists in subjective expectations that are founded in our experiences of past events as organized in our stock of knowledge at hand.' (35) Notwithstanding the problems of Tiresias, of knowledge of the future without the hypothesis of transition, there is nowhere for the leaders to lead the led, and clearly no reason for the led to legitimate leadership. There remains only the administration of things-as-they-are. Common sense is traditional individualism - the definition of reality in accordance with one's own perceptions and one's own share of the stock of collective knowledge. In this case, state-protected capitalism would seem indeed to be the natural state of man. If qualitative change has the material limits associated with 'the level of development of productive forces', it also faces the ineluctable limits both of cultural level and the logical and scientific limits of the 'if ... then ... method of forecasting (fantasizing) the future'. (36)

Gramsci's modernity was clearly an attempt to relate this fantasizing to concrete possibilities, but it thus lacked the element of political-imaginative transcendance. If that must logically be so, it involves revising the notion of Marxism as the movement changing the future, by removing the validity of any rational or goal-oriented status for that change. It makes Marxism utopian, fully accounted for in the conditions of the present, or an explanatory and integrating aspect of social knowledge. Utopia, in the first instance, has failed to break the bonds of existing society: in the second instance, Marxism successfully explains social conflictuality, but social reality is able to contain its levels.

The production of new social images, the emergence of new dominant levels of social interpretation and the recodification of social symbols is only implicit in Gramsci. A comparative failure to develop these aspects of 'modernity', and hence to deal with traditionalism as the ground of present and future and with the logical problem of 'knowledge of the future' was widespread in Italy. This is not unrelated to the rejection of sociology as 'modern thought', in Gramsci's critique of Bukharin's 'Sociology', and to Croce's description of sociology as the 'infirm science'. (37) Sociology was regarded with suspicion by Marxists, who generally preferred to discuss its ideological and political implications without studying the bases of its conservatism. Panzieri and 'Quaderni rossi', who saw that the Left was in danger of becoming subordinate through theoretical weakness and deficient in knowledge of concrete social conditions, were the exceptions. By the mid-1960s sociology was almost wholly institutionalized and academicized and, without American support, its condition rapidly became symbolic of the impoverishment and social disconnectedness of the mass university. It is widely misunderstood as being concerned with public punditry on social 'problems'.

The lack of faith in capitalist rationality is therefore only partially informed by a study of capitalist society. 'Americanization' of the economy, in Gramsci's terms, tends to be taken as given, although the reality is equivocal. The contrast between traditional and modern gives no guidance as to which modernity, and on what theoretical basis, is to be pursued. Traditional society ingests modernity-as-technique to ensure its own continuity and modification. The 'modern' Italy of the years of the economic miracle was created by traditionalists who failed to complete modernization in a society of conflictual, corporatist pluralism.

The PCI continues to see in the strength and centralization of state power the best guarantee for social order. The Christian Democrats represent the 'individualistic, barbaric, egoistical impulses' (38) of man (albeit expressed in corporatist forms), and the discipline of the state is required for a rationally ordered and determined society. The state not only provides the order necessary to harness human energies, but might save Italy from the consequences of Americanism in practice, the international division of labour and technology which places the country in a subordinate condition, one in which the strain of intensifying competition and insecurity threatens the whole of society. This competitiveness is related to a social development, not the exhaustion of the mode of reproduction of social relations. It not only makes the search for security essential for individual survival, but enforces further subordination through national indebtedness (continuing competition plus austerity) and technological dependency.

The experience of modernization in the 1950s and 1960s had been that of a limited Americanization, but one based on low-wage competitiveness. The state attempted to 'distribute subordinate functions'; that is, to undertake planned underdevelopment in the South, and allow the superstructure to grow when the productive base contracted. Only in the first two years of the Centre-Left did the influence of Dossetti's 'Cronache sociali', of the economist Pasquale Saraceno and the Christian Democratic Convegno of San Pellegrino, and the neocorporativism of the encyclical 'Mater et magister' suggest the possibility of state planning, especially to modify the North-South disequilibrium. (39)

Both Catholic corporativism, with its notion of 'social capital' which the state might administer in the name of the community, and neo-capitalism assumed that economic propulsion would continue to come from the 'private' capitalist sector. The state might provide it with an infrastructure for further expansion, and might irrigate the deserts it created. It was not the primary function of the state to concern itself with production, but rather to assist it as it occurred. Even the nationalization of electricity companies can be ascribed to this notion and not to any class rancour or commitment to public ownership, let alone control. For neo-capitalism, an alliance with social democracy depended on, and thus guaranteed, its own prosperity, and helped to pay its social costs. The capitalist sector based a precarious unity on the conviction that its prosperity and growth were social and political priorities. However, the association of reformism with modernization died in the recession of the 1960s and in the degeneration of the Centre-Left.

The disillusioning experience of reformism encouraged the PCI to persist in its notion of Togliattian modernization. In other words, not bourgeois reformism but class alliance would form the unit of propulsion for democratic modernization. Yet a Gramscian influence remained, stressing the need to oppose parasitism by modernity, in the bureaucratic organization of intellectuals in the enterprise-nation. Tronti's revision of Americanism painted a picture of America as a highly prosperous society with intense labour militancy. It was a picture of labour striking against capitalism with impunity, maintaining both its own prosperity and that of capital. Only ideological (cultural) backwardness accounted for labour still tolerating the bosses' authority. Gramsci's 'azienda-nazione' (enterprise-nation) and Tronti's 'free market militancy' represent two complementary aspects of 'modernization as Americanization'. (40) Togliatti, on the other hand, was concerned to ensure the maintenance of a liberal, rather than American, capitalism, kept in check by mass activity and class alliances with the middle strata. The current movement towards austerity and restraint represents a synthesis of these views in a modern, managed economy, where the political 'management' restrains the autonomy of both capital and labour. The real division in the 1960s, however, was between the Marxists and Catholics who regarded the economy under capitalist direction as essentially self-propelled, and those who saw in modernization a move towards a more state-propelled economy.

Masella has discussed some of these themes in the debate on historiography, which centred on the PCI's search to identify a healthy, modern capitalism. This concerns a re-examination of the 'failed agricultural revolution' in Italy and the development of a De Sanctis-Cattaneo-Labriola philosophy as an alternative to Anglo-Saxon monopoly and imperialism. In the late 1960s the PCI tended to the opinion that the key connection was that between Risorgimento and Resistance state. Fascism destroyed the liberal, Risorgimento state, and it was the Resistance which forged the crucial link of the masses with the state. Thus, in 1967-9, the anti-institutional students were faced by a party which, tendentially, believed in the affinity of Resistance with national, not class, struggle and the continuity of national history, rather than discontinuous and anti-institutional class struggles. (41)

Thus the strategy of modernization requires coexistence with a higher (if more malleable) form of capitalism, and even an active encouragement of it. To Tronti and to Gramsci, workers stood to gain more materially and politically from Americanization than from native 'assisted' capitalism. Once installed, neo-capitalism did not raise the problem of its control by the state: the state might subsidize it, or tax it, but was not responsible for its dynamics. These images of social development do not anticipate direct state intervention in the productive (i.e., manufacturing) base itself (as indeed 'austerity and restraint' do not). The movement to a continuist view of national history is crucial. It emphasized political continuity, the 'long periods' of crisis-stagnation, rather than the rapidity of creation and collapse of social groups since the Risorgimento. It also left open the question of the role of capitalism in modernity, and of the functional utility of fascism to capitalist protection, by stressing fascism's discontinuity as a political aberration.

As Christine Glucksmann pointed out, (42) Gramsci contrasted the healthy capitalism of liberal monopoly capital with the pathological growth of the fascist economy. She delicately alluded to a 'certain critical ambivalence' in his approach to Americanism, seemingly both healthy and acultural. This ambiguity is strange in an area so central to fascism's capacity to undertake the passive revolution. Yet, in fact, Americanism for Gramsci avoids the vexed question of reformism. (43) The choice of modernization strategy seems to be one of selecting an autonomous economic force. PCI experts can thus approach the problem of reformism free from certain conceptions: reformism seems separate from and foreign to advanced 'American' economies. The merging of the masses in the state (instead of extra-institutional class struggle) had also apparently lost its idealistic, fascistic, overtones. It was the completion of national history.

The shift in the PCI's predominantly anti-monopoly, anti-imperialist stand of the late 1950s and early 1960s is based partly on continuity with the older tradition. In part, too, it reflects a belief that the laws of functioning of the economy have been discovered, and that this has opened it to direct state intervention. These are marginalist, not Marxist, laws and the state is the Risorgimento-Resistance state of popular, not class, consensus. However, the 'spinta riformatrice' of the PCI started to lose impetus as soon as it became clear that there was to be no room for experimentation with economic controls. Two positions have since been developed: one, that the economy has ceased to be self-propulsive, and thus that the model of modernization through growth must be dropped in favour of austerity and rationalization in the public (i.e., the parasitic) sector. The second argues that there is new room for public intervention in the economy, enabling Italy to experience fully her industrial revolution. Both arguments, in fact, are still about the possibilities of achieving a particular type of modern state capitalist society.

Constructing national unity, with a uniform mode of production (both industrial and agricultural revolutions), involved for Gramsci the inclusion of the masses in the state, which the Risorgimento had left narrow and exclusive. His progressivism of technique and economy contrasted, however, with the need for a form of traditionalism in the political agents of the subordinate classes, who, in Magri's words, 'represent the most organic and mature expression of traditions, values, ways of thinking and moral outlook, widely diffused throughout society and operative within it'. (44) This superstructural conservatism is intended to filter acultural Americanism out of the modernization process. This attitude, that Italy can borrow capitalist technique while conserving its own working-class culture (in the minds of its intellectuals), has become a basic assumption for the Party.

The theme of the modern has been crucial in Italian social and political thought, and was one reason for Gobetti's belief that Gramsci was not a Marxist but a modernizer. Gramsci himself moved from a concern, in the 'Ordine nuovo' period, with the relation between technique and production to one in the 'Notebooks' where virtually everything, including politics, becomes technique. That is, all expert practices are combined in the state somewhere at a level below 'science'. The implications have been examined by Mario Telò, and by Luis Razeto Migliaro and Pasquale Misuraca. (45) Telò argues that the Factory Councils were seen by Gramsci as alternatives to the moribund representative state. However, (46) the worker

> is identified with production, is identified with the factory: the proletarian cannot live without working methodically and in an orderly manner. Division of labour has created the psychological unity of the working class, and created class solidarity in the world of labour. The more the proletarian becomes specialized in an occupation, the more he feels the indispensability of his comrades, feels himself to be the cell of an organized body ... feels the need for the whole world to be like a single, enormous factory, organized with the same precision, method, and order which he recognizes as vital in the factory where he works.

Passages of this kind in the 'Ordine nuovo' period led Gobetti to question the communism of the group, and account for Agnelli's overtures for collaboration. But Telò is correct in stressing that ideologically the group was not open to a 'capitalist takeover'. (47)

This is not the whole story. Telò argues that productivism and the notion of worker as producer is the basis of Gramsci's theory of socialism in the early period, and that 'Americanism' is the basis of reflection and modification of this theme in the 'Notebooks'. Here, combined with a critical reflection on the experience of the Factory Councils, there is an elaboration of the role of production in transition. Hegemony is based on the social critique made by the collective worker, not the destruction of the realm of necessity. The Councils here are not the substitute state, but the link between autonomy and the new hegemony. Technique is separated from the interests of the dominant class, and indeed becomes that of the subaltern classes. The search for the 'original' system of life is not a copy of the American. (48)

Gramsci is criticizing here the naive productivism of the 'Ordine nuovo' period, the Soviet importation of Fordian techniques. Production organized for the sake of consumption, for use value, not for its own sake (exchange value) makes a qualitative break with capitalist productivism. However, it is important to notice that this new formulation avoids the question of capitalist crisis. It avoids both crisis theory and the hypothesis of 'catastrophe'. Second, while it deals with a theme central to the Third International debate on the conditions and organization of labour, or the conversion of state capitalism to state socialism, it does so in abstraction from the international setting. How was the Italian economy to produce for use as a part of the international capitalist system based on exchange? More significantly, the transformation of the concept and function of the Council is not here addressed to the question of the relation between technique, 'factory-ization' and modernization. The Council becomes an intermediate, articulating level in the elaboration of a theory of hegemony and transition. (49)

Gramsci in prison avoids naive productivism: but clearly productivism is the condition for modernizing the economy and producing the collective worker. The earlier image of society as factory is replaced by the expansion of technique and specialization to include not merely productive, but administrative and political, functions. He discusses administration as essentially different from what was normally referred to in the Third International as synonymous with bureaucratic degeneration. Thus, the 'state is the complex of practical and theoretical activities with which the ruling class justifies and maintains not only its dominance but manages to secure the active consensus of the governed'. (50) In this sense, the state is the directing activity of society (in this case, concerned also to reproduce the division between ruling class and ruled classes). Yet the distinction between ruling and ruled remains, for politics, a 'primordial, irreducible fact (in certain general conditions)'. (51)

Gramsci says this is not merely a technical question, but raises the basic question of a bureaucracy formed to destroy this relation. (52) His answer calls for the diffusion and generalization of technique. At first, the overlapping of the bureaucracy as a separate body with intellectuals who see themselves as independent, separate, is maintained by the recruitment of traditional intellectuals to the bureaucracy. However, the qualities of the modern bureaucrat and the 'organic' intellectual coincide. The organic intellectual becomes the new political-administrator. The party, and the party leader, is the basis of the 'state spirit'. The parties and the intellectuals 'enter the state'. (53) Thus, bureaucracy as dominance and separateness from civil society is transcended by the technique of the intellectual-administrator. Traditionalism (individualism and corporativism) is eroded by the parties, which elaborate universal-national perspectives prior to entering the state.

This constitutes a pre-vision of how the 'organic crisis' of the bourgeoisie may be resolved. Organic crisis is represented in the tension and disequilibrium between representative institutions (including the parties themselves) and the bureaucracy. This is the internal conflict between the bourgeoisie as dominant class and its role as organizer of class representation, of socially diverse and conflicting elements. Three replies to this crisis lead to the predominance of the bureaucracy: Stalinism, fascism, and Americanism. (54) The crisis is not resolved by these. On the other hand, Gramsci notes that in 'modern societies' of the democratic-bureaucratic kind intellectuals in large numbers are becoming the techno-bureaucrats, linked with the spread of industrialization. Now, clearly, Gramsci is alive to the dangers of industrial development plus techno-intellectual bureaucracy in 'modern society', as in the USA, the USSR and Italy. His speculation concerns the possibility of creating a new, non-parliamentary state. The logic of Gramsci's argument is equivocal regarding the universal characteristics of this modern state, and how far this resolution of organic crisis is 'socialist', rather than a process of modernization (industrialization plus the diffusion of technical competences), of organic intellectuals entering the state and of parties entering the state. This 'modern society' is not 'socialist' society, but all societies based on industrialization and a relationship of governed-governors. What Gramsci hopes for is for an administrative technique which destroys the latter relation. That must remain speculative, though, since his historical-analytic method leads him to explain the apparent ideological and social diversity of 'modern society' as universally confronting the same problematic. The political necessity of bureaucracy is at once the limit and the precondition of modernity. To avoid the separation of party-state (bureaucracy), the Gramscian party must end the distinction between state politics (of consensus-coercion) and civil society politics (class organization-ideological universalization). Yet the organic intellectuals, by leading the parties, must enter the state as its technicians.

Then the characteristic governed-governing relation may cease to reproduce itself. Italy, in Gramsci's view, must move towards socialism via this equivocal modernity, by way of 'modern society'. 'Italy is the country which, in the conditions created by the Risorgimento and its mode of development, has the greatest weight of parasitism, of people who live without taking any part in productive life: it is the country with the largest proportion of small and middle rural and urban bourgeois who consume a large part of the national income and leave a portion insufficient for national necessities.' (55) The conflict between those who see Marxism as a strategy for development based on equitable reward and those who see it as the means of liberation from the constraining necessity of division of labour and mechanical production has become profound. Gramsci still tried to keep both perspectives active, though his chief interest lay in the process of diffusion of technique and discipline as principles of production, transposed to the state and administration. For him, the process of modernization was concrete: the transformation of the modern into the post-modern and democratic is both less clear and less certain.

Gramsci, of course, also spoke of 'modernism' in the ecclesiastical sense, as a movement capable, for instance, of reconciling the Church with the popular masses, 'hence favourable to reformist socialism and democracy ... or generically to liberal currents.' (56) However, modernity, 'modern society', related primarily to the USA. Though beset by social and economic crises, Americanism and Fordism derive from the need to 'add to the organization of a planned economy ... links of the chain which can follow the movement from the old economic individualism to the planned economy'. (57) It is not opposed by the workers but by the backward, the marginal, forces. This is because the USA has a demographically rational structure. But traditional European society was marked by 'the existence of similar classes, created by the "richness" and "complexity" of past history which has left a heap of passive sedimentations through the phenomenon of the saturation and fossilization of the state employees and the intellectuals, of the clergy and landed property, of extortionate trade and the army, first professional then conscript, but always professional for the officers.' (58) Where Italy has vitality, it is unproductive: unemployment and parasitism contrast with the demographic balance and the lack of historical and cultural traditions in the

USA. Gramsci's America is itself a 'social image', not a reality. He believed, for instance, that 'hegemony begins from the factory and for its exercise has need only of a minimum of professional intermediaries in politics and ideology.' (59) Nor is his criticism of 'Ordine nuovo''s 'Americanism' convincing, for it takes as its target not the demographic and industrial aspects of 'modern' society, but rather the caricatured 'trained gorilla' of Taylorism. (60)

To Gramsci, industrialization meant the difference between cheap and dear, the satisfaction of basic needs or the reverse. Industrialism at first is Puritanical and represses animal, primitive instincts. However, the repression of psychico-physical aspects of labour, of imagination and fantasy, is seen as related to the distorting influence of Taylorism. Despite its attack on sex, alcohol and culture, Americanism does mean high wages, cheap goods and high consumption. (61) To Gramsci, the basic form of post-war crisis is productive backwardness, especially as shown by 'the disequilibrium between progressive industry (in which constant capital has been increasing) and stagnating industry (where immediate labour-power is important)'. (62) Taylorism, in fact, provides Gramsci with a theory of the crisis which is closer to the 'disproportion' thesis than the classical 'falling rate of profit' one. Taylorism evades the law of falling profits (rising costs) by introducing falling costs. The crisis concludes when the supply of material runs out, when the supply of automatic machines ends or when world industry is saturated. (63) The movement from Book 1 of 'Capital' to Book 3 is seen as an explanation of technical innovation as the only way to avoid falling profits: innovation 'determines a contradictory process of development, one of whose aspects is the tendential fall'. (64)

This is not properly an equilibrium theory: crisis can end in explosion or in passive revolution. However, Italy's parasitism is not 'modern': it is based partly on exploitation of 'mezzadri', partly on parasitism on state revenues. Europe needs the advantages of Fordism but, by 'maintaining its army of parasites' which devour surplus value, raises costs and destroys competitiveness. (65) Thus, to Gramsci, since all economic laws are tendential, capitalism may reach its Pillars of Hercules when indeed the world is unevenly, but capitalistically, developed. Then 'the economic contradiction becomes a political contradiction and is resolved in an overturning of praxis.' (66) 'Modern society' in its American form is thus characterized by the possibly long process of erasing traditionalism, expanding production for use, and recomposing a degenerate 'demographic' structure. In this process, how is passive revolution to be avoided, especially as certain aspects of modernity (entry into the state) are so ambiguous? A clue is given in his comments on Weber, where he criticized the quality of the political class, and a bureaucracy which by default 'became a real political party, the worst of them all, because the bureaucratic hierarchy replaced the intellectual and political one: the bureaucracy indeed became the state-Bonapartist party.' (67) Much depends, that is, on the political-intellectual elite: if new intellectuals 'present themselves as a direct continuation of the preceding intelligentsia ... *[they]* are a conservative and fossilized re-creation of the historically transcended social group.' (68)

The problem of innovation is clear in his remarks not only on Michels, noted here, but on Guicciardini, the model 'moderate Italian'. (69) Certainly, this is Guicciardini according to De Sanctis, seen in relation to Gobetti's political scepticism which holds 'traditional forces' as 'impossible to develop and reorganize'. Gramsci's pessimism, of course, is 'of the intelligence', not a diplomat's conservative resignation like Guicciardini's. (70) Yet what distinguishes the traditional 'moderate' from the modern intrigues Gramsci. For example, it would be interesting to study 'the technique of common sense, the philosophy of the man in the street, and the technique of the most developed modern thought', (71) thought which, as science, is not class bound but has 'its own place'.

Aware that progress is an ideology, he qualifies this by saying that true progress involves the rational domination of nature. (72) All the same, (73)

> the official 'bearers' of progress have become incapable of this domination, because they have aroused destructive, contemporary forces much more dangerous and anguishing than those of the past ... like 'crises', unemployment, etc. The crisis of the idea of progress, consequently, is not a crisis of the idea itself, but a crisis of the carriers of the idea, who have become the 'nature' to be dominated itself. Attacks on the idea of progress in this situation are very biased and tendentious.

One cannot be optimistic or pessimistic regarding history: one can only be active. How then does one determine what is to be conserved from the past? Gramsci says the test of rationality is historical conditions: yet he also says, 'if technical progress permits a greater profit margin, this will not be distributed rationally, but always "irrationally" to shareholders and businessmen'. (74) Yet, in fact, this is historically rational. The relation of reason to historical development is his 'open question'. A possible key is the 'problem of political leadership in the formation of the nation and the modern state in Italy'. (75) This is especially linked to the formation of an 'urban' bloc of Northern workers and industrialists, interested in protectionism, as opposed to the semi-colonial Southern market. Indeed, the South's 'active element' became the 'instrument of Northern policy', rather than an explosive force as in popular mythology. This active element was threatened by the function of bureaucracy in a context of 'social passivity'. (76) '"Productive" unemployment determines "inflation" of services (multiplication of small business)'. (77) In short, the bureaucracy is a reflection of the passive element, as against the productive Northern component, which, being active, approaches more nearly the normal human condition. Bureaucracies are the general staffs of the (traditional) parties, and risk destroying the parties themselves by their conservatism. (78)

This process of subjective recovery, of the need for vigorous, rational and decisive action, is constantly referred by Gramsci to technique in the productive forces. As regards Taylorism, for instance,

> When the process of adaptation has taken place, one finds in reality that the worker's brain, instead of mummifying, has achieved a state of complete freedom. Only the physical motion has been completely mechanized; the memory of the trade, reduced to simple movements repeated at an intense pace, is absorbed into the muscular and nervous layers which have left the brain free and unencumbered for other occupations.

Working, that is, becomes akin to walking. (79)

More advanced technology may be profitable for capital, and will allow higher wages to be paid: primitive technology and cheap labour, that is, is not good business for capital. However, this too may produce industries too advanced for internal consumption, and too costly for internal accumulation. (80) The answer is not simply the importation of high technology industry but of the intellectual as professional, with his specialized machines and 'Taylor system'. Intellectuals have the capacity to secure consensus. Indeed, they are even overproduced for this purpose, and, by mass production and standardization, are connected with the need to organize professionally 'defence, unemployment, scholastic superproduction and emigration'. (81) The intellectuals, that is, perform subaltern functions for the political crisis of the dominant class - unlike the factory technician who has no political function for 'their instrumental masses'. (82) The parties provide intellectuals on a smaller scale than the state, making them political intellectuals, qualified leaders, organizers. (83) Gramsci, in short, is arguing that a combination of neutral technicians in production with political intellectuals, first in the party, then in the state, can make the new political class a political class more capable of leading a modern state.

The old political leader, trained in juridico-formal activities, would be replaced by leaders with a minimum of technical culture, able to choose between different technical solutions. (84) Political technique is already suffusing the bureaucracy. The technical-political intellectual still lacks a frame of reference without the party. As we have seen, party spirit is the basis of state spirit. It is also modern, contrasted with individualism, which is 'an animal element, "admired by foreigners", like the activities of the inhabitants of a zoo.' (85)

The crisis itself has 'technical' origins, 'in respective class relations', and not in conjunctural factors such as legislation. (86) Thus we see that Gramsci first contrasts production with bureaucracy, but then brings together the technique of production, the political-intellectual in the party, the political-technical-bureaucratic intellectual in the state and the resolution of the crisis of the ruling class itself. Subjective regeneration has at this point relative autonomy from the quantitative level of economic crisis and development. The question of power has been posed. 'It is true that there is a problem of "bureaucratization", but all continuity presents this danger which must be watched. The danger of discontinuity, and improvisation, is still graver.' (87) Thus Gramsci conceives of the emergence of a new political leadership by way of the modernizing conditions produced by technical development. In the nature of things, it is impossible to 'resolve' the question of what happens when the party of the working class enters the state and bureaucracy. It is significant that Gramsci places little weight on reformism in this context. Indeed, Gramsci's concern is with the spontaneous production of a new technical intelligentsia and the prospects for party-political training of a new political class. Stress is placed less on class alliance, which is imperative where the dominance of an expanding mode of production has not been established, than on consensus and efficiency.

On the other hand, Togliatti insisted on the need for political mass action as a means of self-protection and show of influence. Where Gramsci saw society becoming more homogeneous because of the development of productive forces, Togliatti's idea of modernization was political, that of mass mobilization in a party-movement. After 1956, he recognized that 'modern democracy' was more complex than simply organization of the masses, more open, sophisticated and, once established, a relatively stable phenomenon. Thus, Chiaromonte writes: (88)

> however, it seems to me that one cannot speak of a 'transitional phase' as discussed in the Marxist and Leninist literature before victory in the anti-fascist war. One can and should rather speak of the opening of a new period in which, much more so than before, it would be impossible to separate democratic and socialist successes, and of the tracing of a perspective in which such separation will become increasingly difficult and ultimately impossible. Clearly we are dealing with the prospect of a type of socialist society based on the widest extension of democracy (from that point of view it seems to me doubtful, for a variety of reasons, that one can still use, as it seems to me Vacca does, the expression 'transitional phase towards the victory of the proletariat').

Togliatti had developed the idea of the new, mass party in terms of an anti-fascism which would lay the basis not only for a self-government of producers but was itself a 'long-term historical process, which is the form of the Italian road to socialism'. (89) Again, structural reforms were important, but the main aim was to establish a 'long-term dualism of powers and an irreversible and growing mass protagonism'. (90) This could be accomplished without smashing the 'machine' of the bourgeois state, if the relation between economics and politics were inverted, and the producers 'politically recomposed' for greater autonomy. Dictatorship of the proletariat was not a principle but a question of experience. (91)

The lessening of emphasis on economics and the future of the productive forces was evident early. Togliatti wrote to Terracini in 1932 that though the present crisis should be seen as one of decline, there was always a way out for capitalism. This 'way out' was the object of the political struggle of the proletariat. (92) He thus saw alliance with interested elements of the bourgeoisie as a political objective divorced from any question of the rising or falling crisis of capitalism. He also discussed the state in more mechanical terms than Gramsci's view of it as a series of activities, or organized class relations, and instead saw it as a terrain to be occupied by the parties, in the name of different class interests.

This diminishes the role of masses and intellectuals to that of the participants in a supreme party plan. Indeed, Bocca's discussion of Togliatti's attitude to culture enforces the conclusion that Togliatti's world, and his world view, were Party-centred. (93) His concern was to construct the largest and most disciplined Party possible - to delay awkward discussions, to be frank in defeat, conciliatory in uncertainty and firm when the authority of the Party could be effective. Though there is in Togliatti a notion of social image, and of the modern, this is less strong than practical and tactical considerations. Lacking Gramsci's sense of the equivocal and the paradoxical, he relied on the cautious advance and solutions proposed by a party leadership he knew well and had largely selected himself.

In the middle 1930s he criticized the Bordigan formula that fascism had grown because of the backwardness of Italian capitalism. He pointed instead to its links with the most advanced structures of Italian capitalism. Fascism by 1935 had passed into a bureaucratic phase, its original political support having been ruined economically (the small and middle rural bourgeoisie of Emilia, for instance). (94) In 1944 he stressed the politically reactionary character of fascism, and its exclusion of the people as a whole from politics. (95) Generally, as Jon Halliday has implied, (96) he felt there was little to be gained by discussing abstractly which structural reforms were anti-capitalist, and which were modernizing in capitalist interests. Socialist structural reforms must assist some section of the capitalist economy, and in that way become non-socialist. In 1946 Togliatti wrote: 'It seems clear, therefore, that we are not proposing a reconstruction of our economy on communist or socialist principles. For such a transformation the country as a whole is not yet ready, even though some specific sectors are ready, and even though we all know that throughout Europe, almost without exception, economic development is in the direction of socialism.' (97)

Togliatti came to give to political intervention the task of modernization Gramsci assigned to economics, save that for Togliatti economic development was a spontaneous, inefficient, process. (98)

> There are on the one hand areas of substantial development and growth, not always independent of state aid and customs protection, which is a burden for the whole country. Alongside these there are areas of failed development and of decline ... Economic development has taken the direction of giving monopolistic structures prevalence, both in town and country, and the preva-

> lence of these structures has created contradictions of a new kind, caused growing disequilibrium; it has not led the country to harmonious development of its resources and potential, and has not allowed it to move towards solution of the basic problems, which are those of the labour and well-being of the citizens, the historical imbalance between North and South, and so on. There is therefore no need to ignore the progress which has taken place, but at the same time it would be wrong to ignore the backwardness of whole regions which continues to be the most serious characteristic of the country.

The problem is put beyond economics, leaving the stage free for the party leadership to pursue a political strategy. If neither the more advanced nor the backward sectors of capitalism and state capitalism carry implications for socialist interests, they remain essential but problematic questions. In 1964 Togliatti seems to ask: how can we know what a 'socialist structural reform' would be, were it to become the order of the day, especially when it is virtually impossible to analyse a 'capitalist structural reform'? The same uncertainty is to be seen in the 1964 rejection of wages policy: for the associated question of the relation of wages policy to planning is left untouched. (99) What we see, in short, is the decline of the Gramscian vision of modernity, and of modernity as transition. In the 1970s this concern was replaced in the PCI, after disillusion with economic planning, by an emphasis on growth, and criticism of the cultural degeneration of 'Americanism'.

Togliatti placed emphasis on the Party as the arena for selecting technical-political intellectuals, but few advanced into the state, or into party leadership. Only in the 1970s did the technical-political intellectuals begin to move from party to state, and thence to have a direct influence on production. By this time, though, the discussion of the relation between modernity and advanced capitalism is moribund. It is, for the PCI, either too 'ideological', or, as we have seen, simply unanswerable.

To speak of the 'backwardness' of the economy and the 'advanced state' of political consciousness is to say that Togliatti's choice of the primacy of politics was crucial, but does not present a convincing social image of transformation. We have seen the difficulty of fitting 'reformism' into the discussion of 'modern versus tradition', or politics over economics. When the signs of decline seem unequivocal, modern democracy too is problematic. Even without decline, would not 'further development of the productive forces' against 'ancient privileges no longer compatible with the spirit of a particular epoch' tend also to create new privileges? (100)

The debate on modernity and economy of scale was central to the Third International. Gramsci and Togliatti both interpreted 'modernization' as a cultural and political problem, concerning social relations as well as productive techniques. It was the Socialist Party, however, together with such influences as the 'Comunità' group of Olivetti and the publishing house of Il Mulino, which tried to encourage the importation of 'American' techniques and reformism, based on alliances between social scientists, factory technicians, technocrats, neo-capitalism and the Socialist Party.

The PCI thereafter insisted that only firmer political initiative could avoid the compromises and fiasco of the Centre-Left. (101) Modernization was not reformism plus techniques, but the 'technique of hegemony'. As Cerroni has put it: Marx 'did not give us a theory of transition from capitalism to socialism, though, as can be easily understood, it was already not only of scientific importance but indeed political urgency. We may suppose that Marx's own political interest was centred on the arousal and diffusion of the critique of capitalism both in the form of theoretical analysis and in that of practical struggle, in the certainty that, as it were, the law of the object, the objective contradictoriness of capitalism, would provide and clarify the object of the law of transition.' (102)

In Cerroni's account of Gramsci, two elements of modernization were seen as missing from Italian society: a national bourgeoisie and modern cosmopolitanism in the popular masses. This double absence would help to explain the areas of space available for the parties of the subordinate class, the exceptional, 'anomalous', feature of Italian politics. The problem remains, however, that modernization by interclass alliance is ambiguous, contradictory and precarious, while modernization by the subordinate classes, the repositories of traditionalism, is like squaring the circle.

Discussion of the institutional form of transition when capitalism is too weak, and traditionalism too strong, to allow modernization often evades the question of bureaucracy not as structure but as the formalization of legal power. As Weber said, 'The whole process of development of the modern state ... is identified with the history of modern functionaries and the bureaucratic enterprise, as the whole development of modern capitalism is identified with the growing bureacratization of the economic enterprise. Participation by bureaucratic forms of power is increasing everywhere.' (103) Democratization is an area 'particularly favourable for phenomena of bureaucratization'. (104) Indeed, like Gramsci, Weber speaks of the modern state being 'like a factory', an enterprise. (105) Gramsci's conclusions suggest that 'what is euphemistically called "socialism of the future" is really universal bureaucracy', and in this he remains close to Weber. (106) For Weber, like Gramsci, argued that the parties were in movement towards bureaucratization, towards the state. The only alternative for Weber was to select a democracy based on non-charismatic leaders, that is on professional politicians who would not be 'chiefs'. (107)

Gramsci may have sensed that, to modernize Italy, the rational-technical behaviour required would be that of Weberian bureaucracy, learnt both in the party and the factory. This is paradoxical, being based on the administration of backwardness. The Italian Left, with a strong ideological disinclination to identify socialism with bureaucracy, was caught at the threshold of modernization, its confident talk of alternative political solutions negated by the impossibility of reconciling productivism, bureaucracy and 'mass' democracy. In addition, Gramsci's modern (bureaucratic) state, and Togliatti's modern (mass) democracy implied contrasting images of modernity which in practice could be destroyed by corporatist, traditional-sist, bureaucracy because of the continuing weakness of the capitalist mode of production, even after the economic 'miracle'.

Part two

Chapter 3

THE ITALIAN CRISIS: change or transition?

One school would suggest that the concept of 'crisis' belongs to cultural history, as a sense of inadequacy, futility, defeat or threat. It argues: the state is a complex of activities, institutions, 'separate bodies', of practices and ideology which cannot be 'smashed' or collapse as though it were a single machine or organ. The Italian state appears to be in perpetual crisis because it is really three states thrown down one on top of each other - a paleo-liberal state, the fascist state, and the mass democratic, anti-fascist state. None, however, is a developed bureaucratic-rational state. In the economy, neither rapid growth, slow decline nor headlong decline stimulated an effective economic plan. They encouraged ad hoc, corporate reactions. If economic reform follows only political reform, it will have long to wait. For the political system is caught permanently between two incompatible principles, mass democracy and bureaucratic rationality in the interests of economic-political elites.

The authoritarian prefectorial system gave way to the transfer of responsibility to an impoverished and overburdened communal government, and thence again to impoverished and ill-prepared regional governments. The argument runs that it is clear that corporate institutional and ideological solutions are preferred to inefficient authoritarianism, chaotic and utopian mass democracy or administrative rationality. The problem of Italy, particularistic corporatism, is really the solution to its attempt to pursue universalistic economic and political goals. Capitalism is in decline, not towards socialism, but towards a barbarous competition between the precarious haves and the dispossessed. Not collapse but corporatism is the Italian destiny. Institutions are concerned to maintain their places in the hierarchy of collective 'clientela' and 'parentela'; they are not organized, or to be judged, in terms of systemic performance. The parties will always tend to de-ideologize themselves, as a prerequisite for obtaining and retaining power.

Parties are ultimately concerned with power, status and hierarchy - not performance. Power in the political sphere does not necessarily mean power over the aggregate society, whose divisions and needs are remarkably impervious to political intervention. Society is undergoing a combined movement of slowing modernization and regression. It is impossible to return to old values, and the new ones do not 'fit' the material possibility of achieving expectations. True, this argument continues, there is a crisis, a climacteric, in the economic system. However, the Christian Democrats are probably correct in their assumption that other countries will continue to help Italy. The country has insufficient power to reverse international influences: a strategy of survival and improvisation is better than wasteful crisis planning.

Italy now faces problems associated with a developing society, but from the standpoint of a partially and rapidly developed one. Hence the strains are more sharply experienced, and scepticism regarding modernization is pronounced. Old structures disintegrate, the new ones are adapted neither to growth nor to decline. Italy, in short, prefigures the decline of capitalism, but not its collapse; it is a corporate society which resists socialization, and still more the achievement of higher ideological, socialist objectives.

What follows is an attempt to consider some of the structural and conjunctural phenomena typical of the social, economic and political 'crises', and to measure them against the above 'cultural' explanation of the 'Italian case', conceived of as sui generis. Finally, the argument for the 'autonomy of the political' is examined in terms both of the extent of transformation of institutions so far undertaken, and of the development of the modern democratic (representative)-authoritarian state.

Donolo considers the above case, and argues persuasively for the cautious polarity of 'change or transition'. (1) It is plausible to suggest that the period 1968-76 was that of the digestion of the 1968 experience. 1968 showed that conventional politics were not the only means of effecting social transformation. However, this period also saw the gradual absorption of the new Left into the historical Left or into traditional political (party) experience. In the elections of 1976 the state and political power seemed again at stake. What had not been learned was a means whereby the primacy of the political leads to action, instead of the immobility of the (permanent) crisis. (2) Change is 'the social and institutional aspect of capitalist accumulation' which in Italy produces strong elements of socialization and leaves spaces for political control. Transition is the process of development outside the capitalist economic formation. The Leninist and revolutionary paths no longer apply, as the development of new social forces lead to new political forms. (3) Donolo is also correct in his suggestion that, while transition remains a possibility, the most likely choice is between 'workers' reformism', in its union or PCI versions, or capitalist reformism (i.e., modernization schemes and technocracy). Compromises on the first position should be made only on the basis of full recognition of the representative legitimacy of the PCI. (4)

However, some qualifications must be made. First, the new Left is not only involved in a practice of gradual transition. There has also been considerable activity of psychological preparation for a post-bourgeois phase, much of it within Leninist and insurrectionary terms. The insurrection of the tertiary, and the social margin - the industrial reserve not absorbable into production, and hence not a competitive threat to organized labour - reflects an antagonistic relationship expressing the non-reproducibility of production relations, through the collapse either of material production or of authority. Unemployment, underemployment or non-employment manifest both the 'command' power of employers and the organic weakness of their system of production, their continuing dominance of the mode of production, but also pathological symptoms of social disintegration. Second, 'workers' reformism' sidesteps the considerable problem of the role of state institutions, and the present ineffectiveness of that role, in any reformism. Recognition of the PCI's legitimacy could be meaningful only within the state, and to justify its claim the Party would need to strengthen the state institutions considerably. Yet if such recognition depends on a compromise, is the compromise not inevitably on the essence of the reformism and the objectives of the PCI's experts? What will strengthening the state on the basis of compromise accomplish for the socially marginal? The problem for institutional politics would seem that of securing the consensus of the employed workers for any scheme of restructuring. But we are speaking of structural, organic, crisis, a journey into the dark where the institutions and alliances put together for the purpose may neither hold, nor be effective.

Any proposal would certainly build on existing extended corporatism, legitimated by the association of public and private institutions. Restructuring is thus likely to be a process accentuating uneven development still further. Fragmentation is a sign both of cellular strength and of resistance to external forces. The cells are small and divided enough to be manipulated by the centre, but also strong enough to sustain sub-cultures.

So long as the PCI represents an institutional, social alternative, the appearance of change and choice persists, even though it does not, of course, fully represent the socially critical or marginal elements. As Donolo points out, there is an emblematic use of general social categories - the young, women, the unemployed - when really one is referring to parts (usually the educated) of social categories who are 'marginal' in different senses and for different periods. (5) By definition, they have no 'organized and institutionalized consensus'. Thus we have a situation where the Christian Democrats seek to secure consensus of the workers through the PCI, or simply to enjoy the political rewards of keeping the PCI non-legitimated. The PCI competes with the Christian Democrats in order to secure legitimation. Neither can really compete to 'solve the crisis'.

Though the Christian Democrats have appeared anomalous in a modern capitalist state, centralized rationality would be difficult to apply in Italy. The state form has been more effective at expressing the interests of varying segments of the dominant class than mediating social conflict by representing interests. The party form in Italy promises ideological solutions, but in practical terms is determined by its patronage functions. The 'movement', on the other hand, generally lacks the professional rewards of institutionalized parties. It offers activity and rhetoric but no regularity, or division, of power. Further, a relatively poor country cannot 'offer' alternative lifestyles. They have to be struggled for, and struggled for in the name of the whole culture. Thus, essentially sub-cultural objectives constantly divert attention and energy from the broader task of articulating social groups, and much effort is expended in creating the 'climate', the 'area' in which particular kinds of political activity or ideology flourish.

Donolo's own conception of probable change could be interpreted as 'change-reformism-transformation' as against the alternative 'destabilization-recomposition'. Is there, then, an Italian 'subject' of the first process? Italy's dependent role in Europe is symptomatic of general crisis, but makes it harder for a local resolution to be found. One enquires: 'Transition to which socialism?' - but also remembers the relative defeat of the Left after 1968, its next effort an electoral push in 1975-6, absorbed in a few months into the sponge of parliamentary manoeuvres. The eclipse of 1968, and its consideration as a possible source for unlearned lessons, was also a setback for a 'new social subject'.

Now, in the decline of the 1970s, those who are the victims of the functioning of the state and civil society lack any 'moderate' solution. There is no possibility of re-creating traditional structures, and no apparent future in cautious modernity. The corporatism and 'privatization' of the public employee is an institutional reaction to the withering of authority, which in the 'marginal' may take the form of diffused subversion or petty crime. Both these groups suffer from a crisis of modernity: the 'modern' public employee is trapped in archaic and frustrating structures. The 'marginal' are, ideologically, attempting to escape from the 'modern' world to a post-modern one. There is still vigour on the Left, but it lacks an outlet so long as the fragmentation of the economy produces social disintegration and labour induces a sense of futility.

The improvised and reactive forms which this fragmented corporatism takes immediately involves politicians. Rather than discussing the consensual basis for modernization, politicians have to negotiate with public employees, in ad hoc groups as well as through unions, with tenants' and small owners' groups, and with the public administration.

In Italy the only way to secure attention - if one is poor - is to have a specific organization. The 'political value' of the individual is diminished. Organizations of the above kind become corporately mixed, heterogeneous and attract more powerful manipulators. The vision of totality, and the command hierarchy required for planning and pre-vision, are fragmented and paralysed.

The responsibility of the parties exceeds their capacity, and the available consensual and institutional resources, to act. Politics in turn become 'party-ized' - based on party loyalty. The destruction of a rural and particularist culture in the last century has not been compensated for by a materially vigorous source of positive cultural values. The economic miracle was bewildering and chaotic rather than the source of lasting productivist faith. The height of the boom was reached in 1962-3, followed by recession, the first union challenge to catch up with past increases in profits and productivity, and the abandonment of centre-Left reformism. In other words, 1964 to 1969 saw the first crisis of (unplanned) modernization. Hence the student movement of 1967-9 was in part the revolt of representatives of the 'new subject' against technocratic modernization, as well as for politico-cultural modernity.

The 'autunno caldo' of 1969 marked the second 'push' of organized labour to catch up on economic growth in the intervening years. Thereafter, checks on the relative position of capital and labour were to be made on, at most, an annual basis. Between 1970 and 1972 there were signs of a re-stabilization based on a strengthening of the Right, and, indeed, in the South on rightist populism and localism. 1973-4 saw the end of the political reaction to 1969, when the international economic crisis hit. Between 1975 and 1979 the institutional Left grew stronger, then weakened, and a typical progression of intense crisis with increasingly brief, weak, phases of recovery set in.

Although the recession of the 1960s was not as severe as that of the 1970s, it did introduce three new features. First, it discredited 'modernization' when the miracle was not turned into social investment, investment planning or rationalization of the superstructure. Second, it raised the notion of the 'Italian case' - emphasizing the fact that recession seemed deeper and longer in Italy than elsewhere. Finally, the test of institutions in 1967-9 was as severe as in any European country, probably excepting France. Institutions in Italy had been crisis-tested, if not crisis-proofed in the 1970s. Neither centre-Left nor centre-Right guaranteed lessening conflictuality. In the 1970s, corporate conflict began to replace class confrontation, and the organic crisis increasingly took on sectoral forms, though the conjuncture of sectoral crises has an exponential effect.

In this context, the 'modern authoritarian state' is a product of decline. Re-privatizing economic functions, putting social welfare on an actuarial basis and repressing social conflict where opposition cannot be turned into corporate claims made against other corporate interests are all attempts to overcome the fiscal crisis, the legitimacy crisis (devolution to corporate interests) and the rationality crisis ('efficiency is what works'). These are all 'weak solutions', temporizing. Despite the 'backward' aspects of the Italian case which help to account for its sluggish response to stimuli from the centre, the crisis is now clearly and primarily one of the modern structures, even though these are able to shift some of the effects on to other sectors. Large-scale capital is unable to reproduce itself on a national scale in manufacturing industry, and in forms compatible with Italy's position in the international market. This puts Italy superficially in the position of a developing country, but only because it stands near the frontier of development. In so far as the limit of development has been reached in a relatively developed country, Italy's 'strategy' is instructive for developing countries.

In this context, the conversion of an influential section of the PCI's leadership to a more optimistic view of the crisis gains significance, and is surprising. This refers not only to Berlinguer's policy of austerity, but to Amendola's call for raising productivity, for restraint defined within marginalist parameters, and for Ingrao's proposal to move from sterile discussion of planning to a search for a model of development. 'Optimism' is a relative term. It refers to the belief that by conventional means it may be possible not only to slow down decline but even restore Italy's competitive edge. This implies too that labour has a responsibility, indeed an interest, in not pushing its claims too hard.

The attempt of the PCI to penetrate the state before December 1978 was a political objective rather than an ideological commitment to consociational democracy, though certainly that has been debated, notably by Luigi Berlinguer, and opposed, notably by Federico Stame. The objectives are limited, partial and not attained. Indeed, Bobbio has succinctly expressed the view that overall immobilism can be attributed to the political crisis, where the socialists are neither alternative government nor liberal opposition, and the PCI 'has no possibility of taking over government on its own', hence is concerned not with alternation of parties, but the conquest of power. (6) The PCI is drawn towards a role in the state, since it has abandoned hope of revolution, but at the same time is drawn away from that position through a belief in radical transformation by its own efforts.

There are, however, other forces confirming the structural-competitive trend towards immobilism. Politicization itself makes all proposals for change potential threats to power, and scrutinized as such. It is also clear that though the economic crisis is international, international recovery would not fundamentally change Italy's structural weakness. International realities are in the last instance decisive, but real initiatives must be national. The Christian Democratic 'honeycomb' of power may shrink, but the strategies of the historic Left fragment it. The ultra-Left has combined the PCI's discarded Leninism with the Socialist Party's notion of counter-power. This internal contradiction, combined with a real powerlessness, makes the ultimate choice one between the collectivist, consensual, statist democracy of the PCI, and the particularist, corporate-parochial system of the Christian Democrats. In effect, since both represent different aspects of the polity, both are essentially representative solutions; that is, they recognize aspects of reality, not transformation. In the last resort, both the PCI and the Christian Democrats believe that the long-term answer will be given globally: for the PCI, if capitalism collapses it will do so internationally, while national structures can reach a higher productive level. For the Christian Democrats it seems that the die has been cast: in decline or in growth, one must provide for one's own, and keep one's 'bella figura'.

In the crisis of the 1960s the PCI held a dualistic position, that the crisis was due to insufficient development, but also to an excessively high development of monopoly. The relation of monopoly to imperialism produced the socially harmful phenomenon of consumerism as the local form of dependence on monopoly, and thence on imperialism. However, in 1969, the organized workers 'caught up' with the development of monopoly, while it was the students who had led the movement against consumerism. Though the generation of 1968 was largely recovered by the PCI, the experience implanted the notion of the danger and unreliability of the uneven development of political subjects when involved in a 'vanguardist' 'fuite en avant'.

The analysis of the second crisis was different. Political mismanagement of the crisis had led to insufficient and pathological development. Outside the visible economy, however, two developments occur: that of the national improvisation of small-scale industry, and that of American-style social marginality. Having failed to export the monopoly form as a viable one, from the USA came the association of urban marginality with crime and terrorism, an alliance between sub-proletariat and visionary intellectuals. Clearly, the picture of American as well as Italian reality is approximate. The emphasis, however, is clear: the PCI abandons the global level in favour of the national 'solution' of the small and middle enterprise.

Small industry, with an element of workers' participation, co-operative financing or regional investment, may indeed spread industrialization in new patterns. Meanwhile, the Party underestimated the implication of the decline of large industry (and the fate of large unions), and the relation of new political subjects to the party system. The economic consequences of its strategy cannot yet be assessed, as it exists largely as a de facto approval of autonomous developments. In the long term, it rests on an alliance between techno-bureaucrats and small capitalism, between big state-finance and small entrepreneurship, with the former in theory able to set terms for labour at the outset. This would decrease the need for militancy, and secure higher levels of productivity.

Support for this formulation is given by Chiaromonte. (7) Arguing that the main problem of the crisis is unequal distribution of income and the diminution of the active population, he disputes Sylos Labini's conclusions. To Sylos Labini, the disturbing features of crisis are the decline of the old petty bourgeoisie, the direct cultivators, and the rise of the new - the employees, especially public employees. (8) Chiaromonte, while acknowledging these aspects, noted the growth of professional and commercial activity, the stability of the artisans, the reduction of 'braccianti', the slight increase in workers (up 4 per cent since 1951) and the large increase in dependent workers in commerce. Admitting that Italy has a 'deeply distorted social structure and one that is, in some respects, "monstrous"', he related the rise in parasitic bureaucratization not, as does Sylos Labini, to the political stalemate, but to historical features such as high semi-illiteracy and the close interconnection between positions of parasitic unearned income and 'modern' positions in 'advanced' capitalism. (9) The attack on inequality, and control of movement from the land and the South, involve investment direction of large units. However, this 'new type of development ... cannot be, in the present situation, a socialist development, but rather an advanced democratic one, in which space and room for capitalist profit remains, only in the framework of ... a general democratic control of the investment policy of big industrial and financial groups, both private and public.' (10)

The counterposing of 'democratic' to 'socialist' control shows the extent to which non-Marxist conceptualizations determine discussion which is superficially within the traditional vocabulary of Marxism. Reichlin dealt with the problem thus: 'We are no longer in times when the Right deluded itself that it could enter the "control room" to operate the levers of economic power of a "neutral state" and thus use the margins of the "miracle" to make some rationalizing reforms of the system, of *this* system; while the Left (so to say) used the same scheme, albeit upside-down, and thus did not celebrate but cursed the capacity of Italian capitalism to absorb every reform.' Then he turned to argue that 'reforms, the relation between economic intervention and social structures, the whole theme is beginning to become not only our patrimony, but that of a wide arc of trade union and cultural forces.' (12) The economy was not only reformable, but the idea of the 'vendetta of the system' against the Left was dropped. Democratic planning, in short, lowered the level of social conflict. Second, while economically based on a new type of development, politically the concern was to exit from crisis by 'cutting the roots of fascism'. (13) This approach was taken up in successive numbers of 'Critica marxista' by Napolitano and Amendola, in terms of the Chilean-style danger of Right-wing coup blamed by Amendola on 'extremism' of the Left, and the need to pacify the middle strata ('ceti medi'). (14) That the policy of a 'democratically-influenced' mixed economy had the political aim of attempting to diminish class conflict is clear. Implicitly, it also involved an alliance with sections of traditional economic and political power. There was an obvious fear, in a worsening economic situation, that institutions would no longer be capable of bearing the strain of a social restructuring similar to that experienced in the 1960s.

For Chiaromonte, the notion of 'democratic planning' dates at least from 1971, at the time of rightist reaction in the South. (15) The subsequent economic debate, whose main lines concerned whether planning decisions should derive from demand (public spending and services) or supply (industrial planning), has lessened the emphasis on political consequences of such a project. Clearly, the right of the Party prefers to stress 'planning without socialism' as an opening to the Right and 'ceti medi', while the Left prefers 'planning towards socialism'. Chiaromonte speaks of democratic planning as leading to consequences of a socialist, not consumerist type. At the same time, elements of political defensiveness, based on a realistically low assessment of the strength of institutions, determine economic policy. This is, of course, also clear to the Christian Democrats. What is involved, in fact, is an overall attempt to strengthen institutions against the rival extremes of Right and Left, and to attract 'moderate traditionalism' to 'moderate modernity'. Is moderation enough, and is there 'moderation' in the crisis and its political management?

Zolo has described the PCI response as follows: the 1973-4 crisis helped to convince the Party that existing economic and political fears were justified. The crisis destroyed the grand vision of economic design, leaving only political caution, which was why 1975 and 1976 were seen as justifying caution and compromise, rather than a leap forward. This response was different from suggesting that capitalism should or could continue to function while its laws were being broken in the superstructure. As Zolo comments, there is a contrast between the proposal in the late 1960s to use the state to expand and manage oligopolistic, narrow capitalism, and the argument that the distortion of the state was a function of economic narrowness. But the working class, being more politically advanced than in Germany or the USSR, would not permit dirigisme or passive insertion into the state. This leaves the working class with unusual autonomy within the state. However, this state has the power to mediate between class interests, though it is neither an organizer of production, nor simply the instrument of class power. Its purpose is to govern. (16) Both class and parties have their own spheres of autonomy, and must respect the autonomy of each other's functions. The state, by this argument, can indeed provide moderation. The view that the present crisis is one of the welfare state, curable by the political maturity or organizational pluralism of the working class, sees no threat to the formation of a project for transformation by the insertion of workers into the state. In any case, this has already occurred in a secondary or indirect subordinate manner. The point now is to actualize the 'revolutionary function of a new "garantismo"'. (17) Emphasis on governing underlies the distinction between ailing capitalism and the powers of resistance and organization of the working class, which now asserts its rightful claim to management capacity.

The 'extremist' case, on the other hand, sees the crisis as one of mature capitalism, not a local variant of the inability of a de-legitimated state to spend or save its way out of crisis. State intervention increases instability, while socially-produced wealth cannot be generally distributed, leading to intensifying crises of social integration. Thus, Zolo says, as the fiscal crisis, inflation and unemployment are not casual phenomena but organic elements of the functioning of the state, social disintegration becomes inevitable. The attempts made by the state to re-integrate the socio-economic system and to cover the costs of its own administration are resisted by the separate units, both in the state mode of accumulation and in the private one. (18) The state becomes a terrain for the struggle of heterogeneous interests. In addition, the apparent indifference to 'marginal society' is in fact a symptom of the organic crisis, of fear and of the loss of legitimacy.

The 'extremist' case as outlined by Zolo faces the same problems as we have seen in other 'crisis theory', that the political outcome has sombre and uncertain prospects. The effect of legitimation crisis is to transfer state managerial functions to the parties. The formal functions of the state, representation and legislation, become minor. The legal system is expelled from the state system to the party level. The parties assume the administrative functions of the state, and share out administrative and legal powers with other corporate institutions, public and private. (19) Following this scenario, we may ask whether the attempt to set up a modern democratic-authoritarian state is a reaction to disintegration, or to the proliferation of 'separate bodies'. If the diffusion of legal and police powers of the state is accompanied by a continuing paralysis and withering of the representative-centralizing state, these powers tend to become part of a plural and disintegrated authoritarianism, attached to the protection of corporate and private interests, and to the law-and-order policies of the parties. This model of 'partyocracy' produces corporations in the parties themselves. The mass attaches itself to convenient corporations, and recognizes that 'politics' is now impossible, has become administration. 'Government by referenda' is too cumbersome and exhausting a substitute.

The parties devise their own 'rules' of the game to maintain the system. Thus, in this corporate war of each against all, consensual laws prevail. The intrinsic weakness of the system of the state-of-law enforces caution and prompts alliances between the parties. Consensus is organized through participation of the mass of citizens at the lowest and most powerless local levels, in the quartieri, the schools and community services. Here, social tensions between private citizens can be diffused. Micro-decisions are reached by micro-units with micro-budgets. The decisions are generally proposed by technicians of the administration, by whom they are later co-ordinated and implemented. (20) This community pluralism is thus mainly consultative. It encourages apathy, and makes identification of 'subversives' easy. Indeed, the diffusion and disintegration of state functions makes criticism of the parties, of the administration or of conforming neighbours an act of verbal subversion. This is not the German model of the modern state, but its poor cousin.

Though PCI spokesmen react fiercely to the suggestion that this may be more than a fantasy, the three main theoretical currents in the Party take it seriously. The Gramscian organicists argue that social homogenization and recomposition re-establish the organic ties between state and civil society. The combination of this organic (for Rodano, even interclassist) 'organized democracy' with the autonomy of the political, however, raises doubts about the real centre of decision-making. Is this participation or 'decisionism'? (21)

The Party's Right sees economic restoration as the immediate task of the state, or the pre-condition for halting social disintegration. The operaisti note that the need for social recomposition is one also shared by capitalism. As against the Right, they argue that the problem is not the backwardness of the economy but that of the state. Tronti, for example, has argued that in order to start the process of constructing a unitary democracy, capitalism must realize that social recomposition is in its interest. The working class cannot begin the process by itself. (22)

There are two forms of criticism of these positions. The first is that to restore a system which continues to crumble despite the efforts of the parties shows that a long and confused process of transition has already begun, but lacks appropriate leadership by the appropriate political subject. Restoration of the system can lead only to increasing repression, and ultimate futility. Either, as for Stame, the corporate competition must be rule-contained, or the state must be considered to have lost its legitimacy. The other response is to point to the inherent conflictuality of the solution itself. It is not a triumph of moderation to persuade both capital and labour to bring their conflicts formally to the level of the state, but a further stage in the development of class conflict. True, capitalism and the historic Left have immediate interests in avoiding a disorderly and catastrophic future. Zolo, for example, foresees a successful and subordinate integration of Gramscian organicism into capitalist unity. Class conflict atomizes society, late capitalism tends towards homogeneity and an organicist solution itself. Therefore, inserting the working class in the persona of the PCI into the state is the prelude to inserting it more firmly into the criteria of authority and efficiency of the state capitalist system, chaotic though the latter's future appears.

The PCI, this argument runs, has ceased talking of representation and guarantees from the state, and increasingly emphasizes strength, authority and efficiency. Many of the elements of the 'corporate-consensual state' have already been discussed, and may be empirically demonstrated. For example, we might cite tendencies to the refeudalization of the public sphere (technico-bureaucratic relations between private and public corporate bodies), links between political-administrative bodies and the state-regulated productive system, the closing of the political-administrative system to the immediate influence of the base, and the organization of agencies for legitimation, production of consensus and of manipulation. This institutional feudalism needs to be fought by 'late-capitalist guaranteeism', using law against the state, organizing a social opposition to the failing political opposition. (23)

Zolo's argument, however, permits different conclusions. If the weakness of the state lies in lost legitimation, then he is correct to say guerilla warfare accomplishes nothing, but simply reflects loss of legitimacy. (24) However, he is surely too optimistic about the possibility of mass mobilization outside the corporations. The importation of class struggle into the state, even though the PCI proposes to limit its intensity and negotiate with capitalism for an orderly transition, is more complex than Zolo suggests. Gramscian organicism and capitalist rationale may be united in a regime of co-existence, of proletarian capitalism, but another possibility, given the decline of the productive system, is that class contradictions will be magnified within the state. Precisely because the conflict in relations of production and of distribution enter direct political formalization, the PCI's attempt to find rules for co-existence may succeed, but may accelerate the process of disintegration and intensify conflict. Second, to this scenario of increasing disorder we must add a counter-tendency. Zolo is overoptimistic about the politicization of a social mass, using law against a corporate state, and not itself becoming a corporation.

As regards the first point, Salvati and Donolo showed that the economic crisis was aggravated by Italy's long-term position internationally, and by her internal tensions. (25) On the one hand, exports were weakening and international competition strengthening: on the other, the closing of the labour market imprisoned relations of production, while, especially in the South, the tension between growth and decline tended to increase. Backwardness, in Donolo's words 'is an integral part and product of development'. (26) It is often said that times have changed, and backwardness is now an obstacle to, not a product of, Northern development; but that is to confuse backwardness with underdevelopment. (27) We are speaking of a process of social disintegration, of uneven development within classes, of lack of jobs and income. This is not only economically derived, but produced by, and productive of, the legitimation and fiscal crises. There may be profitable economic development in the South, but it can be profitable only so long as it is accepted as uneven development. It can only be uneven if labour does not reproduce the conditions of (large) Northern industry, and so long as Northern industry survives. These are vital and precarious conditions.

As regards the 'counter-tendency' to mass mobilization, Zolo underestimates the historical impulse to the formation of corporations. They are not merely signs of the weakness of the state and of quasi-feudal improvization. They are also socially integrating and legitimating forces. They belong only as subordinate elements in a centralized, liberal, efficient legal state. Now, however, they form a capillary quasi-opposition. They do protect interests against the state, but generally they are not concerned with the rights of the social collectivity. They swallow smaller fish, and thus survive. The rising corporations represent development, just as the declining ones the reverse. In other words, the legitimation and fiscal crises of the state are being bypassed by a capillary series of alternatives. The tendency to shift power between state and parties has also been offset by the shifting of power to a mass of corporate autonomies. They will be joined by corporations (like the autonomous unions) which present interests more radically. This is a scenario of a highly competitive society, in which the rule is: that no corporate entity be strong enough to aggregate interests to the point that socio-political zero-sum games are possible, and second, that zero-sum games between corporations are impermissible. (28)

The idea of permanent conflictuality leaves Zolo's social, mass, opposition as simply the sum of those who cannot attach themselves to a corporation, an association of the powerless and oppressed, a ragged army of the marginal. The PCI response and the so-called 'extremist' cases lead to a variety of political conclusions, all consistent with the interpretation of the crisis of decline of the world order. It is the crisis where philosophy and praxis go separate ways. This is not catastrophe, but corporate recomposition does characterize the decline of a culture, and social disintegration the decomposition of universalistic world-views. It is also attractive, in that it stands for a certain order, even vitality, as against collapse. In this sense, conflictual corporativism is not an 'Italian', cultural, response to crisis, but a form of disarticulated society in which traditional ideology tends to lose its power to mobilize. The prospects favour 'change' rather than 'transition'.

Chapter 4

SOCIAL 'DISINTEGRATION' AND ADAPTATION

In a period of regression, of the reassertion of Third World 'Levantine' characteristics, social analysis is centred on the 'emerging' groups most affected, those whose aspiration to 'modernity' has been most sharply reversed. In Italy, the narrowness and resistance of the labour market, education and the South are most fully covered. These are studies of frustrated hopes, of the reassertion of traditionalism, and an accompanying decline in the practical viability of traditional roles. Women and youth are again forced back into reliance on family structures, and on precarious employment. Schools and universities which were once areas of politicization have become centres of anomic violence, the corporate discontent of teachers and their 'precarious' colleagues and non-teaching staff has turned into resignation and apathy. There is adaptation to slower rhythms. Finding a suitable job, or accepting an unsuitable one, may take a decade. Though much is written about unemployment, and there are retraining and remotivating 'pilot-projects' and official unemployment lists, until recently there was doubt about how many were unemployed, underemployed or non-employed, and little information on how these survived. The South is waiting for development to 'trickle down' from the North. City administrations, with few exceptions, borrow barely to survive. Problems of public health, housing and transport, even public order, are dealt with, if at all, on a hand-to-mouth basis. It is a situation typical of the Third World, where 'advanced' ideologies do not necessarily address the question of whether further industrialization is feasible.

This is the familiar picture of an Italy heading towards the social condition of a vast Cairo. The interpretation of the phenomena is, none the less, more difficult. For alongside the picture of unserviced 'borgate', child labour, political and criminal terrorism, and the implosion of public services there is a framework of 'positive' interpretation. This ranges from the vague moralism of the 'vigour' of the response to crisis, to optimism based on high levels of politicization, faith in the parties and the political system, and on such apparently 'modern' features as strong unions and high job security. The end of the dominance and the lessening of the prestige of the 'literary intellectual' and its replacement by a proliferation of 'technical', 'administrative' and 'professional' intellectuals is not seen unequivocally as an eclipse of the 'critical intellectual'. Dissent is even regarded as a natural accompaniment of the development of a more complex, interdependent and potentially more socialized mode of production.

In the 1960s the mass production of intellectuals was greeted by the Left as a sign of the emergence of a new mass of 'intellectual labour power', a qualitatively advanced proletarian stratum. In the 1970s, in contrast, it is clear that the extended reproduction of 'intellectual labour power' involves the mass production of formalized, subaltern intellectuals. These did not necessarily perpetuate the tradition of the critical intellectual, nor did they necessarily react critically against their 'traditional' privilege. Many have rather reacted in a corporate manner to their relative subordination, while their attachment to the administrative, state, sphere has tended to attract them to 'statist' political solutions.

The concepts of the 'diffused factory', the 'worker-student', the 'mass worker' or 'society as worker' recall the hopes of the 1960s of identifying a new revolutionary subject. Unlike the 1960s, this argument runs, the workers who take university-sponsored courses under the 150-hours scheme (for workers' further education), and the student who works in the 'black' economy, no longer have the class differentiations and the differential privilege and social objectives which in the previous decade separated organized workers from students. There is a large area occupied by potential workers, student-workers, and precariously employed workers, no longer concentrated in an archipelago of big industries, but in the 'diffused factory' on the scale of the entire society. This is not a traditional reserve army, in tension with employed workers. Whether unemployed, precariously employed or illegally employed, this mass exists tangentially to the conditions and expectations of a stable career. It can neither claim nor assert privilege, and, even if its condition is temporary, it represents the exhaustion of the practice and ideology of traditional productivism, and the limits of the 'welfare state'.

However, the group is internally diversified. Though the overall causes of the condition of marginality are the same, a crisis of capitalist development, a crisis of the state, the 'margin' is heterogeneous. Any potential homogeneity depends on organization, not on an economism based on the condition itself. Yet it is precisely the debate on organization which demonstrates the political and ideological heterogeneity of the 'area' of autonomy, the political margin. This begins at the level of the debate between exponents of 'no organization' and those of 'new organization'. 'Autonomy' may become privacy, or the growth-point of new, fragile, corporate structures. To take an example, though mass-communications are an equivocal 'area of autonomy', a study in Emilia-Romagna showed the majority of private radio stations to be Christian Democratic or conservative-traditional in orientation. The periphery is not the negation of society, but both its past and its future. 'Autonomy' may refer to individualist atomism or to private property, as well as to a self-sufficient political subject.

The possibility of re-absorbing the marginal depends on expanding the black economy, accustoming the young to reduced expectations, directing job-training and -finding schemes to sensitive areas, and upwardly revaluing the qualifications of the potential proletariat in the very schools where they are now devalued. It can be argued that these are self-defeating measures. For example, job-training means creating expensive consultancies and expanding the tertiary sector. Reduced expectations must still be referred to a consumerist ideology. A zero-growth economy must still produce and consume, but for all to produce may be too expensive. In a few years, Italy may be able to borrow micro-chip technology, but only to find herself in a relatively backward position in relation to advanced technological societies. The creation of expensive new jobs will also lead to unionization and homogeneous wage levels. In short, to re-absorb the margin into a declining economy may lead not to recovery but to an accentuation of the problems which initially created it.

In the short term, however, there is considerable space for manoeuvre without large-scale planning or solution of major problems. The short term is long enough to make alliances between state technicians and capital. A really disintegrated society would, after all, have alternative forms of social life, rather than unemployment and parasitism. So long as these persist, they are a paradoxical sign that room for partial re-integration exists.

We must look not only at the collapse or resistance-recomposition of social structures, but also at their place, or context, in global society. As Ciafaloni writes, the causes of the crisis are rooted 'in the total military, political and financial predominance of the USA over the capitalist universe', (1) and now in its waning and unstable hegemony. To most social analysis, a deep assumption is that, for good or ill, modernity does not collapse. Social analysis builds into itself an image of that modernity, so that object and science are both 'modern'. However, a society where 'too much' modernity has destroyed agriculture, and 'too little' created a situation where youth in general is excluded and feared, puts social analysis itself in a dilemma. 'Critical space' can no longer be filled with those concerned to expose social evils as a lack of modernity, and to encourage state action or reformist participation to redress them: these are part of the sociology of affluent progress, of the ideology of growth.

In this regard, it is instructive to re-read Sylos Labini's 'Saggio sulle classi sociali', (2) written when the key problem seemed to be that of relating a trend towards proletarianization, when the traditional working class itself was declining, to the political danger of a reactionary new petty bourgeoisie. Sylos Labini argued that though there were trends towards embourgeoisement in the working class, and to proletarianization in the middle strata, these remained separate entities. The working class was diminishing in numbers, but rising politically and economically. This made political relations with the pathologically swelling new petty bourgeoisie of crucial importance. Intellectuals had previously made alliances with the working class only on the basis of its political disadvantage, but now there was a foundation for political alliance between the new 'ceti medi' and the working class, with special emphasis on employees in the tertiary sector. Thus, 'the area of agreement grows not in consequence of a process of economic proletarianization, which does not exist as a general process, but of a process of civic growth and cultural maturity, which does not happen in the clouds but certainly belongs, in Marxist terminology, to the superstructure more than to the structure.' (3)

Sylos Labini painted a picture of a highly differentiated society, not notably affected by increasing immiseration, not tending economically to a two-class model, not ready for, and indeed retreating from, economic dominance by the interests of the working class. Indeed, (4)

> Petty bourgeois clientelism is in danger of taking over those parties which in theory should, primarily, be the expression of the poorest peasants and the agricultural

> wage-earners (sickle) and the workers (hammer). In reality, these parties, at least as regards their central bodies, are managed and led by petty bourgeois, more or less enlightened: the eulogy of the proletariat, and the proclamation of its hegemony, often become a mask for the real situation, where the hegemony belongs to the petty bourgeoisie: many books, few hammers, fewer sickles. The truth is that the petty bourgeois have won over the electorate, active and passive, while the men of the sickle and hammer generally have only the active electorate.

Still, despite the pathological signs, the consequences of the decay of production and the degeneration of the subproletariat, or potential proletariat, are not discussed.

Sylos Labini was criticized for classifying social groups primarily on the basis of source of income. (5) However, the picture he presented was indicative. It was one of a society whose decline (agriculture) and hypertrophy (industry) produce a new army of artisans, and especially commercial and clerical petty bourgeois. Marx was wrong concerning their tendential disappearance. Both the proletarianization and embourgeoisement theses were incorrect. The working class was still educationally backward, and the stage increasingly occupied by the quasi-class of the new petty bourgeoisie, particularly the private and public bureaucrats. This educated, ubiquitous class, however, was politically unstable, tending to extremes, especially towards the Right. (6)

Yet 'Americanism' suggested that this bureaucratization was a normal process. In Italy, for cultural and economic reasons, this had been a development presenting a choice between 'fascism without Mussolini' (7) and commitment to a non-revolutionary working class. The working class was a source of discipline, stability and order. But it did not lead: the petty bourgeoisie provided leadership. The working class would not disappear, but it was insecure and variegated. Potentially, it was a source of reformist stability and modernization, but was too poor, differentiated and ill-educated to be its own spokesman. Sylos Labini thus placed his hopes in a 'mass' political alliance, on a reformist platform, between the growing and the stable subordinate classes. He was sceptical regarding the possibility of Galli's bureaucratic-financial aristocracy avoiding further economic decline. The state bourgeoisie might have an inclination towards reformism, but did not possess the necessary impetus, being directed to goals of privatized collectivism and stability. (8)

Other critics found the theory of the political supremacy of the petty bourgeoisie incompatible with its internal heterogeneity and dependency, its lack of cultural and historical purpose. The public and private bureaucracies consisted of both technical experts and feeble placemen. A real political danger, however, in some PCI analyses, seemed to come from the apathetic and potentially reactionary young. Bearing in mind the political calculation of not offending those it was trying to attract, Chiaromonte's judgment on Sylos Labini expresses an authoritative Party view. (9)

> We do not believe in a rapid and irresistible process of 'proletarianization'. The working class today is the only force capable of indicating, through its class interests and the political line of the party which represents its greater part, a way out of the country's crisis, and the forms and objectives of a struggle to attract the consensus and following of large, ever more numerous, popular masses.

The policy of attracting the 'ceti medi' without trying to define their class, or quasi-class, interests (save in terms of general, national interest) was indicative. Strengthening the state was not, for the PCI, a policy of appeasing the state bureaucracy. The state could be strengthened only by the proletariat within. The notion of the autonomy of the political, however, means that only the Party representatives need enter. Danger lies not in the cultural instability of the petty bourgeoisie, but rather in their particular attachment to the strength of the state, which has potentially reactionary implications. Partial insertion of the working class does not end its remaining 'autonomy', or threaten its unions and guaranteed employment, where these exist. The state bourgeoisie, professionals who are increasingly direct employees of public and private bureaucracies, and the petty bourgeois public employees, all have interests in reform of the state, and to some extent in state reformism. They are also interested in their own forms of 'autonomy'. Thus they would be both victims and agents of a state plan. Their flight to extremes has actually been slowed by their attachment to the centrality of institutions. They thus hold the key to the Left's political project, and increasingly their corporate demands are a point of reference which conditions any programme of workers' austerity. We thus see, in opposition to Sylos Labini's thesis of petty bourgeois dominance, that of the formation of a national state-class, with internally varied material interests.

It is therefore hard to accept Accornero and Carmignani's conclusion that the working class, 'despite its internal changes and its virtual numerical stasis', is the focal point of the whole social structure, 'above all in relations with the intermediate and marginal strata'. (10) Internal changes such as the trend to employment in service industry, the fall in construction work and the diffusion of industrial development outside the industrial triangle leave a confused impression regarding the stability of the class and its level of employment. They demonstrate that in construction, marginal labour declined after 1961, but was still above 1951 levels in 1971, while in industry the fall continued over the two decades. (11) As they noted, the decline of marginal labour may not be an index of stability, but evidence of general decline. If one-fifth of the industrial workers are 'precarious', are they an industrial reserve army, or the socially disarticulated in the submerged economy? How much 'black' labour is 'lavoro doppio', and what are the economic exigencies which lead people to take second jobs? The remarkable increase in dependent employees in the years 1971-6, from roughly one-third to just under half the workers in industry, is evidence of the centrality of employee-status, rather than that of the working class.

In the case of the employees, these are inserted into central-subordinate positions in the public service and manufacturing industries. The relation of the traditional working class to the margin is more ambiguous. Emargination is described both as a strategy for capital to decentralize and diversify development away from organized, regular labour, and also as a perverse development of the economy. Is the new marginality a mark of the weakness of labour in a declining economy, not of its centrality? The categories used do not allow us to distinguish between 'decentralized' and 'super-exploited' marginal production. A recent study by the PCI uses the categories of mass worker and decentralized worker, both regularly employed, but with distinctive backgrounds and conditions. Then there are 'marginal' and 'black' workers, often unqualified female labour, working at home and in small factories, precarious and under-paid in relation to the preceding categories of 'regular' workers. (12) Some surveys conclude that the 'margin' is a response to peculiarities of the labour market and its difficulty in absorbing the 'weaker' categories (that is, all who are not male industrial workers aged 30-50). Marginal labour is thus an alternative, supplementary labour market, and does not imply a tendency to the immiseration or emargination of the working class in general. It is thus not a product of decline, but an alternative to unemployment, given the relative geographical stability of the active labour force. At all events, the picture of a united and stable working class, central in an alliance with the fragmented 'ceti medi' seems exaggerated.

Carmignani's conclusions raise important questions, especially regarding the tendency of some agencies to give optimistic readings to data lying in the 'overly narrow confines in which the sociology of labour has tried to enclose it'. That is, if one admits that 'a change which can also be defined as "institutionalization"' of the working class has taken place, then 'the concept of workers' autonomy can no longer remain tied to labour because there has been an influx from society to the factory. Consequently, working-class centrality can no longer be seen only from the standpoint of the productive system; if society invades the factory, the working class invades the political system.' (13) However, just as for marginal labour the 'factory' is equivocal, so too 'institutionalization' hardly applies to the pressures on the marginal. If there is a real influx to the factory and institutionalization, it is above all due to an increase of middle-strata employees.

There are weaknesses in the 'optimistic' case for growth, and for the margin as an area developing the working class as a social and political force. The argument that differences regarding the petty bourgeoisie's relations with the working class are primarily political and ideological seems contradicted by the tendency for middle-strata employees' conditions to worsen, and competition to become economic. The recent study by Accornero and Sebastiani stresses areas of decline, marked by a failure of strategy of the traditional bourgeoisie, by poor collective leadership in big industry, and by greater weight, but also greater insecurity, in the public-financial bourgeoisie. There is vitality in the traditional petty bourgeoisie, dependence of professionals, and a mixed experience in the diversifying middle-strata employees. Their argument runs that when the latter have acted along with organized workers in industry they have been successful, and, in addition, differentials between white-collar employees and workers have narrowed. In the public sector, decline has broken the alliance with the dominant bloc, and created anger, frustration and demoralization. As for the working class, two main types of 'marginality' are noted. One is that of the 'new' (regular) workers, those of the new industrial periphery, the other that of the marginal strata proper. This consists of the traditional sector (child labour, 'black' labour and outwork) and the 'new' form. The latter is at once mediated and aggravated by enforced reliance on the family. Yet the conclusion is mildly optimistic: 'Not all is "black" in precarious employment, not all non-employment is emargination.' (14) Even in decline, working-class unity and leadership are seen as growing, despite the evidence of corporate, not class, competitiveness and petty bourgeois militancy.

There is a political message in this. In a perspective of growth, it would be acceptable to read signs of adaptation and improvisation in an optimistic light. Indeed, even in decline it would be wrong to ignore the vitality of certain sectors, the complexity of 'marginality', the changing form and diffusion of manufacturing industry (the 'Three Italys' case), and the effect on union strategy of publishing data such as Gorrieri's on wage spread (the 'pay jungle'). However, in a context of crisis or decline, features which are temporary in an expanding economy become barriers, or lines of defence, in a contracting one. 'Marginality' means less the economy of the future than illegal, super-exploitative employment, or partial employment. The decline of conditions in public employment brings state employees into confrontation with union strategy, since fiscal crisis for the former means austerity for the workers, and raising productivity, rather than cutting the size of 'unproductive' sectors. The decline of the traditional bourgeoisie tendentially strengthens the state bourgeoisie. Their immediate concern, as for any consolidating political class, is to define 'productive activity', to decide whether the tertiary sector or the marginal economy should be sacrificed, and what relations should be established with the traditional industrial sector. The discourse between public, marginal and traditional industrial employment is not based on stable political consensus or economic strategy. It is also potentially explosive because of the 'openness' (the vulnerability) of the economy in the EEC. The basic problem for the working class is that any political strength amassed is not only mediated through alliances with strata less disciplined, and therefore more able to devise short-term strategies, but also (because the class remains consistently socially disadvantaged) the object of capital. The intensity of the social conflicts involving the working class do not reflect a corresponding strength in the political sphere.

In decline, therefore, the tensions which arise from adaptation to crisis tend to intensify, whereas in periods of growth improvisation tends to lessen conflict. The PCI case has been to extrapolate a cautious growth model, relying on the stability and traditionality of class composition and allegiance. This discounts international indicators of continuing crisis, and the fact that stimulation of traditional sectors, or growth in general, would in fact encounter traditional tendencies of conflict from the subordinate classes. (15) The Party's image of society is one in which the marginal economy balances the expansion of the tertiary sector. In fact, it cannot: as Cassano says, 'From the school ... there arises the dimension, both economic and political, of the commodity form of labour power, the very close relation between state, devaluation of labour power and the capitalist division of labour.' (16) Failure to investigate the 'new' marginality is an admission that marginal and tertiary employment do not eliminate the novelty from marginality, that it is a socio-political category resting on the declining value of labour power, and especially that of intellectual labour power.

The new 'marginal subject' has some kinship with the new revolutionary subject of the 1960s, but though its social origin is more nearly proletarian, relations with the organized working class are harder. The PCI grants the status of worker to all working people, while implicitly admitting substantial autonomous interests for those who do not produce commodities and surplus value. In theory, then, the 'marginal' present it with no problem concerning class membership. Donolo, on the other hand, argues that the PCI's moderation and state-centredness reflect and accentuate the weakening of the working class in times of decline. Space for anti-authoritarian and anti-institutional activity exists, but the PCI and the unions have been slow to grasp both the growth of unsatisfied social and political demand - especially crucial in the marginal - and the phenomenon of social collapse. Donolo links the administered decline of the mode of production to the growth of parasitism, and the role of the 'ceti medi' as consumers of more wealth than is produced. To reduce this parasitic exploitation of the productive sector, it is not enough to defeat the 'crisis managers' politically. A model of development, ideological as well as economic, is required. Otherwise, the tendency is for features of collapse to be reproduced on a growing scale, within the weakened working class itself, so that '"class" unionism' ends up 'experiencing the model of corporate clientelism, which is the most modern form of disintegration'. (17) Thus attitudes towards the 'marginal' of all types become crucial to the maintenance of the unity, let alone the potential hegemony, of the working class.

Examination of class structure after 1969 was generally based on the experience of restabilization, which possibly led Sylos Labini to overestimate the normality of tertiarization, though the Italian rate remains relatively low, and its pattern distorted for an advanced industrial society. The emphasis was placed on a redistribution, on the basis of political consensus, between traditional working class and the new petty bourgeoisie, productive as well as parasitic. In the 1970s, however, the submerged economy's size established it as strategically important. It provided a new, living model of development, an area of production, and hence pushed aside discussion of an agreement between the workers and the 'ceti medi' regarding income distribution. Second, the 'ceti medi' did not rise as expected. Their forms of protest became more institutionalized, less movement oriented. On the other hand, large areas of militancy among both middle-strata employees and workers assumed corporate, 'autonomous' forms. The 'ceti medi' assumed forms of working-class organization through union federations and also autonomous unions. Some sections of the working class reradicalized their organizations on a corporate basis (autonomous unions). The new political subject, 'autonomia', found that the space for a movement presenting the most radical class demands, or statements, had been narrowed by the competition and conflict between collective-corporate organizations of the 'ceti medi' and the working class. It now became unclear whether fragmentation, divide-and-rule and backwardness were after all in the interests of the Christian Democrats, as is often claimed. A corporately conflictual and competitive society, without stable reference groups and routinized status hierarchy, at a time of inflationary and political instability, was an unpromising condition for the future of the Christian Democrats or of capitalism. It would seem opportune for the Christian Democrats to introduce stricter rules of corporate competition if the level of conflictuality and social fragmentation were to be contained.

The PCI attempted to maintain that its line and academic analyses were compatible. However, D'Antonio is surely more correct in pointing to the lack of effective policies for transition, or of philosophico-ideological frameworks in most academic analysis. (18) Most 'solutions' require powers over unions and capital which are not available, and in any case fail to take international factors into account. Carlo Trigilia divides the analyses of society in the 1970s into two periods: the first is dominated by non-Marxist analyses of class structure and stratification (Sylos Labini, Ruffolo, Salvati, Pizzorno) and the latter by discussion of the labour market followed by examination of the concept of development (Donolo). The picture is of an inconclusive series of political, economic and now only occasionally sociological studies.

(19) Thus there seems little hard evidence for any party to argue that its experts have a solid conceptual base for policy-making.

Outside the efforts of a few prominent sociologists, continuity of analysis is provided by a handful of reviews ('Aut Aut' and 'Quaderni piacentini', for example) and a few institutes and agencies (Censis, Cespe). Other journals ('Inchiesta', 'La critica sociologica'), reflective though politically committed, party publications ('Rinascita', 'Mondoperaio') and the PCI's theoretical journals ('Critica marxista', 'Democrazia e diritto', 'Politica ed economia') tend to react to issues rather than discover them. Thus, the movement from discussion of class stratification (distribution-occupation) to development (the relation of backwardness to 'modern' disintegration, and thence to social recomposition-diffuse growth) was ultimately derived from the studies of the dominant marginalist economists. Basic phenomena lacked definition: marginality is not separation from society but a state of total or partial dependence. Autonomy may involve a search for a space to exist in, not only to move in.

A good example of the disadvantages of politicized sociology was Asor Rosa's notion of the 'two societies'. (20) This grew from a view of the crisis as 'the sum of elements which prevent this (political, social, and economic) system maintaining its past balance', a situation the PCI had itself helped to create. (21) Now, on the other hand, Marxism had been 'transcended', in that it had been fully confirmed in 1968-9. The PCI must now make use of the negative element of the crisis, using it as creative disequilibrium, dialectically reincorporating the crisis into the strategy of the Party. 'The kernel of extremism consists precisely in believing the democratic and socialist development of this Republic to be impossible.' (22) Consequently, acknowledging this, the Party must recognize that the second society 'breaks off from the rest of society and counterposes itself to it'. (23) Thus if to the second society 'the present is already constitutionally represented by poverty, indigence, uncertainty, and precariousness, then the slogan of austerity obscures its political significance and potential for transformation, beginning directly with problems like that of unemployment.' (24) As a criticism of the PCI's general strategy and attitude, this is important, especially coming from an 'operaista' whose point of reference is the organized working class.

As social analysis, this does not convince. The theory of the second society is really based on optimistic beliefs about the future of the Republic. If the characteristics of the second society are those of economic deprivation, it lacks any other principle of sociality. It is an asocial, impoverished function of the 'first'. Asor Rosa's political case remained, of course. What was still lacking was an answer from the side of production to the marginalist discussion of distribution and development (the search for a state plan) and, from the side of social relations, class relations rather than a 'second society' without societal being, without a socio-economic formation. It is not only crisis-as-disequilibrium that the PCI has helped to create, but also the destruction of traditional relations, replacing them by high expectations. That it may also introduce new forms of cultural and political subordinacy, as these expectations decline and the Party replies with administrative gradualism, is also a risk. A ragged and competitive 'modern' world no longer provides the space for escape from traditional structures. The 'first society' now appears as the area devoted to generating exchange value. This aspect too the PCI has helped to create.

A recent round table (25) addressed itself to the problem of terrorism either as a consequence of the social context or as a psycho-social inverse moralism wherein the dominant moralism (claiming to oppose non-legitimated violence but in fact condoning and practising it) was tried and sentenced by a counter-moralism. This latter 'religious' explanation is really only a function of the first hypothesis. Indeed, given the elements of stasis and regression, and prospects for further decline, one must ask how the PCI can to such an extent have abandoned the analysis of social dissolution in decline. Even Asor Rosa's dialectic is moralistic. It has 'negative' and 'positive' sides for which the PCI is partly 'responsible'. This subjectivism and moralism, when faced with the objective consequences of the dilution and dissolution of sociality and social organization and production, is deep and diffuse. One thinks of the slogan of the 'struggle against inflation', and the hypostasis of class relations this implies. This moralism is also part of the conservative tradition. Pellizzi, for example, speaks of the crisis as a cover for the fact that Italians consume more than they produce. (26) Crisis, in this argument, is a state of mind, aggravated by self-indulgence and sloth.

The PCI's moralism has long been outdone by the Censis analysis, in which there is a growing sense of triumph that the crisis has eroded the state, leaving the way open for a return to genuine (parochial) sociality and individual responsibility. The reports in the 1970s provide a continuous assessment of crucial developments which other individual efforts lack, fulfilling the same kind of reflective function as the reports of the governor of the Bank of Italy do for the economy. (27) In 1967 the picture was of 'an increasingly modern and difficult society, with an essentially complex evolution of the major economic, social and cultural phenomena; it manifests itself none the less in characteristics which put in crisis the myths of radical changes and decisive initiatives.' (28) The problems of society were those of modernization: individual improvement, participation and more rational social initiatives. The negative element was the 'marginalizing' of the less fortunate groups. To overcome particularism and backwardness, the answer was to concentrate and aggregate organizations and causes, though all too often this was done by groups 'decaying, or at least becoming marginal'. (29) The marginal categories themselves, however, were heterogeneous: bourgeois youth, women workers, the old, emigrants (abroad or in cities), areas of high emigration and the provinces, as against the cities.

The model was of uneven but effective modernization, with 'traditional' marginality. Modernization stimulated the state to move from welfare paternalism to the welfare state proper. Only a year later, the report spoke of 'some fermentation of social discomfort and pressure [which] have become almost endemic in the social body'. The rapidity of changing interpretation is remarkable. Rivulets of discontent 'emphasize the endemic character of the sickness of the social body, without reaching their own, even partial, solutions.' It is 'not only, and not so much, that this increases exponentially the distance between civil society and political society, but that these same subjects working directly in civil society (unions, associations, etc.) progressively lose their power of interpretation and their representativeness of the demands of their members.' (30) From being a crisis of uneven modernization, the new pathology is the separation of representation from need. Are mass movements 'a safety valve and outlet for the mechanism of development of our society'? (31) Are they, that is, a representative element of civil society, or a mark of frustration and competitive disfunction?

In fact, all the 1967 features, whether of modernism or traditionalism, seem to have turned pathological. Competition is becoming more egoistic and particularistic. Marginality precludes 'an awareness of the generality of the process' of social change. There is less interest in participation for its own sake than in securing objectives, and to these the public sphere is not responsive.

Many of these observations are moralistic responses to unstated social causes. Participation for its own sake, marginality which might in some circumstances raise consciousness and the strictures against egoistic competition are all ethical concerns. The remedy was seen in not letting pluralism degenerate into corporate particularism, or 'categorialization'. (32) The moralism is typical of Christian Democratic social philosophy, with its fatalism concerning 'capitalist (egoistic) moralism', and a belief that the 'public power' is not responsible for corporativism but is paralysed by it. Fear of imposition of subcultures by intermediate groups which believe in systemic confrontation and accept 'neither mediations nor syntheses' is marked. (33) These groups are weak, but so too is the response, as there are no social forces capable of exercising control. The solution to egoism is overall motivated change through intermediate levels of 'unitary consideration' and 'partial synthesis' - interest groups, that is, which sound remarkably like corporate bodies. All social evolution, even when conflictual, is, nevertheless, seen as 'an enrichment, a step forward'. (34) In a year, the emphasis shifted from a self-propelling modernity to the realization that, lacking state and intermediate, representative bodies, society was quite formless, undirected and egoistical. The evidence was that of a society either already disintegrating or never properly articulated. Yet the emphasis lay on introducing principles of sociality to consciousness, disciplining the individual.

The report's accent was placed on the need to produce a 'collective consciousness' in Italy. The new contestation wanted an impossibly rapid transformation, but was prevented by traditional group interconnections (the existence of independent workers, their assistants, employees and professionals who mediated between basic classes). Now, the relation between modernity and growth was seen as changed. Traditional egoism asserted itself against modern, movement egoism. Ultimately the need was to replace broken traditional bonds by the solidarity of neo-egalitarianism. This was a slow process. For example, the students were led by a declining, or previously declining, element, the middle or upper intellectual bourgeoisie. Union struggles, on the other hand, had now been adopted by the bureaucracy. Despite this, 'power' had changed little. The ruling classes 'favoured dialectics over struggle, discussion over commitment, verbalism over individual and collective concrete action'. (35)

This is a view of society where on the one hand 'power' continues its own discourse, while at the same time institutions change capriciously from modern to traditional, struggling both for change and for egoistical relief. What is lacking in the analysis is a theory of the relation of socio-economic to political power, and indeed of social dynamics and articulation. Why was it that modernization produced so many signs of traditional regression? (36) Why did various forms of institutionalized and non-institutionalized struggle turn into corporativism? The answer to this would seem to lie in the fragmentation of relations of production combined with the state's capacity to resist and absorb universalistic (ideological) challenges to its power. In fact, the state is seen as having 'elements of regression or at least of stasis, almost a convenient alibi for maintaining or backing aspects and groups which the economic and social reality of a modern country ends almost automatically by transcending.' (37) In other words, the conflict in society is one of egoism versus backwardness. Later the 'lack of collective consciousness' became one of conflict between public and private.

In short, the moralistic categories and the inappropriate criteria of a 'modern normality' prevent the articulation of a model of social and political development, or underdevelopment. Instead, there is a lack of vital force: in 1971 there had been a decline of forces 'which have been at the root of post-war development'. (38) There were more strikes than in 1968. Were we then to understand that the declining 'forces' were the entrepreneurs? The state, it seemed, could not take initiatives, perhaps because local authorities saw their own role as multifunctional. The parties could not make syntheses, the regions had no powers and the state had lost ground to pluralism, the multiplication of atypical centres of power. Lack of strategic options reinforced the privatized and traditional conceptions of power.

The 1972 report confirmed that since 1967 modernization had been put into reverse, so that the prospect of reform was more distant, and the margin was essentially a backward, traditional area. Non-occupation, patriarchal support of the young, women and the old, along with falling employment all led to further slowing of development and loss of unitary vision and responsibility. The crisis was especially severe in the tertiary and agricultural sectors where the situation was 'less dramatic but harder to resolve'. (39) There was lack of faith in development, and a probability of explosive phases. On the one hand, old themes of reform and public spending were no answer, on the other, crisis itself produced 'an egoistical search for particularistic solutions', (40) a split between pragmatic and political objectives, and between politics and reality. Traditional remedies, in other words, could not be applied through traditional structures, whereas new proposals were frustrated by pragmatic egoism.

1972 saw the crisis accelerating. Employment and purchasing power had suffered. There was 'political incapacity and inability to control any of the old and new distortions in the distributive sector and public employment'. (41) Lack of control, low personal qualities, seemed to demonstrate that the state, in mediating conflict, met an immovable obstacle in the temperaments of conflicting groups. At this point the reports begin to speak of reforms which involved the central state only peripherally: regulation of the submerged economy, raising the standards of the tertiary sector and controlling public expenditure. This involved not making 'false avant-gardist evaluations': for instance, guaranteed family income 'deresponsibilizes' and the 150-hours programme simply sends workers to the schools of the 'ceti medi'. (42) The virtues praised here, of responsibility and 'keeping to one's class', are notably conservative, even in a context of declining modernization.

In the new strategy, a kind of unsteady optimism concerning decentralized, unambitious and re-motivating proposals outside the state, the parties and the 'egoistical-ideological' movements began to emerge. 'Spontaneous drives' are lamented in their absence, and criticized for their effects when present. The latter lose unitary vision, lack analysis of how society is articulated, in particular as regards the relation between state and civil society, which is both pragmatic and ideological. The reports, however, praise the working class (the only 'European' area in Italy), and lament the absence of a liberal bourgeoisie, as well as the petty bourgeoisie's search for privilege and status. The 'ceti medi' swell at the expense of the state and form a self-interested coccoon around it. In 1973 the solution seemed to be social pluralism and alternative powers to 'unblock our society'. (43) What, then, was the real choice before society? It could only be that between social and individual discipline and away from institutions, from corporate expressions of individual egoism, away from state and parties, and away from the vain, uncultured 'ceti medi'. This is no analysis of social and political structures, but rather makes a virtue of institutional decline as promoting a social, interclassist collectivism.

The sense of living 'in penultimate times' is still stronger in 1975. There is 'too little sense of history, too much ideological simplicity, too churchly a sense of life and society, too great a tendency to follow fashions and take refuge by running ahead, too generic an approach to the knowledge of problems, too much de-responsibilization in transferring to other periods and powers the duties of development, perhaps too much cunning in demanding that everything should change so that then nothing changes.' (44) This is a fine example of the confluence of idealism (or moralism) and common sense in traditional, blocked society. In 1974-5 society was regarded as tendentially de-qualified, tendentially non-European. Yet, the author argued, was this not a possible strength? Was it not better to die from progressive 'slowing-down' than from violent crisis, and might that not provide time for the reassertion of a civic sense? (45)

Again, the psychological commitment to collective life and the moral one to sociality are seen as the ends of social individuals. Their absence defines the existence of crisis. The society is still alive, though with the 'schizophrenic coexistence' of a 'mechanism of adaptation and a continuous prospect of change'. (46) The means of transformation is no longer the state, but 'development', as opposed both to pre-industrialism and bourgeois enlightenment. One must now rely on social vitality, on the 'self-sufficiency if not superiority of real society vis-à-vis the cultural and organizational superstructures which try to dominate it'. (47) The idea of a society relatively independent of its own superstructures, and superior to them, is a remarkable image. It is a logical inversion of the autonomy of the political - the autonomy of the social. It reverses the earlier notion that the state was distant and powerful, and that corruption came from society. Again, however, less radical remedies are proposed than reliance on popular vitality. They are to broaden the productive base in alliance with the productive petty bourgeoisie, encourage social mobility and control the efficiency and costs of public intervention, accepting tertiarization as a 'modern' development. (48) More responsibility must be given to all, yet the problems require unitary interpretation, and the desire and tolerance to experiment. Unfortunately, the message contains its own critique. For spontaneous development de-institutionalizes the public sector. For instance, assemblies prolong 'rigid positions typical of the old cultures and decision-making procedures'. (49) In other words, centralization runs the risk of 'decisionism', and spontaneity leads to ideological rhetoric and stasis, frustration and a private reaction. Who, then, is to orientate society, but not to possess it?

If the basic difficulty is Italy's lack of 'real maturity in culture and collective behaviour', (50) how do pragmatism, decentralization, tertiarization and the submerged economy create it? Given crisis in housing, youth employment, entrepreneurship, investment and public finance, how can collective conscience maintain resistance to regression? The report inverts cause and effect, as society is seen as determined by individual will, not vice versa, by an individual impulse to the collective. In a situation where everyone lives in a constant state of 'generalized intersubjectivity', (51) egoism becomes a form of Italian original sin.

The report for 1975-6 concluded that, despite the picture of shipwreck, resistance and selfishness, 'our crisis is a crisis of identity more than of emergence, it is a crisis of inability to connect the effects of the past to present tensions and hopes for the future.' (52) Italy is presented as a society de-culturated by modernity, with regression and confusion regarding the future, but still imperfectly modernized. The reader's question recurs, however, as to where this new modest, conservative, political class is to come from, committed to central reforms, sound accounting principles and the commercialization of public projects? The Christian Democrats seem to be locked in the state like the princess in the tower. The ultra-Left is really ultra-conservative and, implicitly, the PCI is rhetorical and dirigiste. By 1977, the blockage seemed complete. The cycle of development was over. The present and future, in a 'blocked' society, were characterized by differentiation of lifestyles through the growth of subjectivity and 'everydayness', or day-to-dayness. The new skills of living in the interstices of society, in 'the other Italy', were part of a process of 'constant adaptation and making do'. The crisis was no longer one of development and regression, but of floating half-way between 'the will to survive and the courage to exist'. (53) Society had learned to adapt its needs and ambitions to an economic system determined by fifteen years of a policy of conflict. To maintain standards, people would take second jobs, return to the family and accept a lessening of social mobility. Social consensus was now more open to homogenization by the mass media. Politics, it was argued, no longer innovated but reacted so as to absorb innovation. It had become an interclassist mechanism for social reconciliation, reflecting society without leading it. (54)

Visions of reform had been replaced by relief that, after all, society could survive its tensions, and improvise outside its institutions. Initiative now lay with society, its 'almost anarchic vitality', which now offered 'the prospect of a long cycle of submerged, molecular growth'. (55) This, however, would be accompanied by the continuing collapse of institutions, and a crisis of the machinery of (potential) planning. The unco-ordinated growth of public bodies had led to overexpansion and underresponsibility. In turn, the demoralization of the public, or the privatization of the public, sphere caused a recurrence of the old tension between 'civil society and political society, between the autonomy of the social and primacy of the political, between molecular, spontaneous development, and planned, directed development, between the vitality of individual and collective initiative and public intervention, between the conflictual management of pluralism and the nostalgia/search for hegemony.' (56)

The hypothesis of de-institutionalization needs to be more closely examined, since the collapse of institutions may also imply the abandonment of the needs they were designed to fill. The loss of the state also implies a transfer of power, a social movement, rather than a weak, interclassist, reconciliation. Society seems instead to float along without politics or administration. Social tension is resolved without the state, and outside the public sphere. The danger is more of 'micro-conflictuality' than of terrorism due to the 'marginalization of marginality'. (57) The danger of collapse continues, but the future lies once more in the subjective responsibilities of individual spheres of autonomy. Perhaps 'the public' can be revived by interaction between autonomies and the state, by 'assisted processes of equilibrium'. (58) What, then, was this equilibrium? Was stability the bottom of the trough, and was re-institutionalization probably beyond reach?

The Censis introductions deserve attention because, with their fatalistic and deferential interclassism, they reflect attitudes common to the 'ceti medi' of all political complexions. The spectre of crisis and decline is counterbalanced by relief that society can float without the state, that the country can 'make do' despite a worsening internal and international situation. In 1978 the report concluded that the country had reacted to its extraordinary year with 'a clear and conscious rejection of injustice'. However, there was 'not a loss of solidity and consistency, but rather of the steady strength to put things and everyday responsibilities in order.' (59) Yet the social fabric of the country was not dissolving, and there was an active process of decentralization. The submerged economy had, in fact, produced a boom. This could not be measured, but was observable from rises in savings, the ability to meet price rises and to travel, even to buy second houses. (60) The argument ran that Italy was now taking more rational economic steps to catch up with the rest of Europe. Again, the basic national and international situation is ignored in favour of the work ethic. Admittedly, the report said, there was no effective link between state power and more complex needs, the sectoral crises and planning. The 'middle layer' of authority was still missing, hence the base did not 'feel governed', and from the summit came only rhetoric. (61) All hopes were pinned on small and middle industry. Big industry was conflictual and rigid. The burden of tertiarization increased, and the vital, non-parasitic, sector continued to carry all the rest. (62) However, the problem of concentrating on an interstitial 'boom' is twofold. First, such a boom is a response to intensified crises in other areas, and it tends to reproduce their crisis conditions. Second, it is a chaotic, undirected, strategy. As the report quaintly puts it, the lying-low of a ruling class prevents the emergence of leadership, and emphasizes 'certain ancestral characteristics of our social behaviour: the need for security and political pretexts, the obscuring of collective consciousness, and the privilege of corporative and localistic logics, which compete to produce a perverse socialization of the economy.' (63)

The moralism and individualism of the above views resolves itself into trusting civil society to tackle the havoc caused by the imperfect functioning and legitimation of the state. It seeks a principle of collective responsibility outside the political, state, sphere, save where the state can act as organizer of social services. The movement to incorporation of social strata into the state is overlooked. That we are witnessing a stalled, or inconclusive, battle at the threshold of the state is also minimized. We might instead describe the situation as one of 'imperfect statalization'. Horkheimer described the completed process: 'In integral statism, socialization is required ... But the producers, to whom capital juridically belongs, "remain wage workers, proletarians", notwithstanding all the injustices towards them.' (64)

The PCI, on the other hand, continues to propose the traditional 'remedies' of party and state power. 'The Constitution generally contains precise guidelines to encourage the workers' movement to make itself into the State, and guarantees wide spaces for what is described as "protagonism of the masses".' (65) Extremism is held to rest on a Catholic notion of a negative, critical society, opposed to regulated society. (66) The state is not simply a class state, despite certain pathological features in the relation of parties to state. Despite the confusion of a mass of agencies, participation and 'democratic administrations' have changed the state's nature. Direct democracy is not sufficient, however. A 'vertical element' is required as well, to ensure 'the vertical channelling of the directions and decisions of both assemblies and executive'. (67)

Luigi Berlinguer admits that the 'unitary recomposition of society', the 'social development of consensus' and planning the 'economic healing of democracy' run the authoritarian risks of consociational democracy. The real threat, however, comes from the 'closed society', from conservatism and traditionalism. (68) The proposal to concentrate power is clear. It is less clear how this is to be done, and what the criteria for calculating changes in the state should be. (69) Rejection of the state is taken to be peculiarly a mark of Left Catholicism, involving also an attack on the working-class movement and its aspirations to become the state. Yet the association of attacks on the state with Left Catholic, or 'subversive', criticism, and belief that the first phase of the transformation of the state has already occurred does not address the real problems. Vainicher, (70) on the other hand, raises these in the context of late capitalism. He argues that the tertiary sector is not absorbable into one of the basic classes, though that does not mean the sector is unproductive or parasitic. The sector does, none the less, develop in response to difficulties in distribution (not, be it noted, in production). The real crisis is one of stagflation, or under-use of resources, problems due to the 'openness of the economy' (balance of payments problems) and the undersupply of jobs in the private sector. Pathological development in the tertiary sector is thus related to the crisis, not to the tendency to produce a larger quantity of tertiary workers in itself. The latter is an international phenomenon. Rather than concentrating power in the state, which means in the tertiary sector, some response like Ingrao's workers' hegemony in pluralism is more appropriate. (71)

This is not a solution to the problem of gaining power from a position of subordination. Yet it does try to confront the relation of productive and unproductive labour as a generalized systemic problem by suggesting that modern capitalism can support much heavier tertiary burdens than the Italian and, with proletarian hegemony, the class alliance of the tertiary sector is resolved in favour of the working class. The tertiary sector must not increase at present. More production, not more state power, is the answer, and only the working class can devise articulations to make the tertiary sector productive. For tertiary employment is 'the basic generator of crisis for the capitalist system'. (72) At present, capitalist dynamics are weaker than those of neo-feudalism and its clients, so to develop capitalism further has no future: it produces parasites and a 'crisis' tertiary sector.

The problem is that social analysis is interrupted by triumphalist and optimistic political solutions. Ingrao was more cautious and realistic. He noted the 'incessant action of corporate re-equilibrium', (73) and the slowness of political reaction to crisis. This lag naturally aids improvised recomposition, and encourages ad hoc strategy. Yet where Censis bases its hopes on social recomposition and ingenuity, the PCI stresses its political, statist skills, and proposes the formation of a divided, or dual, state class whose new elements are recruited from sensitive areas of crisis itself. In fact, the PCI's efforts to enter the state make it a part of the problem of the state form. It is true that 'there is no longer a space empty of institutions which is "occupied" by the knowledge of intellectuals': (74) one of the problems of the new subjects of the 1970s is that indeed these spaces have been filled. The PCI, or certain currents within it, has in fact staked heavily on the largely untried political, statist, skills of its political intellectuals. As Tronti put it: (75) 'Politics is no longer the state but the party, and not only the party but the movement, and not only the movement but whoever lives without organization in the folds of society, as non-acceptance of the state, widespread discontent, objective antagonism, the will felt, but not yet thought out, to change ... The autonomy of the political is thus the mature form of a new antagonism, a more advanced terrain of struggle, and the grasping of a more complex articulation of class attitudes in the capitalist crisis.' The claims of the state and the diffusion of politics tend to create two basic, conflicting classes, in which the one wins which 'knows how to do politics better'. (76)

This does not exclude society, as Censis Introductions tend to dismiss politics, power and the state. However, by avoiding questions of social composition, the relation of state power to reconstruction in the economy and the effect on the 'unproductive' tertiary 'ceti medi', the omissions are serious. This replaces the manoeuvres of unwieldy, heterogeneous, masses with the 'supreme game' of political generals. Yet the traditional 'masses' are themselves now organized, to the extent that extra-organizational politics is assumed to be contra-organizational.

Once the working class is organized and partially inserted into the state, it is dependent on its representatives, who are only autonomous in a manner of speaking. If the class tries for confrontation, rather than subordinate power, it will be because it has failed at the latter.

The aim has been to bring the machinery for the reproduction of class relations under the joint control of the politically organized. At the same time, it is now impossible to reproduce these relations on an extended, and expanding, scale. Those 'outside' the system are collectively powerless. They observe that the system reproduces, and does not transcend, class relations. The idea of a counter-society, a subversive state - or the armed party - cannot conceal the dependent character of the margin. The struggle thus becomes one for survival, not transcendance. Even at the height of 'autonomia', there seems to have been a mood of intense personal disillusion and disorientation. Action was once more localized ('autonomia' in Padua, various collectives elsewhere, diffuse subversion in general) and scaled-down (the gang, or groups keeping in touch through local radio or the underground press).

At the national level, to the marginal, terror is another disappointing ritual of retribution which changes nothing. Terror against the state becomes reprisal rather than subversion. 'Organized sociality withers: subjectivity, in the processes of self-construction, of "wild" socialization, grows in importance, is inflated. But it is a sick growth, fed by organized poverty, not social wealth.' (77) Indeed, the harshness and abrasiveness of life on the margin is in sharp contrast with the prospect of a post-labour society of sufficiency. The struggle against demoralization, in collective or individual forms, becomes predominant. For marginality is not only a material condition, it is a cultural one, experienced by worker-students, women, the unemployed, prisoners, young workers - all those disoriented and deculturated by the rapid changes in urban cultures in the 1970s.

In the 1960s, the 'new subject' had been hailed, provided with an ideology and a mission, though these gifts were promptly rejected. At that time, the new subject appeared as the bearer of an optimistic future. Even in 1975 it was still possible to speak of the homogenization of the young, the liberating relaxation of traditional values and openness to new ones. (78) This, however, was still based on the notion of the 'youth as student', in a relatively protected cultural environment. This tutelary situation had been challenged in 1967-9, in the face of attempts to maintain or instrumentalize this subordinacy.

A decade later, a different subordination has returned. Social repression is not simply repression by traditionalism allied with techno-bureaucracy, but by the winding down of the machinery which reproduces the social hierarchy of production, replacing it with structures of command. The formal 'learning arena' and that for self-education have both sharply contracted. Being a student has come to mean studying in seclusion, and 'education' is not a protected environment so much as a desert or, at times, a jungle.

It seems unlikely now that a Communist leader could criticize students for attacking universities as the defenders of culture and tradition, as Chiarante did in 1968. (79) Still, it is hard to see prospects for a rapprochement with the margin, so long as it is seen as the political negation of the PCI's strategy, and identified with 'autonomia'. The margin does not 'fit' into the technical elaboration of the PCI's authority. It represents the end of faith in organization, in sociality, in alliance and in technique. Politically, this does not constitute the basis of a movement, and indeed 'autonomia''s chief theorist, Negri, has always denied that this is a movement of the marginal. By itself, the margin is an underbrush of sporadic or clandestine 'subversion' or anomie. Experience teaches that it is unlikely jobs will be created, security provided and collateral services developed to offset a decline in employment, even though this may be masked by the 'uneconomical' processes of tertiarization, foreign borrowing, parasitism, low productivity or even dependent industrialization.

Another traditional link with the aspirations of the young has also been weakened. The intellectuals in the late 1960s and early 1970s who intervened in politics have for the most part been co-opted into administration, or form part of the historic Left's ideological apparatus. They are 'technicized', no longer peripheral. If they occasionally speak up for the periphery, they do so from another cultural and social world. They do not represent the periphery, and their distance from it is a greater setback for the Left than the distance of 'privileged' students in 1967-9 who ran ahead of the workers' movement. For the periphery now is a broader social mass, tendentially isolated from institutional politics and also from intellectuals.

In the early 1970s the PCI was changing the basis of its economic and social analysis, stressing that the priority was for Italy to defend her status as an industrial nation. It proposed the democratization of the schools, making them areas of adult participation and involvement. Educational policy must be seen not only in its political context, but as part of a strategy for maintaining the skill level of industrialization, and an area which, unlike investment or public spending, was accessible to the Party. Scepticism about optimistic forecasts by Svimez and Censis of the need for graduates led to a proposal for greater occupational qualifications for school-leavers. It was unclear whether that was a general cultural principle, or whether this would fill vacant positions, or create new ones, and raise the value of qualified labour. By the mid-1970s participatory democracy and decentralization had ceased to be mobilizing slogans and had become limited administrative realities. Yet where the issue of the early 1970s seemed to be that of curriculum reform and the school system as a whole, the prime question soon became the reorganization of the teaching body. This shows a more practical, less generic, approach, but it is also a tacit admission that settlement of the professional position of teachers must precede an approach to the students' interests. In fact, mass citizen participation, (80) like mass student or marginal movements, has been less effective in innovation than in corporate defence. In times of weakness of the student movement, the PCI attitude has tended to be: 'We cannot abandon the students and the students' movement to their fate, nor can we leave ... the student movement's banner to be carried exclusively by groups which from time to time may inherit the leadership of the movement.' (81) Thus political considerations have tended to dominate the technical question of the preparation of the skill-base for a new process of industrialization.

In part, the problem is that 'mass intellectual labour' is not proportionately raising the quality of the labour force. By common consent, the tertiary sector needs higher qualifications and fewer personnel. The distinction between the intellectual as technician-leader, as subaltern (teachers) and as mass of potential labour power is once more intensifying. The PCI has established itself as a force, if a lesser one, in universities and the professions, but 'mass produced labour power in formation' tends to resist incorporation into institutional politics. The underlying reasons are becoming clear, as data such as those for Southern graduate employment become known. (82) Graduates, as elsewhere, are forced into the public sector as there are so few scientific and technical jobs. Mass schooling here means mass tertiary education as an alternative to unemployment. The die is cast by the nature of local society, leaving only the alternative of restricting entry to the university (which would increase 'active' unemployment, or passing intellectual labour power from mass university to the dequalifying state sector). In this situation, neither the PCI nor organized labour offers protection. In 1969 the student movement seemed a permanent feature, capable of shaking the ruling class, a force for modernization, part exploited, part general intellect or general proletariat. (83) A decade later, its consistency, continuity and promise are compromised. It is a murky and obscure area of frustration and bitterness, regarded by the PCI as part wounded animal, part mad dog.

The university is still the instrument of social mobility or social confirmation to the professions. In addition, for some, it is the means to a humble career in reproducing already attenuated values and prospects in the school, and for others an initiation into the sub-proletariat. In an overcrowded and prospectless situation, the only economically viable 'solution' is the self-destructive one of removing surplus graduates. In 1969 Giovanni Berlinguer estimated them at one-third. (84) The students, in the PCI view, have nowhere to move in the present system, and are still less a modernizing force.

In relation to today's employment prospects, the children's comments on their teacher in the 1967 'Letter to a Teacher' read even more ironically: 'She has studied so much Latin, but she has never seen a statistical table.' (85) Now, not only are school and university not integrated into the productive system, a fear in 1968, but they are not integrated into the productive classes, a hope of the 1970s. In 1969 the PCI urged the student movement to escalate its demands to the level of the whole society. That path has been followed fruitlessly, the choice lying between direct action and apathy. (86) The 1968 PCI solution of democratization no longer operates for an institution in decay, and which seems to pose a threat to other institutions. (87) Nor can this intellectual labour power be seen as a producer of cultural alternatives, in the 'Angelus novus' sense of a non-bourgeois culture. (88) It is the culture of a sub-proletariat, quickly learning the conditions of other sub-proletarians.

Since the 1960s there has been a division among intellectuals of the Left between those following the traditional policy of bureaucratic intellecturals, that of forming consensus, and those who, rather than advocate class war, withdraw to professional concerns, or critical and sceptical positions. The historic Left offers leadership, organization and stability (also place) and leaves its intellectuals a considerable space for proposing policies. Yet, as the case of Salvatore Sechi shows, the role of an intra-party critic is thankless. (89) Intellectuals are needed as consultants. There has not been a massive influx of professionals to the parties of the Left: the large gains, especially in the PCI, have been made among the administrative staff. Yet as a handful of intellectuals, as administrators and consultants, have become more organic to the parties, the workers become increasingly the unqualified base whose function is to applaud the decisions reached by the leadership.

The key intellectual figure of the 1980s is likely to be the technician in public or semi-public service. This figure is highly specialized, in the sense of having access to small areas of information, and is also a subordinate part of the decision-making process. His indispensability to politicians transfers to him a minor part of their power: he is both servant and brain. Though, like traditional intellectuals, he may diffuse his findings, he is a part of the apparatus of power, of the chain of command, to a higher degree than the consensus-producing, ideological, intellectual. The function of the technical intellectual is not to reproduce intellectual labour power, but rather to administer the consequences of its overproduction. A decade ago the concern was to change the orientation and philosophical background of the PCI's interlocutors, to open the channels of communication to new voices. Now, however, the generalists are plentiful. Indeed, their job can be done by intellectual-journalists, in addition to the few philosopher-politicians who have sought their platform in the PCI. The crucial articulation is not, as before, at the level of great intellectual/Party, but expert/Party. The expert, of course, may also be a politician, in which case his value is much increased.

The PCI, with its first congress of administrators in 1979 (90) and the first attempts to devise regional investment planning, is in the process of equipping itself with governmental expertise. Expert-politicians, being in short supply, rapidly establish themselves in careers combining Party, government, and professional or bureaucratic elements. Alongside the technicization of politics there is a reciprocal politicization of strata of technical intellectual labour, such as journalists, cultural operators and employees in publishing, often by way of union activity. (91) In short, the 'crisis industry', its management and analysis, has a growing occupational structure. It is a structure close to forming part of the political class itself than the old, committed intellectual, or the intellectual as loyal Party member. Cerutti describes this as a process not of proletarianization, but of a 'strategy of politicization for the scientific intelligentsia'. (92)

This politicization is in part a direct result of the crisis, and the search for security and corporate protection. Yet it manifests a distance from the mass of labour power in formation. If the school is the immediate place for the production of (labour) value, it is clearly ineffective, or reflects at least the declining value of labour and the difficulty of 'valorizing' it in contemporary society. (93) The figure of the technician mentioned is that of the social analyst-administrator working, for example, to enlarge the labour market. It would be wrong to see the technician and the student as divided by class antagonism, but rather than the 1960s discussion of the lateral process of proletarianizing student labour power, the crucial relation is now the vertical relation of technical crisis-manager to 'devalued labour power in formation'. For the former, the concern is to 'get out of the crisis', and push for 'full employment for intellectual labour'. The argument about students as an 'autonomous division of the working class' is no longer appropriate when there is neither autonomy nor work. (94) Now, students are increasingly representative of the disprivileged of all social classes, with their potential labour value depreciating in the training process itself.

Education traditionally commands respect, confers power and determines social values. Mass education means the universalization of responsibility and the respect public opinion confers on it. Now, however, the evidence of low morale for teachers and administrative personnel, the overcrowding of faculties such as Magistero, Lettere and the social sciences, which offer few job prospects (especially for women, who are the majority of those enrolled) is eloquent. Those already vulnerable seem to gravitate to those areas which will unequivocally confirm and reinforce marginality. Working-class students tend to concentrate in the 'democratic' faculties of Magistero and the social sciences, where declining prospects add a political particularity to the social one. The technician must be optimistic because it is his function to solve (or minimize) the problem. (95) The margin, on the other hand, must exaggerate its size, as this is the only way of increasing its power. On social fragmentation of this kind, the literary intellectual can impose no coherent image. (96)

The relation between intellectuals and mass intellectual labour power was formed by crisis. There can be little optimism concerning the spread of technique to the mass intellectual as a political subject. The PCI's loss of influence among the young in general implies difficulty in establishing organic links with the cultural development of this section of society, not so much because it is a counter-culture, but because its culture is improvised, non-historical, non-literary, and certainly non-commercial. The PCI instead has wooed areas of technical and managerial expertise. The relatively privileged are attracted, while often the precarious worker is considered a potential extremist, to be avoided. The PCI's strategy for decline has concentrated on the administrators of crisis, rather than its victims. It has, at least for the moment, to aspire to be a Party of government not simultaneously with but as an alternative to being a Party of opposition.

Meanwhile, the margin has no part in the culture of literary-political intellectuals. The long preliminaries of approaching the masses by way of the artistic avant-garde now seem archaic. Literary intellectuals have yielded their place to organizers. (97) 1968-9 showed that 'culture' could have pre-vision of social need and demand, but exercise no control over them. This is a 'modern' trend, in that literature stops trying to provide an imaginative vehicle towards the future, and becomes one of many modes of communication within, and sometimes between, classes. It is the technical, administrative and publicist intellectuals who model the future. The margin does not share the values of intellectuals, therefore it cannot enter their world.

The 'silent victims' exist outside the 'new autonomization' pf technical-intellectuals as producers and distributors of integrated cultural values, and outside the reach of their communications. As Barbagli points out, this situation dates not to the early 1970s, but to the 1950s, and Alicata's observation that Italy was a society with too many teachers and too many illiterates, and too many doctors and too few hospitals. (98) For a generation, there has been an oversupply of nominally overqualified people only partly absorbed in the tertiary sector. Non-crisis periods have also contributed to the creation of a 'margin', which must increase in periods of decline. Optimistic forecasts have consistently been wrong, as in the 1961 Svimez report of a 1.2 million deficit in graduates by 1975. (99)

The crisis society lacks the social repositories of values which have traditionally sustained it, such as the idea of the Nation, of the people, the peasants or the workers, of 'culture', and of thinner figures such as 'responsibility'. (100) Initially, the Left could explain the contrast between its cultural conservatism and its faith in modernity by a rather unreal dichotomy between values and technique. (101) This also involved a de facto recognition that production of ideology was a social function, not a party monopoly. The question was to what extent the Party should, or could, intervene and influence that production. Since 1965, the consensus in the PCI has been that the Party should let its political prestige speak for itself. (102) This recognized the diversity and vitality of intellectual life and also its incorporation into a cultural industry where the PCI could not follow. Culture was no longer even mythically 'self-organized'. Now, however, both 'traditional' and 'plural' culture have lost their resonance.

This phenomenon reflects a breakdown in social articulation and communication. Society cannot identify its constituent parts (for instance, the size of the submerged economy) (103) or justify its own usefulness, its rationale (for instance, parasitism, corporativism and tertiarization). The search for cultural identity is hindered as much as helped by the absorption of intellectuals into Party circles, and thence into official or even administrative positions.

Indeed, as regards science, Giovanni Berlinguer's pessimistic forecasts show every sign of being fulfilled. (104) The prospect of a 'democratic control of science' seems even more distant, in an industrial context, than democratic control of management. As regards the latter, there tends to be a belated move towards a higher degree of public statement. The era of consolidation of family firms is now followed by efforts to expand Confindustria into the educational and political fields as spokesman for a national, not merely a sectoral, interest. The growth of the submerged economy changes the basis of alliance between the state and the private bourgeoisie. In addition, the state petty bourgeoisie provides the upper strata with opportunities for a new alliance, as well as for conflict. If the new petty bourgeoisie is not assimilable into a basic class, it none the less becomes crucial in determining if there be a renewal of the economically and politically dominant class, based on the lower level of conflictuality in the submerged economy. The new petty bourgeoisie is also a test of the organizational capacity of the directors, managers, major technicians and upper bureaucrats.

In 1973 a quarter of the labour force was in public administration, and relations between base and summit were described as 'tense', if not conflictual, by 1976. (106) In the 1970s the state bourgeoisie is becoming less speculative-political, more interested in identifying entrepreneurial skills and more concerned with partnership with private industry. It dominates social capital by controlling the banks and commerce, as well as major industry. (107) The PCI has always hoped that the decline of separate fractions of the dominant class would not be reversed by a new lateral alliance between state and private bourgeoisie, and a vertical reconciliation between the new petty bourgeoisie and its managers. The barrier to such a recomposition, apart from the overall prospects of the economy, is the fiscal crisis of the state, which perpetuates a division into 'public' and 'private' spheres which in other respects is no longer valid. In so far as the growth of public administration marks in itself the difficulty of the mode of production in 'proletarianizing' intermediate strata, or making them productive, decline will further accentuate the economic burden (and centrality) of the public sector. The aspirations of the state petty bourgeoisie are thus ambiguous. If the state bourgeoisie could devise a way of tapping revenues for the public sector, it would provide a means of uniting the upper and lower portions of the state bourgeoisie in a joint political and economic strategy. Such an alliance would involve strategies for overcoming limitations such as the illegality of the submerged economy's operations (notably fiscal evasion), and the fact that alliances within bureaucracies tend to be passive or inert. (108) Bureaucratic rationality de-mobilizes and de-ideologizes by becoming an ideological end in itself. Only in crisis does anti-capitalist (anti-private) sentiment in the bureaucracy take a democratic and radical turn, although the impulse to turn the private into the public is endemic.

It also seems that any appeal to reconstitute the petty bourgeoisie on the basis of the unity of intellectual labour is not at present feasible. De Castris is correct in saying that the 'democratic' movements of parents, teacher and students do not overcome the trend to 'the reductive management of social conflictuality at an eminently technical and corporate level'. (109) 'General intellect' has had a poor recent history.

Political administrators, like the career state bourgeoisie, suffer in their ambitions and efficiency from the discontent and inefficiency of their staffs. Thus, the first objective of, say, a Communist assessor is 'getting the system to work'. When this objective is translated into a regional plan for economic revival, the least perilous projects and scale are likely to be those of the 'Emilian' development, decentralized, small and middle industry, often based on social truce. This form of development is more conducive to the development of intellectual elites, backed by, if not actually composed of, institutionally organized technicians. The image of an interlocking decision-making structure, stretching from administrators to bankers to industrialists, is articulated by the bureaucratic, but institutionally distinct, organization of technicians, not on any horizontal articulation of the stratum of 'intellectual labour power' or technique. (110) Intellectual labour power is thus functionally reorganized, not on the basis of politically 'advanced' elements, but according to the various branches of public and private technical bureaucracies. It loses its last general qualitative and critical attributes, retaining vestiges of these only in the limited horizons of technical responsibilities, in the service of a superior political direction. Bobbio's remarks on the acceptance by intellectuals of politicians' arguments without discussion being a form of betrayal or desertion move to a new context. (111) The 'modern', technical intellectual, organized according to his skill and value in the making of consensually acceptable policy, does indeed discuss with politicians, but characteristically in a relation of apolitical complicity.

In 1970 Napolitano was still able to refer to the intellectual as moving upward from ideological (subaltern) tasks to leadership. (112) One of the features of social crisis is the failure of the working class to absorb new elements, whether of the middle strata, the margin or intellectual power in decline. This is of course because the working class, as a function of capitalism, is defined by the level of activity in the mode of production. For Marx, overproduction was the precondition for revolution: in decline, the class declines. It is not the working class but capitalism which recruits its members. The intellectual 'leads' the working class through control of its productive activity: production itself becomes a public sphere, and labour a public resource. Yet, for the intellectual, this is not a move 'upward' from an ideological function but a change in function which involves both submersion in the political, and subordination to the political.

If there is space for Gouldner's 'revolutionary intellectual', (113) it is not a general condition. The problem for the committed, literary, intellectual was how and what to oppose: for example, the cultural industry as an instrument of the dominant class. Now the image is fragmented and there is no agreement on what to oppose. The 1978 discussion of the 'courage or cowardice' of intellectuals, conducted in terms not too distant from Hegel's master-slave dialectic, was an indication of how divided intellectuals were about their political commitment in so far as it implied also a commitment to the state unto death. Did one risk one's independence, or one's life, for the (Italian) state? In the 1970s, the certainty that writers could express themselves as political dissenters has been overlaid by the search for a 'dissent also against politics', a verbal assault on the nexus of intellectual-politics-state. Left-wing politics now seems to be leading not to the class but to the interclassist state, not to the destruction of the state but its life-and-death defence. The old, anti-fascist certainties (114) no longer seem pertinent as guides to action. Hence too the charges against Negri involved the whole intellectual Left as demanding a response and formulation of personal conviction, which in its early stages seemed to develop towards an alignment of 'intellectuals versus the state'.

Effective space and effective choices diminish in decline. Though the social relations of the productive, subaltern classes are 'generalized' in abstract labour, the search for social identity may end in a generalized recognition of subordination. (115) Or, rather, intellectuals incorporate abstract labour into the state form itself, and are themselves incorporated. They are thus 'systematized', and are at once the managers of the state and subordinate to raison d'état. Politics then becomes a technical discussion of whether there is a crisis, and how it can, or should, be managed. This area of political calculation was nicely expressed in the discussion of the 'due tempi' (i.e., whether reform should precede or follow economic recovery). (116) If one cause of crisis is alarmism, waiting in silence for a short-lived recovery is an excuse for doing nothing. Productivism becomes more plausible than reformism, and may evade the artificial or partial recovery (the 'ripresa drogata'). (117) Crisis politics increasingly rests on the range of dispute among economists. Whether one waits to see the second stage of the 'due tempi', or attempts reform when struggling out of recession, the results are fore-ordained to modesty because of the structural limitations and the social interests to be mediated. The choice between apocalypse and austerity is mirrored in political discourse by the argument concerning concentration of power as against the proliferation of counter-powers. This is an argument not on what the state does but on what it is: is it the barrier to collapse or an unnecessarily concentrated expression of social powers which should be diffused among responsible social subjects? Should it oppose legal rationality (rights) to administrative rationality (corporations)?

This scenario is not that of Marx, with its optimism about growth, infinite resources and unlimited human ingenuity, and a revolutionary subject historically wise amid the mountains of unpurchasable commodities, from whose production it has only recently been excluded. In declining industrialization, the margin must grow. Yet improvised forms of elaborating new values and restraining social conflict, though inherently unstable, are not necessarily volatile. The 'traditional' margin may experiment with militant protest (organizations of the unemployed, for example), but its material situation inhibits strategic dissent. The 'new' marginality is divided between a political form of autonomy and an economic form of precarious dependency, which are not easily reconciled.

Thus, Italian youth, with slender connections with the past, and minimal hopes for the future, is confronted by an apparently uncaring (and in any case impotent) society. It is consequently attracted to 'thanatos'. In such a context, social disintegration is neither a necessary prelude to reintegration nor a condition of growth in which social ties must be weak to permit mobility and the acquisition of new skills, needs and values, even though these in turn must be transitory, and easily annulled or devalued. (118)

Social disintegration is the mark either of loosening social ties in a developing society, or a failure of a social system to reproduce and integrate on the basis of reciprocal social relations, of multi-laterality. Both cases excite an anti-authoritarian response. However, anti-authoritarianism leads either to new authority (with command), or to further social disintegration. When it leads to the latter, there is a need for command to confront challenges to command, such as the armed party, which is destructive not of authority but command. The 'narcissism' of the margin is thus either one of personal annihilation (death-wish, drugs, suicide), or a violent rejection of integration (the gang, the paramilitary group) which challenges command, and has its own command and authority. We see in Italy both the privatization of individualism into a personal, apolitical form, even to malaise and self-destruction, and the direct challenge to social command.

Meanwhile, the old petty bourgeoisie is experiencing a modest boom, although the success of the small-scale tends to produce a fresh movement towards dependent labour. The state petty bourgeoisie is in part a victim of the narrowness of the productive sector, but has no prospects save that of corporate organization. The traditional organized workers have re-elaborated their qualitative demands, the quantitative limits having apparently been reached. They cannot articulate and direct the new strata, even where there are income and organizational similarities.

This society is less organized on its own account, more divided, and less authoritatively governed than could have been foreseen in the post-miracle Italy of the 1960s. Can there be a steady reconstruction in the economy which also reverses the trend to the constriction and sclerosis of social relations? Is it even feasible to consider autonomous economic measures in an economy so integrated into the international division of labour, and so open to international pressures?

In the transition from feudalism to capitalism, a feeble capitalism not only attempted to dissolve the bonds of customary authority and mutual dependence, but relied heavily on the stability and adaptability of feudal structures. Its relation with feudalism was one of symbiosis. It too had its 'margin' of sturdy beggars who were centuries from forming an industrial proletariat. The analogy with other periods of decline-transition may in fact be instructive.

Chapter 5

THE 'ARMED PARTY'

Terrorism, grand and petty, may be fuelled by social and psychic marginality. It is, however, one response to the incapacity of the state to impose its claim to legitimacy in the form of either consensus (authority) or deterrence (command). The armed party is a political rather than a social phenomenon because it is the product of a state with weak legitimacy. It may sometimes behave like a party, in a system of parties, but it is really a shadow-state. Since the state lacks the capacity to produce consensual authority relations throughout civil society, the social margin provides a tendentially growing constituency for an armed party. However, as a quasi-state which challenges the authority and command of the state, it must base its claims on a much broader class constituency. By extension, it requires to be judged by the criteria applied to states, and not to parties as their sub-systems.

It is assumed here that terrorism is not merely anomic, and that it is not wholly ideological (for example, Catholic-millenarian or Leninist-Stalinist). It is also assumed that there are substantial differences between the shadowy 'area of autonomy', often described as suspended or defunct, diffuse physical militancy and the clandestine paramilitary movement, even though there is inter-penetration on a substantial scale. In the case of the paramilitary movement, the Brigate rosse have most openly discussed strategy and tactics. It is a further assumption here that the existence of the 'autonomous' movement and paramilitary organizations helped to deepen the legitimacy crisis of the state. These are responses to the political incapacity of the Italian state to maintain authority by acting either as a liberal state with 'decisive neutrality' or as a bourgeois democracy by admitting producers to the political terrain of discussion of the distribution of the social surplus. The state becomes a primary target at this point, since in the economic sphere 'private' capitalists can no longer retain hegemony (now seen as command), and 'state' capitalists can no longer effectively intervene in the economy (exercise authority). The legitimacy of the state class becomes the focus for attack at the moment when the distinction between public and private (formerly 'political' and 'economic') becomes untenable.

It is not easy to analyse a submerged politics with a range of behaviour including militarily planned attacks on the state and its symbols, as well as petty sabotage and intimidation often related to local concerns. Theorists legitimizing political violence have tried to appropriate the classical Marxist tradition of the armed class. Other interpretations of the armed party or armed movement have included international conspiracy (even a black and red one), 'common criminality', an anarchic, petty bourgeois confusion of ideologies (Stirner, Stalin, liberal individualism, Nietzsche, Sorel - a pot-pourri for the desperate and semi-literate), and a crisis in radical, anti-capitalist Catholicism. (1)

Political violence in Italy has taken so many different forms, and been theorized on so many different grounds, that it seems essential to account for it in terms of broad, structural causes. Second, there is an important difference between the claim for terrorism, or political violence, at the state level and that for diffused violence against the private, ranging from self-protection to 'street justice' and intimidation. The debate on the legitimacy of the state, and the claim of its opponents to be acting as a state, and demanding to be treated as members of this second, hidden, state is more serious than often admitted. It is basic to the dialogue between a paramilitary movement (like the Brigate rosse) and its presumed social constituency, the movement. This remains the case even if links between the 'strategic command' of the Brigades and the movement are established. For if the case for 'armed counter-power' rests on the impossibility of a class state being legitimized by its class opponents, what is the status of an interclass state? If the PCI inserts the formally organized part of the working class into the state, and secures the class's approval, can this state not be legitimized by the working class?

Terrorism normally has as its objective destabilization so that long-term counter-organization can take place. It justifies itself on the moral-political grounds of the non-legitimacy of the state and the moral iniquities committed in its name by its agents. The terrorist, however, in rejecting the state's legitimacy, does not reject the concepts of rights and law. Theoretically, his respect for these should be higher. This leads to inconsistencies. The Red Brigades, for instance, have refused to recognize state justice, and have also demanded that the state recognize their rights, as a kind of recognition of future state by present state.

The argument against political violence on the ground that Italy is a politically 'open' society, not one which has restricted political rights, is in reality complex. We may agree that using violence against individuals as possessors of guaranteed rights is not legitimate, but still argue that this does not resolve the question of the legitimacy of exercise of differential powers in society in the name of the state. In the latter event, we may also argue that the onus is on the guerrilla movement to prove its legitimacy, as the Resistance movement in Italy had substantially managed to do in the North by the end of the war. Until it does so (and so far it has progressed little beyond retributive justice, with military flair but political bungling, as in the failure to 'try' Moro publicly and indeed surrendering the initiative to press, parties and Moro's own letters to the Christian Democrats), the state-in-occupation is presumed to be legitimate. Yet the Italian state has a poor record as a representative, guarantee state. The exclusion of the PCI from the government ran counter to the spirit, though not the letter, of the Constitution. It encouraged the view that the state, while it had elements of liberal and social democracy, was primarily a class regime in the early 1970s that itself used subversion to retain power, in the policy of the 'opposed extremisms'.

If the state is open, and representative, it protects individual rights. It does not have rights of its own. If it cannot guarantee the social, economic and political rights as set out for individuals and groups in the Constitution, does not its partial protection of rights destroy any claim to be open and universal? If the state is open, it cannot be a victim. In the open, non-class, state, only individuals can be victims, though the state acts as victim when it charges terrorists with crimes against itself. Recognition of political crimes admits a moral personality in the state, and thus, theoretically, supplies criteria for contesting its morality. What is the moral personality of an open, liberal, state - one, that is, where conservative structures are in decline, and where individuals, organized into self-protective institutions ad hoc, still inhabit a vast, unregulated, human market-place where individuals are free to sink or swim, enjoy themselves or be frustrated, legitimize or not legitimize? What, for instance, are we to make of the non-guaranteed 'constitutional right' to work? What is the moral basis of expectation from the state, or indeed from sociality itself? What guarantees and reciprocal responsibilities operate?

The decline of liberal and social-democratic states, and their economic and social systems, does not logically or politically justify armed insurrection. Both types of state were based on the (rising) expectation that they would be able to guarantee sociality during periods of growth and of temporary decline. Now these rules of (implicit) state obligation are being rewritten in Italy where the prospects are of decline, rather than in hegemonic states such as Germany or Japan where authoritarian measures are seen as legitimate to ensure reproduction of social relations and maintain the status hierarchy in times of recovery.

Italian social democracy and the PCI developed within an ideology of growth. The current debate, on the other hand, turns on whether to institute a liberal, market, model of decline, seeking institutions outside the state which will guarantee a minimum of civility to competition, or a conservative, authoritarian, model, enforcing order even at the expense of free competition and without attachment to tradition and community. These processes of transition envisage social recomposition under consensual rules. There is a case, on the contrary, for saying that under the rules of former liberal-welfare democracy both models are tyrannies, curtailing or abrogating rights and expectations formerly enjoyed. Their legitimacy derives from law and order, not the hope of satisfying material needs and securing individual protection.

What, then, can the basis of legitimacy and guarantees in the future state of armed party or armed movement, be? Scalzone, discussing relations between the unarmed movement and a military arm claiming to act on its behalf, provides some criteria for the legitimacy of the latter's claim. He argued that subjective armed struggle was based on false consciousness or anomie. We might extend this to say that persistence in armed struggle despite the criticism of a (presumed) constituency is also de-legitimating. Second, armed struggle as the reaction of new social strata, the young, precarious, insecure and educated proletariat, is merely a social reflex, not a political strategy. Armed struggle is legitimate only as a radical extension of the class struggle. (2)

It remains doubtful whether the Brigades have state-legitimacy in the eyes of 'autonomia', even though other forms of politics seem static and unavailing. This is not only because of the wide divergences of opinion in 'autonomia', but also because the activities of the Brigades have curtailed so much of those of 'autonomia', which in any case is the antithesis of a disciplined, dirigiste organization. 'Autonomy' itself is a style of life, often of aggressive, physical response to, and rejection of, institutionalized life. It is not an ideology or political movement so much as a spontaneous, bitter and even brutal attack on the most immediate representatives of 'normal', capitalist civilization, the teacher, the shopkeeper, the policeman. Politically, it is of the Left, in the sense that its opponents are presumed to be fascists. This form of 'autonomia', as opposed to the 'intelligent "autonomia"' of universities and the older generation, does not claim to be part of a 'historic' Left. The young 'autonomi' of the sub-proletariat practise a politics which is essentially one of cultural deprivation (sometimes manipulated by 'intelligent "autonomia"'). The social background is that of the slums and the concrete jungles of the urban periphery, where employment prospects are meagre, at least at the level of professional qualification they are theoretically being prepared for.

Their alternatives would seem to be to remain as a cultural margin, anomic and violent, essentially composed of life's losers, unable to articulate widespread and coherent political action, harried by the police and feared by those in contact with them, or to become militarized. In the latter event, this would mean accepting that only diffuse guerrilla action and the destabilization of the 'integrated' working class are feasible options. Guerrilla warfare does not destabilize the political system, but it does destabilize, or rather immobilize, the organized working-class movement. For 'autonomia', political discussion has its limits in the cultural apparatus at its disposal. Over those excluded by the system, the system, of course, has absolute power, at least till the moment of revolt or dissent. This observation provides 'autonomia''s links with an intellectual heritage with which, by definition, it should properly acknowledge no connection.

Socially, the identified leaders of the Brigades are not marginal, and this helps to account for a political consistency and determination which the 'autonomia' of the socially marginal lacks, as well as partially explaining the differences of objectives and strategies between their organization and the amorphous autonomous movement. The former has a history, and an international and theoretical context and tradition: the latter does not. The former represents a discussed response to the failure of mass insurrection, and the radical movement of 'bourgeois' students in 1967-9. It developed on the basis of analysis of the strategy of tension from 1971 on. The movement, however, shared the shadowy and shifting character of the marginal, the proletarianized petty bourgeois, as the sea in which the Brigades fished for sympathizers and minor recruits. The establishment of close links between the Brigades and 'autonomia' would justify the PCI's political, if not its social, analysis. It would also restore the prestige of the state. Yet, at another level, it would also show how hard it is to find effective political space to the left of the PCI, and it also continues to show that the present and future direction of Italian society is contested not by a few ideologues but by a substantial social and political stratum.

Negri has most intelligently expressed the spirit of the new marginal, with its combination of millenarian justice, of disgust with 'legitimate society'. He combines social analysis (the 'societal worker' or society-as-worker, the diffused factory), with utopianism. (3) He proposed a vision of post-labour, that is, post-necessity, society, a dictatorship of the proletariat alternative to the forced division of labour and the essence of capitalist authority in the state plan. The analysis is based not on marginality and the marginal, and is a proposal for the whole society. It is a project for a state, not a party, and a verbal declaration of war on both state and party form. It is not, however, a contribution to the theory of the socialist state.

Of course, the Brigades have attacked the state form physically, in the symbolic figures of managers, union leaders, magistrates and police, politicians and journalists. They have hit the modest employee of the state and the 'statesman'. The strategy of symbolic retribution has been completed. This can now only be repeated, or replayed on a grander scale, as there are no bases for compromise, only an interchange between concessions and intimidation, for the state cannot recognize the Brigades as also a state. The Brigades' attempt to combine armed insurrection with mass movement would normally rest on an alliance between an active nucleus and a passive, repressed, mass of sympathizers. Thus it is not because the sociaty is 'open' that the guerrilla movement is not legitimate, but because it is covert, and its supporters must be silent and passive.

As Stame suggests, 'autonomia' has flourished not only because, in a blocked society, class conflict is not openly and decisively expressed, but also because 'autonomia' is a way of actively 'doing politics' when there are no prospects of power or place, and no organic links with conditions of production. The choice of clandestinity artificially emphasizes the tendential passivity and disillusion of this mass. It seems, therefore, that since the clandestine party can never openly instrumentalize the movement, and vice versa, the elements of a long-term but inconclusive, submerged, dialogue are present. Leaving aside the academic question of legitimacy, the political impotence of the movement has its counterpart in the maximalism of the armed nucleus which yet has no public, political, discourse or debate. It is a nucleus which, unlike the Resistance, fights a civil war in the name of a class which does not accept its right to hegemony.

Certainly, 'submerged politics' is not restricted to those culturally deprived and excluded. It runs through areas such as common criminality, the secret services, interlocutors in or close to the political system and a variety of non-violent but non-legitimated and non-institutionalized politics. These areas are not only part of an endemic social pathology, but a natural response to the blockage of the state and of institutional politics. In this situation, 'social pathology' simply refers to lack of consensus that no objective has priority over keeping the rule of non-violence, and this becomes 'political pathology', which means simply the non-observance of the rule that sabotage is not a valid response to power or dominion. The less efficient the state, and the more the mode of production declines, the more attractive politics outside the state becomes. This then ceases to be a question of 'marginality' and becomes central. To counteract inefficiency and incapacity, the state resists non-legitimated and non-institutionalized powers (autonomy). Repression stimulates the claim that the rules of civil war be observed. But civil war destroys the mass base by making the movement powerless, and thus de-legitimizes the clandestine forces themselves. Valerio Morucci and Adriana Faranda, and the alleged 'movement' faction in the Brigades, accused the Brigades of ineffectiveness and of rigidity caused in part by the lack of realistic concern for, and contact with, mass support. (4)

The difficulty of securing change through non-institutionalized movements has not lessened since 1968-9. Indeed, the most effective innovation in the past decade has been the use of constitutional referenda. However, 1968-9 is not the only 'movement' phenomenon which can be claimed as a legitimizing model. The relation between mass and armed party is part of a tradition which includes the Carbonari, certain aspects of the Third International and pre-industrial terrorists and bandits. Obviously,

Bocca exaggerated when he linked modern terrorism to the central tradition of class politics: 'The tradition of the workers' and peasants' movement is one of political violence.' (5) It is not one of terrorism, and it was not the prospect of mass violence that initiated the process of formation of the Brigades and the Southern, often prison-based, Armed Proletarian Nuclei, but experience of defeat, of governmental manipulation and reaction after 1969, and the decision to form a 'resistance' from 1971. The choice was of defensive warfare from a position of weakness, and the use of violence at least in part was a direct response to fascist terrorists. The first phase of Brigade activity was of 'exemplary justice', not killing. (6)

It is important to stress the political calculation behind the formation of the Brigades, not social pathology or spontaneity. Clandestinity forms its own supportive margin, while the social margin attempts, with great difficulty, to form its own movement, a quasi-institutionalization of its present, and the only vehicle for its future. The Brigades have a coherent strategy, if it be seen not as organizing revolution but as putting pressure on the state, especially that part of the state disposed to conciliate or instrumentalize them. Diffuse sabotage of minor targets also exerts institutional pressure. It exacerbates the resentment of prison officers who claim they are underpaid and underprotected in undermanned prisons. Intimidation also secures better treatment for Brigade prisoners, and establishes the influence of the 'brigatisti' among other prisoners. The real impact on the state, however, is indirect, in the uncertainty as to whether reprisals represent the action of a nucleus, or a social and political area. Black terrorism and 'red reprisal' is endemic: so is what we might call social terrorism, where kidnapping, threats and sabotage are directed against the wealthy (speculators, landlords) and the influential (journalists, teachers). 'Militant anti-fascism' and social terrorism, with the latter's ambiguous relation to common criminality, do not involve an attack on the state. The state fears not a direct political assault so much as the dissolution of social consensus.

Militant anti-fascism is a practical self-defence against 'squadrismo' moving into new areas of the cities. 'Social terrorism' is a response to the illegal, speculative and exploitative activities of the wealthy and powerful. This type of vigilante action, though it may have a political base, does not claim to redress the social balance. Yet social terror is often the base for the qualitative leap to the level of the state, as it seems to have been for 'Prima linea' and other organizations with a presence in more than one major city. It creates a climate of passive sympathy, as well as insensitivity and confusion.

The attack on the state, though, does not follow easily from 'street justice' against profiteers or landlord-politicians. The public still communicate with the state through its parties, and the parties try to interpret the silences of the state to their followers. However, this social communication is now incomplete, because of general disillusionment and a lack of interlocutors to the PCI's left, an area where the Party itself can no longer despatch envoys. It is significant, however, that it was not the state, which in Italy is really an archaeology of states piled on top of one another, but the parties, which responded to the Brigades in the Moro case. This also explains why the Brigades' objective of attacking the state is so unrewarding. The state is not a summit to be won, but a mass of separate bodies serving different masters and in various relations with the political class and economically dominant class.

The PCI is committed to the notion of the centrality of the state, and hence of the Brigades as its negation, through its appreciation of the 'centrality of centralism', the monopoly of command in the Western state tradition of Hobbes, Locke, Rousseau, Kant and Lenin. The state is inclusive, and democracy requires inclusion in the state. The Socialist Party, with its notion of counter-powers, is capable of a more realistic description of the Italian state structure, though it is hard to see its proposals for an 'advanced liberalism' as a real option. The choices seem to lie between paleoliberalism and the 'modern state'. The centrality of the universal state, as the political form of the total society, explains why the PCI is so uneasy with the concept of social margin, and so adamantly opposed to the notion of the state, or parties, doing deals with armed militants. Other parties are willing to take part in the traditional manipulation-reconciliation in the name, and in default, of the state.

If indeed the state fears political organizations waging war on the summit of the state less than a diffusion of anomic and social violence of Right and Left, it has cause for alarm. The autonomous movement and the Brigades declined after the execution of Moro. Petty insurrection spread. The number of 'left' organizations claiming responsibility for terrorist attacks increased between 1977 and 1978. Attacks on political and union facilities dropped, while in Rome and Milan attacks on individuals nearly doubled (they fell slightly in Turin). (7) In Rome, attacks on school, university and cultural and recreational property more than doubled. The implication is that there are more, younger, and smaller commandos taking part in diffuse violence.

Ottavio Cecchi noted that in Padua, 'autonomy' serves as a focus for poor students, often from the South, for whom the university is central (a quarter of the city's) population are students), and for whom autonomy gives a sense of power, a revivalist strength. The basis of the movement is poverty and messianism, whether Catholic or of the Left: this accounts for the reprisals against public transport after fare increases - a strong sense of the need to inflict punishment, whatever the cost. (8) Poverty and vandalism, social hopelessness and the gigantism of carrying a weapon, being able to damage the people and things which damage one's already precarious existence are recipes for continuing attacks on civil society, its administrators and protectors. The aim is less an alternative state than a 'community of the poor', built partly on hatred and contempt for the comfortable and competitive. Their situation is a forewarning to neo-liberals that at this level the rules of the market cannot be enforced, and to neo-conservatives that it is hard to fabricate organic communities in a declining market society. For the theoretical discussion of legitimacy, blocking the buses is not illuminating. A delight in violence, natural in a society where high-level corruption is so common and blatant, does suffuse part of the movement, and explains why it is so close at times to the underworld, 'la mala'. (9) It reflects too the existence of a covert civil war in which the bourgeoisie finances its own terror. (10)

'Terrorizing' comfortable, corrupt, society is nurtured by the general sense of apocalypse and collapse. Tronti argued that the removal of Moro had exacerbated the crisis by finishing with the last force capable of mediating between social conflict and state institutions. (11) Social conflict, however, is not synonymous with terrorism, which failed to sustain its momentum after 9 May 1978. After the arrest of its 'thinkers', 'autonomia' seems to have settled back into a 'normal' condition of social and political powerlessness. Not only had the limits of street politics been reached, they had been pushed back by, for instance, forcing the movement out of the Rome university campus and by banning demonstrations, but in any case the movement had not brought social conflict on to the terrain of the institutions.

It is still unclear what the links were between 'autonomia''s theorists of diffuse terror and the Brigades' macroterrorism. In Negri's case, he tried to formulate a non-Leninist form of organization and a 'theoretical anti-Stalinism', (12) which retained Leninist formulations of the need for dictatorship of the proletariat. This was an appeal to the class, not to the margin. Others have argued that the Brigades do not rely on a specific social base, and that contact with 'autonomia' is suicidal for the latter. (13) 'Autonomia', it has been argued, should identify itself with the marginal. The subject is not the student-as-worker, but a movement of workers either outside, or hostile to, the institutionalization of the traditional working class.

Therefore, the argument has been, 'autonomia' has nothing to learn from the experience of the Brigades, whose principles are Leninist and military. It should address itself to the problem and phenomenon that it is primarily a movement of marginal workers, of workers who study because they have no work, or work because they cannot afford to study. 'Autonomia' should cease to regard the Brigades as a proxy political wing, and face the consequences of its isolation and immobility. The margin is potentially too large to wither as its political expression has done, but it has failed to address itself to the public (14) and, more to the point, has failed to identify its own constituency. In its state of powerlessness and social disintegration, 'autonomia' became localized and insulated from society: 'society' was happy to leave it in isolation.

Institutionalizing this isolation, however, is a two-edged weapon, as is shown by the parallels drawn by Cacciari and Bolaffi between 'autonomia' and pre-revolutionary Russian messianism. (15) Yet both seem to assume this is one pre-revolutionary movement for which there will, and must, be no revolution. Bolaffi criticizes the notion that terrorism forces a crisis of existing forms of social control, arguing that terrorism loses sight of the centrality of class struggle. 'Autonomia''s ambivalence towards violence undermines its legitimacy. Yet in fact 'autonomia' does reflect a crisis in social relations and social obedience, and it is a sign that it is the PCI that has assumed the task of blocking the traditional route to the Left. 'Autonomia' is thus the movement of a failed revolution, one conscious at the outset that it has failed in its historic mission, since capitalism in decline kills the working class and the perspective of revolution.

The state does not recover legitimacy by suppressing 'autonomia', or by establishing its possible connections with the Brigades. The decline of social relations makes both terrorist and political reactions, especially on the margin, the exception. Normality is to be found in the anomic reaction. The state might guarantee order (reprisal and punishment), and by accommodating the PCI increase its formal, representative, legitimacy. However, in a period of decline, legitimacy based on order (command) does not necessarily recover authority or civility.

We may expect the coexistence and disconnection of the attack on the state by military means, a diffuse 'social terror', and a margin alternating between proto-movement phases and anomie. The conditions which produce marginality prevent the restoration of legitimacy, but the attack on the state does not represent the size or opinions of the margin. Politicians of the institutional order may be able to keep the forms of dissent and rebellion separate, but the various causes of each seem likely to persist, without resolution.

The movement, unlike that of the 1960s, is acutely conscious that the destiny of movements is death. The 'armed party' parodies the generalized, repressive-destructive, state it aspires to replace. The PCI, by proposing to enter the present state, clearly hopes to provide a continuity for the social life and evolution the non-institutionalized Left repudiates. It is thus bound to deny the origins in the crisis itself, or even the authenticity and existence, of these 'new political subjects'.

Chapter 6

STRATEGY FOR DECLINE: the economy

Though the PCI presents itself as the best guarantee for political stability and systemic integration, economists hold out little optimism regarding economic recovery. (1) Almost all major economists are marginalists, and thus seek strategies for re-equilibrating the economy, finding areas of potential growth in the South and in diffusing and directing the submerged economy. A primary issue is the extent to which structural problems antedate the international crisis of the 1970s, and the distortion these produced in the marginalist mechanism of recovery. Low productivity, conservative and countervailing monetary policy and a narrow industrial base were also features of the 1960s. The 1970s added a balance of payments crisis, the congealing of the labour market and an apparent increase in precarious and irregular employment, as well as rising unemployment and a crisis of large industry already suffering from the 'strike of capital' in the previous decade. Italy's vulnerability as an export-propelled economy, with few resources (except labour), especially energy resources, seemed to preclude many 'development' strategies. One view holds that Italy is an economic type peculiarly damaged by international factors. Rich in labour but poor in resources and capital, her future can be only as a low-wage economy tributary to, for instance, Germany. However, rising prices inexorably drag the country into debt, while rising wage costs and low productivity destroy previous advantages.

Another view is that Italy has suffered more than necessary, despite her international situation. Thus, the recession and stagnation of the 1960s were worsened by the Bank of Italy's monetary policies. The 'miracle' gave a misleading prospect of growth, and discouraged modern economic management. It had been possible only with weak unions, old-fashioned and often repressive labour management, and disregard for social investment. The 1960s showed no eagerness to move to the next phase, with planning and rational investment policies. The pattern of Southern development, of public investment in the infrastructure and private expensive 'cathedrals in the desert', raised expectations in the Mezzogiorno which were soon bitterly disappointed. Organized labour, at the beginning and end of the decade, reacted with two wage-pushes to 'catch up' proportionately with their share of national product, and in 1969 had some measure of linkage between wages and inflation. However, the continuing weakness, division and social irresponsibility of entrepreneurs meant that the general picture remained one of industrial conflictuality, with falling productivity as a consequence. Agriculture was drastically reduced as a result of the improvident aim of a totally industrialized Italy, so that now food imports contribute to the balance of payments deficits. Devaluation of the lira was rapidly overtaken by inflation in the 1970s, making repayment of foreign loans more onerous. So long as resources of labour are under-used, the internal market and internal demand will remain weak. Development of the tertiary and public sectors, normal in advanced countries, had a pathological and parasitic aspect, as forms of subsidy or pension, a political strategy to lessen the discontent of the middle strata and provide support for the regime.

Paradoxically, this second interpretation gives grounds for optimism, especially to the Socialist Party and PCI economists. For the implication is that the crisis lies in relations between government and experts, and government and industry. The government did not heed expert advice because it saw public money as a patronage fund to be spent on the grand scale for political motives. Entrepreneurs had no confidence in the government, preferring to export capital or wait for government guarantees for their operations. Now, the argument runs, it is too late, and too utopian, to hope for a master plan. The only hope is for a capillary movement of industry to the centre and South, with regional investment plans based on agreements between regional giuntas, banks, public, private or co-operative enterprises to co-ordinate projects. This, of course, is a 'productivist' solution, and runs the risks of new investment at a time of recession. Its critics argue that a combination of factors make periods of recovery shorter in Italy than elsewhere, and that new investment will simply enter the cycle of brief up-swing and lengthy decline.

Therefore one should begin not with the risk of fresh industrial investment, committing public money to high-wage and long-term projects, but rather cut existing subsidies and the public portion of the tertiary sector, despite subsequent institutional strain and the social cost of deflation. Another 'low-cost' initiative would be to ensure that the 'welfare capitalist' system produced more social benefit. Social priorities should be established as a criterion for lending and public subsidy. This would give incentives to private industry to 'responsibilize' itself.

Others argue that these general answers are unrealistic. The crisis is structural, but its manifestations are sectoral. This necessitates a sectoral approach to problems. Finally, another school of thought focuses on the centrality of the submerged economy, suggesting that the guess of a 15 per cent contribution to the national economy is too low. The 'welfare state' properly means welfare capitalism, and it is for the submerged economy (particularly 'lavoro doppio' (second jobs) rather than child or superexploited labour) to compete on favourable terms with Eastern European manufactures (because of East European payments difficulties) and with the smaller, less adaptable, export industries of, say, India and China.

Most analyses, however, provide over-simplified accounts of social conflict. One assumption is that, in the absence of an enforceable wages and prices policy, labour should see that its interest lies in increasing productivity. Indeed, some union leaders see this as the next phase of their strategy. But this raises the question of conflict involved in the modification of the status hierarchy, and of control and distribution of the newly produced social wealth. It also minimizes the significance of conflictuality in the 'unproductive' sectors and those involved in the distribution of revenue, not surplus value. Raising productivity requires a sociopolitical culture, prospects of growth and legitimation of public control and private ownership, which do not exist in Italy. The guarantee of democracy which the labour movement contributes to the objectives of the PCI is not based on the integration or 'Germanization' of the working class, but on conflict and struggle. Raising productivity may be a rational interest only if labour accepts the rationality of capitalism in the long term, and the aims of public management. Baffi, of the Bank of Italy, recognized the justice of such scepticism, arguing that neocapitalism plus bureaucratic control reduced the whole system to general inefficiency. Productivity in any case was determined not by union strategy and wage levels, but by the efficiency and promptness of managerial responses. Where surplus was absorbed by the unproductive sectors, and by maladministration of backward and uncompetitive sectors, only unorganized entrepreneurial sectors could escape the trend to permanent recession.

There is considerable agreement between economists, the Bank of Italy and the PCI on the key features of the crisis. Indeed, it is instructive to trace the change in the PCI's original class-struggle account of the crisis in the 1960s to a marginalist one. In 1968 the analysis was that the deflationary policy of Carli (the very powerful governor of the Bank of Italy) from mid-1963 was a punishment of the working class for the catching-up of wages in 1962. (2) Carli convinced Colombo at the Treasury that he should pursue the former's deflationary line, and Colombo convinced Moro in May 1964 that economic collapse was imminent, a 'pure falsification'. (3) La Malfa, the Republican Party's leader and economic expert, had, in his 'nota aggiuntiva' in May 1962 already laid the foundation of the notion of the 'due tempi': first, control of the immediate crisis, then social expenditure during the recovery. Even this was sabotaged in 1964-5 when the government exaggerated the gravity of the crisis while contributing to it by economic policies which reduced investment and employment. (4) The failure of the Pierraccini plan marked the end of any pretence at long-term, large-scale planning, and the end of the hopes of centre-Left planning or reformism. (5) To the inherent instability of monopoly capitalism there was added political sabotage, directed both against the claims of labour and the Socialist Party in government.

Between this statement, however, and the new orthodoxy of the 1970s, there is a divide. In part, changes in the economic analysis can be explained by tactical concerns, such as the end of the need to criticize the centre-Left. None the less, the change in approach is profound. In 1974, said Luciano Barca, the Italian economy lost important support. The revaluation of the US dollar hurt European exports. The era of low raw material prices, especially of energy, wastefully used, ended. The era of low wages was also over. (6) Earlier analyses had seen the period of the 'miracle' as the last phase of the 'easy development' of capitalism. The present crisis was not the final crisis of capitalism, but a general worsening of economic conditions. Yet the 1962 Convegno organized by the Istituto Gramsci in Rome recorded the 'general crisis of capital which is becoming more serious, because of the collapse of colonialism, the advance of socialism, and world competition between socialism and capitalism.' (7) Between 1962 and 1966 the PCI debated, and was in doubt over, the merits of struggle over wage claims and those for reforms. In 1966 Longo went further, and proposed a change in the mechanism of accumulation, directing investment to popular, not luxury, consumption, but stressing the role of the market and profit as means of development. (8) Italy was thus coming to be seen less as a victim of capitalist development than as a victim of its decline.

Barca, one of the leading Party economists, argued that there was continuity in the PCI's analysis of cyclical European movements between 1944 and 1974. (9) In the 1960s the Party had been discussing the role of profit in growth, and of the labour movement in reform. However, compared with the 1968 Cespe account, there are important differences, and the case for continuity does not ring true. In the 1960s the assumption was that monopoly-imperialism was a cause not only of development, but of distorted development, and that the difficulties of the 1960s were a direct result of a strategy designed to frustrate reforms which might strengthen the labour movement. 1962-4 was indeed a turning-point, changing the balance of forces between dominant group and subordinate classes, and from 1963-8 the dominant class carried out a counter-attack at the economy's expense. Barca, by placing the turning-point in 1974, and the weight on factors outside national control, shifts the emphasis from class struggle and monopoly capitalism's distortions to international price and monetary factors. True, their importance had been recognized in the 1962 periodization, but as phenomena of the crisis of imperialism, not themselves as prime causes. Their cause was the nature of capitalist development and class conflict.

Between 1969 and 1972 a conversion of senior elements in the leadership and of Party economists occurred, adding 'marginalist' political strategies to the marginalist economic analysis. These can be explained as mere shifts of emphasis, but they were crucial in the PCI's search for universal consensus and legitimation as a national party concerned with national salvation. It was not in 1974 but five years before that the conclusion had been drawn that the economy and political system really were in danger of collapse. 1974 merely helped to convince the Party's cadres that the political and economic situation justified some form of historic compromise to resume development or at least slow the rate of decline. The insertion of the working class could strengthen the state, thereby also reducing socio-economic tensions. The need was for a strategy of development in decline, rather than redistribution and transition in a developing monopoly capitalism.

Other factors played a part. As Graziani pointed out, among economists neo-marginalists were much more strongly represented than marginalists or Marxists. From the point of view of the former, any 'crisis and fall' theory from the Marxist tradition lacked theoretical substance. Reformists too had little prospect of success, as the crisis further fragmented the mode of production, and created fresh imbalances through sectoral crises. In the absence of an overall Marxist economic analysis which promised short-term improvement, the field was clear for capitalist apologists and short-term palliatives. Schemes like the 'Progetto '80' (for 1971-5) proposing full employment, a harmonious urban-natural environment, self-management and production to satisfy needs 'of a higher order' seemed abstract in the light of 1973-4. (10) Thus, though PCI leaders continued to speak of transformation 'in a socialist direction', they were also scanning the horizon for 'ripresini', little recoveries, and viewing the crisis as a mass of separate but interconnected crises. (11) This led to a more pragmatic approach than that of the Socialist Party modellers, moving into a second phase of planning even though the first had not been realized in the 1960s. The prospect had changed from that of crisis as the result of the growth of imperialism to one of decline in the national economy and the model of development in general.

This position is particularly associated with Giorgio Amendola and the economists Barca and Peggio. (12) It may, of course, be replaced by stronger emphasis on capitalist distortions if electoral or Party considerations so dictate. It is also a realistic extension of the Party's tradition of 'closed to the Left, open to the Right'. By extension, Chiaromonte's interpretation in 1970 was instructive. He said there was a danger from alarmism about the crisis. Crisis had been exacerbated by recent wage claims, which created 'serious problems for the general economic development of the country'. (13) The crisis was already seen as 'conjunctural' rather than structural. Alarmism frightened entrepreneurs and created contradictions between workers and other labouring classes. Thus, the 'objective of planning cannot today be a socialist economy, but a kind of democratic development, in which the public interest prevails over that of private and monopoly capital.' (14)

The change in the dominant economic analysis was not unequivocal. Certainly, Amendola's 1971 article is significant. The crisis is seen as primarily governmental. Capital is available, but the government had failed to provide leadership. The crisis is not so much in capitalism as in the Italian government. 'The political crisis conditions and favours the advance of the economic crisis, and the growth of economic difficulties, threatening a radical crisis (the tendency to falling production, stagnation or reduction of demand, worsening of the employment situation and increase in unemployment) makes the progress of the political struggle more agitated, sharper, and more violent.' (15) The danger is of a right-wing reaction, caused not by sabotage but by inefficiency.

Pesenti continued to relate the crisis to imperialism. The end of the US dollar's supremacy started 'a phase of growing economic, and thus monetary, instability, determined by the sharpening of the contradictions of imperialism.' (16) Peggio, however, sought to allay alarmist attacks on the working class, without specifying what part he thought wage claims had played in the recent crisis. Expansion in 1970 was related to 'the mid- and long-term trend already expressed in the past ... the victories achieved by the workers in the last two years have not in fact caused the productive paralysis or the economic collapse prophesied by the Cassandras of Confindustria or the Bank of Italy.' (17) Peggio's analysis was to defend the working class by saying, in effect, that militancy was economically irrelevant to the crisis. The 1973 recovery was said to have been destroyed by VAT increases and devaluation, by government policy. (18) Amendola was directly involved in defence of opposition to a wages policy. The crisis was due to the 'ruling groups of Italian capitalism'. A wage increase required a commensurate increase in productivity. Amendola saw that increase as being still the responsibility of capital, but the argument worked both ways, as he criticized Italian labour for an inadequate response to charges that it was responsible for inflation. (19)

He defended the labour movement's wage strategy on the ground that it was a response to internationally generated price rises, or to internal stagnation and waste. This purely reactive role of labour led to its virtual exclusion from the analysis in 1974. International factors predominated. Faced with world crises in food and energy, the Italian answer should be reliance on small and middle industry. (20) The start of the crisis (dated by Chiaromonte to 1968-9) was carefully placed by Peggio in November 1967, (21) relating not to the Italian class struggle but generally to relations between the USA, Europe and Japan. 'There is no danger of a catastrophe due to the physical shortage of particularly important, specific resources'; rather, there was a need to 'avoid a massive deflation and thus a grave and dramatic crisis in the whole capitalist world'. (22) In short, the working class, having 'caught up' economically, faced a reaction for which it was politically unprepared. The crisis existed, but beyond the horizons of the working class. The Christian Democrats and the Socialist Party were wrong to see the crisis as a moral one, or one capable of resolution by coercing the workers, but it was not a final crisis. What was needed was 'a task of reviving and renewing the state and economy', not by one party, but by a government 'able to unite in a great effort of renewal all the forces of the nation'. (23)

This had already been expressed economically as the need for further growth, and a policy dealing with areas of unemployment and investment, foreign trade and agriculture. Amendola argued that Italy suffered more acutely from the world crisis because of the contradictions between monopoly growth and (until 1969-70) low-paid labour, low productivity and failed reformism. The Christian Democrats had created immobilism, but the key to leaving the crisis behind was realism - the avoidance of waste and parasitism, and sacrifices. (24) Other, generally lesser, figures tried to retain a link with the Marxist tradition. Soriente, for example, examined the counter-tendencies to the establishment of a new equilibrium after the destruction of value, of masses of wealth, by inflation. This created decline and instability, but also prompted a search for new bases for exploitation. (25)

Attention shifted to small and middle industry as the consensus grew that working-class strategy was a reaction to declining purchasing power, not a contribution to inflation. This industry, peasant, industrial and commercial, 'is the real motive power of the country' and 'should be helped to develop all its capacity for initiative, also through a growing and autonomous form of associationism.' (26) Workers and managers in big industry were stagnating and vulnerable. Prices rose, wages followed, and managers could not raise productivity. Elsewhere there was parasitism, lack of research, waste and corruption. For Amendola, the working class was an excessively passive spectator and follower of a damaging and politically reactionary crisis. To Peggio, the class was a victim which had lost its protection and its power to intervene in crisis. He stressed that 1975 was the worst year since the end of the war, 1974 had been a year of zero growth, and that despite predictions of a 4 per cent growth in 1976, that year looked unpromising. (27)

However, the evidence of continuing decline, especially in the areas of investment, borrowing and inflation, did not lead Peggio to predict an offensive from labour. The concern was to argue against a wages policy, since wage control did not necessarily stimulate investment. (28)

The basic need was for more independence and autonomy. Classical Marxist perspectives, we observe, have clouded over in the previous six years. Indeed, to Amendola the declining hegemony of the economic and political dominant class was a national disaster. This is not to say the PCI shared the views of the Christian Democrats. The ill-fated 'middle-term project', for instance, did speak of 'some elements of socialism in the functioning of the economy and society, the adoption of some values of the socialist outlook in the national collectivity'. (29) It also proposed abandoning 'welfare capitalism' in favour of a 'policy of planning ... based on participation and consensus, together with a rigorous technical-scientific design, *[which]* does not counterpose itself to the needs of the correct functioning of the market and the autonomous development of enterprises: on the contrary, it is the condition for overcoming the structural crisis of the market and the enterprise.' (30)

The PCI had moved from a position in the early 1960s where the enemy was the economic system of capitalism itself, to one of arguing that its difficulties were in Italy exacerbated by inadequate political leadership, and thence to that of the 1970s, arguing that the crisis was due to ill-planned national development and hence damaging to the national interest. These changes are quite coherent, and consistent with Togliatti's policy of supporting small, national capitalism. They do, however, demonstrate a crucial change in the notion of transition from an anti-imperialist, anti-monopoly strategy based on equitable growth and class struggle to the attempt to preserve Italy's future as an advanced industrial society.

At this point, the task of presenting the new line as a necessary adaptation to new realities had been accomplished. This was still different from the Christian Democratic approach. Lombardini (a Christian Democrat), for example, admits the failures of entrepreneurship, but points also to its success in the 'miracle'. Thereafter, there was insufficient restructuring and specialization, and insufficient mobility of workers, 'one of the most disturbing characteristics of our industry'. (31) After the miracle, there was 'full' employment, but it was only 'partially productive, and precarious'. (32) The real problem, apart from the failure of planning in the 1960s, was the continuing gap between wages and productivity, requiring 'an ability in the political forces to express public entrepreneurship'. (33) The only solution to the gap of wages and productivity was a policy of productivism. Aside from such things as European fixed exchange policy, productivism could succeed by means of credit for small and middle industry, mobility of labour, aid for large industry and a new strategy for small industry. Labour, in short, was to be moved, irrespective of the cost of social investment in relocation and, of course, at the expense of organization. Another tradition, more closely associated with Dossetti, centres initiative on the governing party and its internal specialists, as against independent consultants. The economic crisis is seen as one of economic policy, not structure. The villain is immobile labour and wage demands, which 'block' the economy. (34)

There is a current among the Christian Democrats which argues that Italian state intervention in the economy is typical of the liberal tradition itself. It is not a principle, but a reaction to a series of separate crises. The association of state and capital is the normal form of Italian development, rather than the English model of non-protection, and the German protected model of alliance between bank-industrial and finance capital. It is an alliance of bank, industry and state participation. (35) Consequently, though often not recognized as such, this model is superior, as it regards a state, or really a social, component of capital as normal. Historically, the economic failure was in (peasant) agriculture, where starving subsistence agriculture of capital forced a choice between low production and emigration. Unlike the 'Progetto' of the PCI, the concern is not with the creation of jobs but with the revival of the enterprise and of public administration. It is a social-liberal alternative to Lombardini's entrepreneurial conception. Italy was a developing country which had always required state intervention, which explains the typicality of credit organizations partly in the public sphere. These are typical of developing, as against developed, economies. Jobs are created by offer (supply) and investment, not through demand for employment. (36)

Perhaps, Saraceno's argument runs, Italy underestimated the cost of urbanization without a central authority. What is needed now is social capital formation to win the support of all labour, especially for a wages policy. The conception rests not on existing demand, but on the question of how to distribute a limited amount of capital. Italy is short of capital, and cannot supply all labour's demands. 'Of the three moments of planning - the political, the union and the administrative - it is clearly the first which generates the others; this moment has always been lacking in Italy, first, when reconstruction began, second with the *[1954]* Vanoni scheme, and a third time in the attempt at planning in the 1960s.' (37) The ideological determinant was liberalism, leading to the exploitation of the country which was never properly a market economy. The final block to the competitive model was the union refusal to accept a wages policy.

This schema, for instance in seeing labour responsible for the failure to recover in 1969-70 and after, is often close to Lombardini. The PCI sees Italian capitalism as a version of capitalism tout court, and the form of state intervention as pathological, an attempt to buy the political advantage of economic control with public money, thereby underlining the weakness of political and productive systems. The historiography of the debate on Italian state and capitalism cannot simply be reduced to polarities between competitive capitalism, public ownership and state socialism, or between interclassism and class struggle. Rather, the Christian Democrats' case is for a restoration of normality to communal relations by productivism plus social capital, in the subordination of living labour to social capital managed jointly by bureaucrats and entrepreneurs. The PCI has recognized international barriers to economic recovery, and aimed at 'change', rather than 'transition'.

In terms of everyday politics, the economic phases of the crisis seem separate. As Donolo remarked, they are really a 'unity, and thus the reciprocal determinacy between the various "moments" of the crisis'. (38) The crisis is not simply because of governmental errors, but because (39)

> there is no longer a sufficiently large margin of manoeuvre in the system, even at the conjunctural level, and ... in Italy we are moving towards an explosive combination of crises in political institutions, paralysis of the instruments of short-term intervention, and of the cancerous, insoluble, difficulties of the structural problems of Italian capitalism, in the framework of a world economic crisis whose seriousness is now beyond discussion.

Since 1974, the crisis, as the organic crisis of the regime, does not seem to contradict this judgment. Christian Democratic 'normality' seems much less attainable than some form of adaptation to the crisis or 'change'. In this perspective, it was really 1969 which marks the start of permanent recession, with the last important attempt by the PCI, and Carli, to face up to the implications of structural modification.

The restrictive governmental policies of the 1960s were dictated by political reflex and monetary conservatism. Any 'state plan' now would be determined by the claims of public clients, which are responsible to a considerable degree for the shortness of the 'ripresini' and the 'riprese drogate'. In the 1960s, restriction of public spending, part of the 'disegno Carli', restricted the growth of the tertiary sector. In the 1970s, however, there is no choice: public indebtedness, a negative balance of payment and inflation commit the government to following its commitments, to inflation and to growth of the public sector. (40)

This is a crisis of the model of development, and of social relations, engineered in the 1950s on the basis of political management of spontaneous development and patronage investment. This was done, Carli implies, by those who had neither the skill, vision nor interest to command the economic instruments potentially at their disposal. There were also objective reasons for this. As Podbielski points out, an export-propelled economy is dependent, without guarantees that export growth will fertilize other sectors. (41) A growth in manufacturing drains agricultural and independent labour, increases the tertiary sector and inflation. Historically, it would seem that wage militancy in the 1960s did not cause but followed the movement of prices. In the 1970s the record of days lost through strikes implies that qualitative demands have effectively replaced 'inflationary' wage demands. It is doubtful whether wage claims can now be used as a means of attacking the status hierarchy.

Other sectors outside manufacturing industry, and especially those overloaded with unskilled and immobile labour, have followed different strategies. The relatively high cost of social services, and concern about the quality of social life, especially as regards housing, health services, education and environment, leave little option but to seek monetary compensation. Some organized workers have been able to use existing resources (the 150 hours), or to compel employers to make up deficiencies in the public services. Yet these strategies are also disincentives to employment and domestic investment. High wages are in practice no compensation for the declining quality of working and urban conditions. The commercial and distributive sectors are both oligarchic and capillary. Prices are maximized by the wholesaling oligarchy and multiplied by the army of independent distributors. Yet to the Christian Democrats these features are inseparable from an open and democratic society.

Carli terms this pattern of development 'Brasilian', where the conflict between wages and investment priorities obscures the need to construct a socially modernized society. Carli blames 'us', the ruling class, for lack of foresight. (42) The Christian Democrats chose to fight a class war where other governments might have chosen prudence, especially as regards the largest, best-organized industrial base. It is true that the Christian Democrats are interclassist, but they are least effectively so in the more advanced sectors of the economy. Carli argued that the Italian political class was typically timid about its commitment to capitalism, and determined as regards its uncertain political hegemony. It had entered the European Community as a backward, protected, member in the process of reconstitution. The independent peasantry had been destroyed as a political force, but at the cost of producing a volatile, culturally unprivileged, first-generation proletariat in the heartland of the historic Left. None the less, peasant or Southern mentality entered public administration and national politics. The rhetorical lawyer-politician provided personal mediation between the formal state and powerless, ill-informed, clients. The ruling class, unable to dominate through economic relations, was forced to manage civil conflict between the public sector and entrepreneurs, and the organized industrial workers. The exclusion of the PCI symbolized the front opposed to the 'European' sector of the working class. Thus the insertion of the working class into the state is not a simple process of social democratization. It would be a partial victory in a situation where the ruling class had always opposed such insertion. This is a victory for only a part of the labouring classes. Clearly, the PCI wishes to take as much as possible of these classes 'into the state', but the material base is so far lacking. What are the prospects for this strategy in prolonged depression? Why did a weak ruling class attempt a frontal attack in the 1950s on the strongest section of the working class? One answer is that in that decade the working class was not in fact strong, and its strength was revealed only at the moment the economic strategy for development was shown to be failing. The government had no alternative strategy to an export-based economy, relying on low-paid labour and a stable lira. At the first sign of trouble, in the 1960s, entrepreneurs 'disinvested'. So, as Olivetti pointed out, the state could not continue to act as a police power vis-à-vis the working class. It had to share responsibilities with entrepreneurs who in turn could not act as paternalists or class warriors in modern industrial conditions. But by 1969 there was no room for economic manoeuvre. Deflation and failed reformism had not been enough to stop the workers from improving their conditions, but at that point the limit of institutionalized capitalism seemed to have been reached.

Italy is a society devoted not to class war but to class struggle: it has little attachment to modern capitalism. In terms of modern capitalist rationality, the policies of a Carli, a Colombo or a Rumor seem self-defeating and restrictive. (43) Yet, as Carli said, 'every kid knows' monetary policy is a political weapon. The aim is less to restructure than to contain. In the 1970s the Christian Democrats had two advantages. They had lost socio-economic ground but not a major political battle. The 'bourgeois' students in 1967-9 had passed a decisive judgment, but the state still controlled the machinery of repression. Second, however, the crisis produced its own methods of continuing class struggle, methods which passed initiatives to the public sector and convinced the PCI that its mediating presence in the state could modify the new strategy. This strategy was one of inflation, not deflation, unemployment, not low wages. The PCI's opposition to this was certainly consistent with entrepreneurial ideology, that inflation and unemployment meant lost business. It was not so much that the PCI had a conclusive answer to the problems of a declining economy as that it felt almost any price was worth paying to secure entry to the political, not the economic, control-room. The working class of the 1970s was strong enough to resist the imposition of the deflationary medicine of the 1960s, but economic decline weakened its position so long as it was outside the state. What price, then, is it worth paying for no longer being an out-class, one of the 'scontenti', the 'magri'?

There is no reason for the Christian Democrats, if they decide to fix a price, to see such insertion as stabilization. Rather, they would institutionalize the threat to their own hegemony. They have no reason to suppose that in crisis conditions there would be a modification of what D'Antonio terms, in his classic study, the refusal of Italian labour to admit the element of reciprocity which maintains capitalist societies, describing the 'diffused disaffection' of 1969-72 as 'the reflection ... of a political crisis which has attacked Italian society, and whose primary manifestation consists of the refusal by the labouring classes to consider "natural" (and thus non-modifiable) the conditions of wage labour' (43) or even of labour tout court in capitalist society. The PCI sees homogenization as the best development strategy for the working class, rather than the compartmentalized, 'non-communicating sub-markets, so that depression and increasing labour costs can be found simultaneously, and even present themselves alternately as characteristic of the economic cycle.' (44) To the Christian Democrats, that kind of 'dependent growth' enables them to prosper not as the party 'of pure mediation' (Tronti's phrase), but a master of a shifting, dislocated class front. If they are not effective in terms of modern capitalist rationality, they are effective in class struggle. This political traditionalism is linked to a particular kind of subaltern economic development, not that of big business or big labour, but one of relative underaccumulation of capital. It involves both subsidy and 'welfare employment' in the public sector. Underaccumulation explains the under-use of labour resources, and the oversupply of labour when productive activity declines and investment remains low.

This accounts for the neo-Ricardian proposals of Agnelli for an alliance of capital and labour against waste and parasitism. (45) Governmental policy sets limits to the development of modern capitalism. It also accounts for D'Antonio's view that the Italian economy is too fragile for Keynesian remedies. It lacks the social consensus the latter required, and traditionally closed its balance of payments gap by emigration (expulsion of labour) and tourism (attraction of revenue, not capital). Intermediate industry increasingly relies on the public sector as its financier. This leads to partnership, rather than straight subsidy. The aim is not that of economic growth per se, but the creation of dependent strata which both mediate class struggle and can be instrumentalized against militant labour. The aim is not, in this perspective, an integrated sociality, but the creation of privileged, dependent middle strata: hence Censis could conclude that structural fragmentation left Italian society 'satisfied'. (46) Fragmentation encourages molecular individualism, while the more homogeneous the category among the subordinate classes, the more likely is discontent, and support for the PCI.

Capitalist productivists lament the waste of the system, whereas PCI economists argue that this marked only a 'natural' movement from the dominance of industrial capital to finance capital. There is crisis, but 'The catastrophic interpretation more generally is thus not only "mistaken" on the analytical level, but often camouflages particular interests in order to paint the crisis in dark and scarcely discernable colours.' (47) That is, the disjuncture between political class and economic class allows the former to wage class struggle under the banner of interclassism, and the latter to redispose of its investment. The 'optimism' of this account allows the PCI to modify the mechanism of this joint operation by inserting itself into the state apparatus, thus fulfilling the destiny of the Party in the state (though not as its sole occupant) with the power to administer the classes of civil society.

In this view, there is no general crisis of institutions in a period of decline, but rather a crisis of institutions unable to control a conflictuality they partly promoted, and partly, by inhibiting 'modern' development, hoped to avoid. Salvati argued that the Italian bourgeoisie was simply too short of ideas and purpose to organize planned production. A double-dual system developed, of 'public' and 'private', of the 'employed' and 'unemployed'. (48) We might extend this by saying that the 'mediation of the political' consists in not letting these dualisms irrevocably separate. Sylos Labini attempts to fit the circular movement of falling profit, rising wages and rising prices into a cycle, with its own dynamic of tendential recovery. Thus, profits fall as direct costs rise and exchange rates are stable. Investment falls, which limits wage rises and reduces the increase of prices, which in turn helps to restore profits. (49) Indeed, since initiative lies not with industry but with the banks, it is arguable that the state is better seen as an agent in investment and spending than as a conscious agent of remedial intervention. Any intervention would depend on uncontrollable, or non-existent, international machinery and factors, and rather than broaden state functions it is probably better to rationalize the criteria for its existing operations.

As Graziani pointed out, most economists are forced to modify classical positions to deal with the Italian economy. Marxists find the market does not set the value of labour, conflictualists lack a theory of conflict and neo-marginalists find too many pathological features destroying the compatibility of the system's components. (50) Hence Barca was consistent in stressing the importance of the parties' input for any scheme more ambitious than the Christian Democratic activity described above. He argued that the parties must be transformed, by dropping their ideological dualisms. This also involves modifying the economic interests attached to the parties. He continued by indicating the crucial relation of 'new strata' to the parties, since Italy's development had been rapid, though uneven, and national. Thus the interests of the old may suffer while those of the new are being accommodated.

Peggio has been markedly optimistic concerning 'spontaneous recovery'. (51) To him, the chief sign of crisis in 1969-77 was an overall decline of investment of 3.2 per cent. True, the signs were that the 'ripresa' of 1978 would again be 'drogata', there was virtual stagnation in the growth rate and in 1975 a shrinkage of 3.5 per cent in the internal gross product. Yet there were signs of 'a certain continued expansion', not cessation of growth, but emergence of disequilibrium and contradictions. After 1976, despite the incidence of inflation, the increase in the public debt since 1970, and unemployment of over 30 per cent in the South, Confindustria had calculated that a rise in investment was imminent. After all, the industries hit by weak investment in the past had often been those of doubtful value, such as non-ferrous metals. Monetary policy would be crucial but, given a recovery, Italy should be in a borrower's market. The implication is that, after a decade of recession and unemployment, firms have been strengthened and can dispense with state aid. Hence, 'thanks to these results, a policy of relaunching economic expansion is possible'. (52) In the last resort, however, the case made is not for recovery being imminent, but for a policy of recovery being necessary.

What is omitted is the tendency for the economy to multiply its distortions. As Peggio remarks, recovery may eliminate still more 'productive' jobs. The recovery will again be export-propelled, and thus not directed towards social investment and rational growth in the tertiary sector. If the submerged economy were only as large as the estimate for the USA (10 per cent), (53) this would account for the rise in personal consumption, but proportionately increase the significance of a fall in social consumption and, indeed, of the poor performance of the 'official' economy. Stressing the importance of monetary policy thus assumed that the submerged economy be free to develop outside other constraints and controls. Yet as Graziani points out, any recovery of the official economy requires that the working class recognize three areas of required sacrifice related to the balance of payments, to inflation and to overmanning. (54) Italian development has always tended to increase unemployment. Would a working class accept austerity knowing, for instance, that this would involve political concessions to West Germany connected with the balance of payments?

The division of employees into public and private, and of the economy into official and submerged, already implies a loss of control and authority for organized labour. New 'official' economic development would take place in the 'third Italy', the expansion of the industrial triangle North- and South-East, in small, decentralized, units. This combination of finance and industrial capital, perhaps with guidance from the regions, strengthens them more than it does the unions. Small units mean fewer union and Party cadres, and smaller-scale conflict. While this need not lead to the situation reported in the South where unions themselves now act as channels for finding jobs and pensions for their clients, decentralized industry makes the union a co-ordinator and communicator for small enterprises, rather than a mouthpiece for shop-floor organization.

Peggio's position has been criticized by Graziani and by Napoleone Colajanni. To the latter, this is not 'a situation for development'. (55) The key to economic analysis is the South, and the internal market generally. However, the tendency is for the whole economy to assume Southern characteristics. Italian 'productive' workers carry a heavy burden of the unproductive. Development, in other words, follows the pattern established in the 1960s. Small industry proliferates, but in the context of falling employment (now lower than in 1962), falling profits and falling productivity in big industry, caused by the high cost of indebtedness, high managerial costs and a high rate of technical obsolescence. In this framework, he concluded, the loudest voices are those of free enterprise (Carli), and advocates of workers' restraint (Ugo La Malfa and wages policy), whereas the Left in general has failed to come to terms with the lessons of the 1960s.

The free market, however, created structural imbalance, while the centre-Left encouraged the decline of confidence and responsibility in the management of industry and finance. The state as distributor of resources to the unproductive sectors for 'subsistence and speculative purposes' ultimately leads to forms of 'organized parasitism'. Colajanni argued that this is not a form of pre-capitalist reaction, but a pathological version of the 'state of mature capitalism' where material production must support a disproportionate quantity of the unproductive. This involves a crisis of the bourgeois order, which Colajanni sees as economic as well as political, though Offe elsewhere argues that only political contradictions now remain. Transition 'runs the risk of being long, and coinciding with a whole historical epoch'. (56) For Colajanni, the basic historical contradiction is not between privileged and oppressed, or public and private, but capitalist stagnation and productive development by and of the working class. Reform of the state and economic restructuring are thus obligatory because of the nature of capitalist weakness internationally, but especially nationally, and the existence of a strong working-class movement capable of protecting itself. His proposal is one of 'democratic planning' as direct social appropriation, not through the state, but through external financing which would allocate a share of profit to entrepreneurial, or rather managerial, efficiency. The state is to be avoided, as 'the highest point of crisis is the state'. (57)

To reward managerial capacity implies that the whole proposal is managerial, which sidesteps the question of the criteria of democratic planning. It assumes too that 'control' be accepted as an adequate reward for austerity, and that conflictuality over distribution, especially likely if the economy were export-propelled, would not disrupt the planning process itself. The notion that planning can take place outside the mature capitalist state makes the assumption that it is too diseased to intervene pending its remodelling. In practice, economic decline strengthens the state bourgeoisie, while economic recovery strengthens the entrepreneurial bourgeoisie. Colajanni also underestimates the effect of the lack of faith in planning, though he does discuss the lack of planning ideas. All this makes the modernization of premodern micro-units of production a likely strategy. (58) This, indeed, is virtually a consensual solution in its 'democratic-pluralist' (PCI) version, and its 'social-entrepreneurial' (Christian Democratic) form. The concern of the latter is to place its client structure in the new micro-units, given that the long-term trend is for big industry to erode its traditional supports, and to aggravate the condition of the South.

The PCI proposes efficiency as an alternative to the bureaucratic-welfare state, a transfer of power from the traditional to the modern sector in conditions of controlled conflictuality - proposals whose limits we shall later explore. The 'Proposta di progetto a medio termine' put this clearly: (59)

> The abandonment of 'welfare' policies - policies of discretional subsidy with public money and credit to support inefficient enterprises - is the precondition for the revival of entrepreneurship, a reaffirmation of the responsibility of the entrepreneur, and the pursuit of a healthy and active management of the enterprise, in order to establish the value of the spirit of initiative in public and private managers. The democratic state, based on the principles of pluralism, can and must influence the choices of private economic operators - respecting the autonomy of enterprises' decisions and management - and perform the function of guiding the total economic development of the country by a policy of redistributing resources, and by the use of the controls of public intervention, direct and indirect, consistent with the pursuit of general aims

> worked out in the planning stage. Any public incentive or contribution acquired by an enterprise must be accompanied by an acceptance of these aims.
>
> To be able efficiently to launch a policy of planning, on the other hand, it is not necessary to extend the whole of the public economic sector: it is essential to put this sector in order, through clearer definition of the areas in which the state's presence is essential, and through a sharper outline of the specific roles of the bodies and enterprises the state heads.

This planning, based on participation and consent, attempts to extend still further the principle of decentralization, though, again, without suggesting criteria of performance, only targets. The 'Progetto' is to be considered in the light of forecasts of recovery, and of the supposed possibility of reformism based on updated figures published in mid-1977 regarding wages and salaries first discussed in Gorrieri's work. (60) These showed the contractual weakness of certain categories and the privilege attached to 'culture' or education. The middle strata were thus presumed to have an interest in conservation. However, between the early and late 1970s, Gorrieri's identification of a trend towards egalitarianism, resisted by the 'ceti medi', was replaced by one stressing polarization within these middle strata, and the cementation of the bottom stratum of low wages and salaries. Given assumptions that capitalism had further to expand, the lower-paid or those excluded from the labour force might plan expansion in their own interest. To promote this idea, 'Rinascita' published confusing diagrams on the growth of a 'Third', industrializing, Italy. (61) 1977-9 was the peak of optimistic interpretations of the economic situation, and of belief in the unity of interest of the lower 'ceti medi' and working class.

Even reports of continued growth, or of 'mixed prospects', in no way simplify the task of 'democratic planners' unless pluralism be equated with a free-for-all expression of interests. In 1977 a conscientious planner might have studied the already mentioned Socialist Party convegno, Peggio's 1973-5 proposals, the 'Progetto', the 1972 and 1975 Christian Democrats' Convegni and Saraceno's 1976 'Il Mulino' article. In the area of the Christian Democrats alone, there were choices between the maverick Carli, and the economists Caffè, Lombardini and Andreatta, as well as Saraceno. There were few overviews, but there was important work by Fuà, Sylos Labini, Graziani and others mainly formulated in the late 1960s. The approach to planning choices plus a 'democratic' component was, in short, a political as much as an economic issue. Optimism, therefore, rested on a conception of participation which did not question immovable structural problems but sought to minimize them by mobilizing opinion outside the state.

The suggestion that Southern development/de-development was a form of capitalist restructuring, or form of subordinate development, raised the question of the extreme difficulty of devising a 'plan' for the South. (62) Efforts to prune the bureaucracy tend to finish by increasing it in the name of efficiency and patronage. Decentralization of industry had to take into account the proposed priority of deflation in 1975-8. Calling for 'relatively autonomous' Southern development, not as a dependent but as an organic development, left open the question of economic model, and political and economic interest. To speak of a 'new entrepreneurship in various forms, including co-operative ones', provides little guide to the real resources and prospects for Southern recovery. For the South, despite having 'intelligence in power', has lacked precisely that 'intelligent capacity' to make North-South relations cohesive. Historically, the initiative for adopting new economic models is Northern. The subordination of the South is a problem sui generis, not resolvable by appeals to democratic participation. Indeed, if it is true that the Bank of Italy issues money to annul the effect of real wage increases, the very idea of planning 'from the base upwards' would be unavailing.

Commitment to the idea of planning was established for the Christian Democrats by Saraceno. The pre- and post-1961-2 experiences of planning, on the other hand, make their notion of democratic planning a last resort, not a first attempt. This is stressed by the mixed, but generally disappointing, efforts to reach planning targets, as described by Polillo. (63) Until recently, the Christian Democrats have preferred the deflationary conservatism of Carli to planning: now they prefer to manipulate inflation rather than to push the 'squeezed' 'ceti medi' into a left-wing plan for restraint. The principles of democratic planning may be unimpeachable. None the less, what its content might be, and what its priority might be, is obscure. In practice, party influence is associated with planning proposals, and the technical choices are left to experts who, in the Italian case, may be sceptical concerning the prospects for success. The PCI case has depended on an optimistic view of prospects for national growth and a movement towards the Left, and, as these tendencies slow, the realities of social conflictuality and institutional dis-aggregation again assert themselves.

Since 1963 the fading pattern of vigorous 'modern' development, with free market competition and integration into the world economy, has been replaced by a growing independence and insulation of personal and institutional systems of power from objective economic priorities. There has been a shift from conflictual consumerism to strategies for corporate survival. Fragmentation of the 'traditional' system was at first accelerated by the mass 'social' phenomenon of consumerism and, conflictually, class organization. Continuing decline, meanwhile, has shifted the balance from these marks of social vigour and aggressiveness to a 'social' dependence on administrative power systems and corporate survival mechanisms, and towards a 'private' pursuit of consumption, and privatized forms of conflict. The attempt to 'modernize' the traditional political class by making workers' productivity the index of the fortunes of both classes has been contested from both sides. Both reject tying their future to 'productivism', and herein lies the special character of the PCI's insistence on production.

Traditionally, a society of high competitiveness and correspondingly intense exploitation had erected a facade of public power to front a personal, private, magnificence. This individual magnificence was shaken in the 1960s first by proposals to soften or mediate class relations through a 'social' state, and second by the refusal of labour to play its traditional role of work-horse, a refusal which also assisted society's opening to mass, modern, urban cultural influences.

The demystification of the traditional power system was marked by the efforts of Carli at the Bank of Italy to maintain traditional privilege while cementing a more skilful and united politico-economic class. The Bank possessed great power and prestige in the 1960s. It had relative political autonomy, and indeed dictated policy to the government. In the 1970s this position was gradually reversed, and the Christian Democrats struggled for mastery of the control mechanisms operated by the Bank. In 1978-9, this struggle was particularly severe, and the prestige of the Bank declined. Carli always had a view of the ruling class as more than a clan of politicians distributing public surplus amassed by the economically dominant class. He conceived of a universalist, homogeneous, class where politics would conform to the general economic interest of the class. He also had a European perspective, seeing Italy's dependence on exports as making monetary controls the supreme guarantee of development and stability. Given strict control of the money supply and a stable lira, the Bank seemed to control all but one of the conditions for growth - productivity.

Carli's philosophy was clearly expressed in 1962. 'Experience has also shown that the faster the rhythm of development, the more rapid is the rate of increase in productivity: this confirms the existence, already confirmed by economic analysis, of the interrelation between development and its precondition, competitiveness and productivity, which is made to generate a self-sustaining movement.' (64) This simple, non-interventionist, view of the natural self-propulsiveness of growth was re-elaborated as: 'The productivity factor has in reality been the one which has had most weight in determining the rapid development of the country's productive activity' in which 'our credit system adequately guarantees the money flow between the various parts of the country.' (65) The first signs of disquiet appear in the 1962 report, prepared in 1963. 'The share assigned to labour has increased', (66) but money issue has been swollen by increased goods and services. The negative signs are of rising prices, weak food supply, the construction industry and a trend to capital export. The end of the optimistic vision came rapidly. The ruling class spent irresponsibly. The workers were unproductive.

In 1964 Carli said the 'levels of pay achieved in 1962 [exceeded] the increase in average productivity in the economic system.' (67) There were also external factors, such as changes in money markets, but the main cause of falling production was the wage 'push'. Wages and consumption were up, and investment falling. The spiral was not controllable by monetary means alone. The 'scala mobile' of price-indexed wage rates had the inflationary effect of pushing consumption beyond production levels. The solution was a wages policy, in the workers' own interests. The policy of the Bank was to deflate, and in order to restore a favourable balance of payments severe measures were justified. (68) 1964-5 promised international recovery, and a subsequent redress in the imbalance of the economy. His analysis was that wages were rising too rapidly (the example given was chemicals), and this was discouraging investment. In 1965, 'our productive system is not in a position to tolerate modification in the distribution of income ... which would increase the proportion assigned to labour.' (69) In short, the negative effects of increased public spending, combined with forecasts of falling investment in 1966, meant that labour would have to be restrained in order that the 'propulsive effects' of external demand could stimulate growth. (70)

The attempt to retain the low-wage, export-propelled economy was not questioned in 1967. The link between rising labour costs and falling investment was seen as direct and simple. Higher wages depended on higher investment per capita, 'accepting the resulting constraints as regards the volume and composition of public spending, the rate of taxation and distribution of income'. (71) In other words, labour depended on capital to satisfy its desire for greater personal consumption, which could only be damaged by rising social expenditure. In 1967 Carli showed concern for the key stabilizing factor of his system - the international exchange rates - based, of course, on American dominance. The devaluation of sterling raised doubts about the inflationary effect of the USA balance of payments, even though Italian exports were growing. Labour costs were rising in 1967, and investment was still poor. (72)

Carli did not analyse the fact that the tendency for labour costs to fall in 1964-6 had not in fact produced the expected rise in investment. The image of a society where the natural growth-processes of capital could be stimulated only by restraining the claims of labour committed him both to a belief in the prospect of recovery and to acceptance of the naturalness of uneven development. In 1969, using the conventional indicators, he spoke of a generally good past year, with slightly higher productivity and slightly lower labour costs, but still failed to explain why the conservative orthodoxy of the Bank's policy, and lower labour costs, should not have the mechanical effect on investment of raising it. On the movement of 1968, which seemed an ominous exception in the 'good year', he commented: 'This fascinating and austere idea, of liberty: there are still those who do not know how to strive for it without emotion.' (73) Liberty is a natural condition in situations of universal competition.

By 1970, when the failure of the Bank's two-class, liberal competitive policy and the thinness of his social policy were evident, he admitted that worsening balance of payments were aggravated by capital export, by the lack of confidence in the economically dominant interests, despite a supportive, politically dominant, element. Still, however, he continued to regard wages as a prime cause of inflation, which would be worsened by expansionist monetary policies. In 1970, contract renewals were seen as further accentuating the inflationary trend, along with other factors such as reduction of working hours and limitation of overtime, and the shortage of skilled labour. (74) The association of productivism with his restricted and restrictive view of socio-economic intervention was not an encouraging basis for a policy of voluntary austerity. Capital export in the 1960s was evidence both of the limits of the Bank's economic assumptions and of social tension which tried to use inflation as instrument of class conflict. The investment strike in reality produced inflation and lowered productivity. With few exceptions, labour in the 1960s struggled merely to keep its place. In the 1970s, labour had no choice but to try to increase its share of a dwindling patrimony simply to stay in the same relative position and attain general European wage levels. In this process, public investment, replacing private, was a salvage operation. Inflation in the 1960s did not register a consistent shift of bargaining strength to the workers. On balance, inflation tendentially marked a social success for the labour movement, as it destroyed the confidence of capital and accelerated the organization of the new, mass worker. Carli's counter, deflation, did not create investment and raise productivity.

In the 1970s, however, the initiative passed from the Bank to the political sector, which proposed using inflationary pressure to 'pull' wages, to neutralize wage demands as an instrument of class struggle by using control of the money supply and public investment to shift initiative to the public sector. The labour movement did not desire a deflationary alternative, but was itself forced to pay the price of low productivity and inefficiency in industry through the combination of political (public) control of investment and inflation. In other words, though much of this shift was dictated by uncontrollable external factors and instinctive response, the 1970s eclipse of the Bank made the working class dependent on public strategy, on state capital, once private capital had fled the private sector. In reality, this flight of private capital was towards the banks or to repatriation as foreign loans. At the same time, the form of its administration had been assumed by the public sector. This accounted for the PCI's view that the restoration of investment decisions to the private (and democratic) sector would defeat a lacerating but effective policy of imprisoning the working class in the inflationary spiral, feeding the spiral with public money, and then acting as friendly banker to the industrialists and a capricious soup kitchen to the rest.

Carli's convictions that inflation was primarily caused by wage increases and government spending (75) and unequivocally represented a victory for the working class, were a dangerous half-truth, and contributed to the weakening of the market sector, the 'private' industry he wanted to protect. The strengthening of the 'public-private' sector in the 1970s he did not recognize as an alternative and potentially successful strategy for ruling-class solidarity. He always saw the economic fraction as necessarily dominant. This created the distance between Carli and the governing party. Earlier than he, the Christian Democrats came to the conclusion that his 1950s capitalism was dead. It was potentially too conflictual, and its own supporters had deserted it. Confindustria and other employers' associations were in any case incapable of coming collectively to terms with new forms of alliance between politics and economics, foreshadowed in 1963-4, trumpeted in 1968-9 and reinforced every subsequent year. Even in 1979 Confindustria had not defined a new role.

Carli saw the growth in unemployment and precarious employment in 1970 as a sign of economic weakness, not as weakening of the working class. He saw the strikes of 1968-70 not as a form of self-defence but as an anomaly, a suicide in the current economic climate. Yet he was aware of the international character and impact of crisis. He began to discuss planning. Perhaps 'different economies themselves possess differential vulnerability to inflationary processes and differential capacity to create them'. (76) On the one hand, monetary solutions were not working: on the other, when they were reversed, there was no recovery. There was continuing low investment and low internal demand (individual consumption was lower than at any time since 1954), but he continued to see wage rises as an insufficient stimulus for internal demand. There was, at this point, a notable modification. Although increased public spending did not seem proportionately to increase internal demand, 'there are no other elements which present prospects of accelerating economic activity save those related to a massive intervention by the public administration.' (77)

In Italy, the classical features of crisis were concentrated in certain sectors of the economy. This limited the power of those workers involved in modern, falling-profit, high technology industry, making the 'backward margin' a crucial element in social and economic development. In this context, Carli relaxed his notion of primitive linear development, of capitalist productivity financed by highly disciplined and low-paid labour. Yet faith in restructuring was lacking on the part of the ruling class. Private capital seemed to face endemic problems, and was vulnerable to international policy changes. The best solution did indeed seem to lie with state-participation industry (the 'partecipazioni statali'), even though this gave excessive power to the political fraction. Higher rates of investment now seem to coexist with, if they did not actually cause, unemployment. Wages still rose faster than productivity, and management replied by raising prices so as to retain their proportion of income.

In short, Italian capital was evading Marx's 1857 'Einleitung' model of collapse through overproduction and falling profits by refusing to expand the productive forces, freezing 'necessary labour', consuming surplus labour as revenue or capital transfer. This strategy for decline, or immobilism, would, without forthcoming state intervention, run down rapidly. This intervention, to Carli's surprise, did not take the classical form of welfare, distributing surplus as a social wage. Indeed, 'the public sector has been provided with a larger quantity of instruments designed to favour production for individual consumption, but not to satisfy collective consumption.' (78)

Carli had thus been overtaken by an improvised, temporizing response to the crisis, aided by the political fraction's crucial intervention. Carli argued instead that when wages rise, prices lag and profits fall. The reverse is also true to the extent that when prices rise wages lag, and profits, in an under-productive context, rise, to be consumed as revenue or exported, or re-cycled through the state as a relatively inefficient form of investment. Carli assumed that inflation was caused by demand pull, not supply push. Demand increases, then investment declines, and profits fall, which leads to unemployment and a fall in demand. Why, then, he asked, could the USA manage to break that cycle by public investment when Italy could not? One answer might be that prices which rise ahead of wages effectively reduce or annul the impact of public sector investment, given too that labour is too fragmented to raise wages faster than prices.

Carli continued to blame the high unit cost of labour for falling productivity. Public investment was of the wrong type to stimulate recovery. Private investment in 1971 fell 7.9 per cent, while public investment rose 34.5 per cent, both in money terms. In two years, labour costs had risen 28.8 per cent and prices 13.4 per cent. Yet internal demand was still weak, and it seemed that industry must have paid out its surplus in the form of wages. (79) Now if the switch to public investment involved an attempt to expand, albeit 'inefficiently', the capitalist mode of production, the phenomenon of inflation without an accompanying classical recession might be explained. We might argue that Marx's scenario of capitalist collapse as a result of expanding fixed capital was a self-delusion caused by confusing the money-value of fixed capital with the fact that 'fixed capital' is written off in favour of circulating capital. The canal is 'fixed capital', but does not enter the equation of capitalist dynamism as such, any more than the river, the ocean or, we might add, the condenser. Inflation simply accelerates the process whereby fixed capital is devalued and ultimately ceases to be a cause of collapse. The difficulties lie not with the part played by fixed capital in the capitalist equation, but circulating or investment capital, and the exclusion of living labour.

The partial recovery of 1972 showed investment returning to the private sector, increased profits and a modest industrial recovery. The share of wages remained stable. Carli again stressed monetary factors, particularly the dollar crisis, as adverse factors. However, he was encouraged to see that some kind of reciprocal arrangement existed between private and public investment, some means of reducing employment if necessary, to reduce the overall share of wages. True, as a spokesman for entrepreneurs, Carli could not welcome the inefficiency of 'bureaucratized entrepreneurship' and the lack of innovation and management skills. Public industry was 'hailed by its employees with exultation, aspiring to become members of the privileged community.' (80) Still, 'overcoming the crisis became difficult, in that it seemed tied, both at the level of the enterprise and of the system, to a reconstitution of relations which could no more be a return to past normality, but the product of a search for a new normality, necessarily difficult since it was not clearly defined in the problems and solutions', (81) proposed, that is, by ideologies and interests. Normality was possible, even though not the one originally envisaged, as public managers lacked entrepreneurial skills and thus could not 'restructure' relations.

The 1973 report speaks optimistically of the recovery, despite the oil crisis, and the fact that Italy had floated the lira in 1973 (February) and borrowed $4.4 billion, although the suggestion was not that the recovery was long term. Productivity was still low, and the balance of payments worse than the worst year to date, 1972. On the other hand, inflation, exacerbated by the depreciation of the lira, had coexisted with increasing investment, easier credit and stronger demand. Italy was still in a weak position, but Carli gave the impression that he was less unhappy with a heavily borrowing but still industrially reviving country. There were two surprising admissions: first, that despite the year's labour militancy, the metalworkers had not maintained their wage position relative to 1966 (as is generally the case for contract minimum wages, as against earnings), and second, that two major influences on prices were not wages but import prices and the non-competitive sectors of state and backward industry. As soon as industry began its recovery, Carli shifted the burden of responsibility from the working class to state parasitism as cause of low productivity. 'The area of high productivity has been hurt by the extension of the pampered parasitism in public spending, by bureaucratic paralysis, by the state bourgeoisie.' (82) Workers' interests still dictated co-operation with capital, and accepting such features of the free market as unrestricted imports: 'today's problem is not that of the quality of life in the factory, but that of the continuity of the life of the factory.' (83)

This shift in emphasis is due to the re-emergence of familiar cyclical movements, albeit weaker and, in the phase of recession, deeper than in the past, and despite the raw materials crisis. Wages were stationary or falling, and unemployment was up. The pattern of a short rising phase of the cycle seemed established, but at least, with a cycle, traditional remedies could be applied. International pressures on the Italian system combined to produce signs of stagnation and decline. However, optimism recurs. Carli felt that restructuring in the productive sector had after all occurred in the 1960s. Though accepting public investment at times of crisis, he believed the private sector, as it moved from self-financing to more modern forms, would establish control of the domestic labour force and re-establish its export competitiveness. The problem was that the state sector had 'commitments of thousands and thousands of billions [of lire]: local authorities are suffocating under an indebtedness swollen over the years,' (84) and the state must concern itself with these debts. Centralized power is dangerous. However, 'in the womb of this system the conditions have matured whereby the old relations between productive forces have been modified: taking note of this is the condition for eliminating the antagonism between social groups.' (85)

Ultimately, Carli believed the challenge to social peace and industrial recovery (even if in a much-reduced world economic context) was no longer derived from the links between wages and productivity, a form of workers' sabotage-suicide, but from the political class and the state bourgeoisie. He resigned in August 1975, and it was his successor, Paolo Baffi, who felt the full weight of these latter elements. Carli's reports had, of course, been designed to defend the Bank and increase confidence. Yet it is still possible to see broad strategic designs and, at least till the 1975 recession, a belief that restructuring, though not planned restructuring of the non-export sectors, was being achieved and could win the co-operation of labour. Labour had not won: rather, weaknesses lay in the obtuseness of the political class.

Baffi stressed the fact that the strategy of the politicians and the state bourgeoisie was internationally damaging. Increased public spending put pressure on loan repayments, and earned criticism from the EEC and IMF. To go 'beyond the crisis' meant moving from the state towards self-financing. Two principles must be observed: first, that labour costs could not exceed those of competitors, and second, that monetary policy must be in line with international competition. This implied wage controls, even though the workers could be assured that a 6 per cent wage increase was worth more in real terms than a 20 per cent increase. Italian labour costs had risen 137 per cent in 1970-5 compared with a 107 per cent increase in Britain. (86) Again, the lines were drawn between the Bank's view of restructured normality and the political forces which shrank from confronting the working class on the wage issue, and had no intention of pruning the administration or retreating from public investment. Baffi put the choice as one between stabilization and a speeding-up of inflation, and stagnation. The danger was of permanently joining the second rank of industrialized countries.

None the less, Baffi's policy of stabilization was not succeeding. It was a policy of austerity, of replacing consumption with investment. 'The programme of stabilization was intended, in addition to its immediate ends, to launch a policy which would again provide space for the further development of our economy.' (87) Inflation and unemployment continued, however. Not only were these pathological, but on the one hand the government was committed to a non-protected lira and a European policy, while on the other, the country was increasingly precariously attached to movements of the European economy. (88) Two conclusions may be drawn. First, that after the early 1970s, conflict between the Bank and the Christian Democrats was increasingly over conflict management. The Bank did not control means of restructuring, and monetary conservatism may have aggravated the problems. On the other hand, state intervention vigorously pursued in the 1970s registered its main successes in 1971-2. Since then, the system has suffocated under debts, national and international, and suffered from lack of expertise. It is a strategy for development not yet agreed on planning, criteria of investment and managements, or on the advisability of a confrontation with labour. It is deeply sceptical of the capacities of private industry, while it is itself responsible for increasing the strain of indebtedness and of postponing examination of structural policies. The Christian Democrats' state plan is a poor cousin of the corporate capitalism of the 'modern state'. It is both derivative and an adaptation to tradition. It is a version, less economically based and less integrated than Carli's, of the attempt to create a ruling class capable of dealing with situations of high inter-group conflictuality. The strategy of the state bourgeoisie is essentially subaltern and co-opting, shrinking from confrontation and structural intervention. (89)

In the 1970s the political choice of state participation in the economy did not assume that a 'higher form' of productive development was possible. It is arguable that the distinction between the Christian Democrats' 'welfare state capitalism' and the PCI's regionally determined, small-scale, industrial development represent differences of degree and convenience rather than of principle and strategy, despite their apparent contrast. Both involve 'beginning anew'. The Christian Democrats must convert their clients into an economically more viable form to avoid the consequences of fiscal crisis, while the PCI will have to re-institutionalize any development of micro-capitalism. In both cases, their plans tend to exacerbate the problem of state and public administration, the Christian Democrats because development takes place with and through the state, the PCI because it depends on an untried 'democratic' element and weak regional governments. Labour market studies, especially of the Mezzogiorno, offer an insight into the type of development which is actually in progress. Mottura's and Pugliese's case is that the decline of agriculture is part of the normal development of a capitalist society, and that the South is now a stable population, not an industrial reserve army of labour. This seems more convincing than Meldolesi's argument that the South remains a reservoir of labour for Northern industry. While Northern development determined, and still determines, the fate of the South, the latter no longer fulfils the function of a resource, labour, for the North, despite a continuing 'seepage'. It is now 'waiting' for a new solution. (90)

The history of post-war Southern agriculture shows how a dominant economic class can switch from one economic strategy to its opposite, in this case defeating the representatives of the working agricultural population, the Federbraccianti and Alleanza nazionale dei contadini. The agricultural counter-revolution of the fascist period, the contadinizzazione of agriculture, was followed by mechanization and a policy of 'modernization' which completed the fuelling of Northern industry with Southern labour. It seems a suicidal destruction of the post-war social constituency of the Southern dominant bloc, but in reality it exported social conflict, creating a new, dependent, sub-proletariat in Southern cities. Mottura and Pugliese refer to the newly impoverished as 'rural poor', perhaps two million expelled from agriculture by the Mansholt plan's final solution for European agriculture as subordinate function of industry. (91) They argue that what is normal for capitalism is too often seen by the PCI as pathological because it is not 'rational'. This might be attributed to the suspicion that there is a secret capitalist plan capable of transcending the limitations of normal development.

Mottura and Pugliese identify three phases in Southern development after the 1950 establishment of the Cassa per il Mezzogiorno. The first, to 1957, is the welfare phase. The second, from 1958 to 1965, they describe as the phase of selective development and, from 1967, a phase of investment concentration and priority for the industrial sector. Thus, from the start of the post-war 'process of underdevelopment', the intervention of the Cassa per il Mezzogiorno has, by treating the South as an internal colony, created a 'bloc of underdevelopment'. Full of contradictions between big industry, small industry and agriculture, mainly agricultural zones, and areas of pauperism, the South has been effectively confined for some unknown future purpose. (92)

This implies that though divisions between Northern proletariat and Southern subordinate classes may be artificial, or created by policy, they are not thereby trivial. Emigration from the South does not necessarily create class unity, since emigration is precarious, and emigrants to the North and abroad may also be 'present' on the Southern labour market. Against Zitara, (93) they argue that autonomous, proletarian, development in the South is conditioned by organizational weakness. Unions are either lacking or tend to be clientelistic. The Southern subordinate classes confront and depend on the state, not on management. This produces political dependency on vertical authority systems, not on horizontal co-operation. As opposed to Meldolesi, the precariously employed or the unemployed 'in a non-employed situation' are not an industrial reserve army, but marginal to production, ignored. (94) Their lavour is unusable. They do not reduce the cost of industrial labour, and if employed in 'modern' industry, do not cut wage levels.

The optimistic Ceres (Christian Democrat) report on 1978 indicates along with other negative factors such as public indebtedness, poor investment prospects and inflation a trend to rising unemployment, which indicates at least a decline in regular employment, if not overall working activity. In the South, unemployment was up, underemployment down. There are signs of a sizeable child labour market, as high as 8 per cent of children, not necessarily full-time, and of rising intellectual unemployment. (95) The drive to escape unemployment by raising qualifications is frustrated by the saturation of the tertiary sector. There seems no reason for thinking that Southern development will be of a higher type, even if there is a continuing spread of industry from other areas. Pressure for public employment will continue, and though the submerged economy may provide some relief, it is unlikely to equalize North-South relations. The 1976 Censis study pointed out that in 1974, 59 per cent of those seeking a first job (and who, nationally, tend to find temporary employment less frequently than those describing themselves as unemployed) and 52 per cent of the unemployed were in the South and the Islands. Of women seeking first employment, 54.5 per cent were in the South and Islands where a smaller proportion of the population tries to enter the labour market (Sardinia, for example, has proportionately nearly half the active population of Emilia). (96)

The submerged economy in the South is not a seed for industrial development, being concentrated in private service industries and agriculture, and various forms of child labour. The submerged economy grows on the margin of established industry. Paci explains this by observing that a transition from overoccupation in the boom to recession does not stimulate the South's 'stagnant overpopulation'. The demand for employment in the submerged economy may be strong among women displaced by the crisis. Yet there are structural limits to their absorption, such as skill levels, location and the types of labour available. With a combination of managerial and technical expertise, finance and the support of government agencies, the parameters of the labour market can be modified or expanded. Despite this, the main structural limits remain. Those displaced leave the market involuntarily and are not redefined as an industrial reserve. The labour market is divided along the lines of disjuncture between marginal labour, working-class labour and intellectual labour. This division reinforces the immobility, the rigidity of the market. Some types of labour are short in the North (hence a semi-clandestine movement from parts of the South), and growth takes place in small industries. The export economy becomes out of scale with both the international economy and internal consumption and services. Meanwhile, the South continues to have an occupational structure disproportionately large in agriculture, construction and public works, and roughly proportional in non-commercial service. In commercial and industrial undertakings it is underrepresented. (97)

Fuà's study of employment described activity in Italy, compared with fourteen industrial or industrializing countries, as 'somewhat (but not exceptionally) low as regards countries with similar age structure.' On this basis, women's employment was 'rather low', but that of men 'exceptionally low'. (98) The tendency to undertake tertiary education, which had been low in 1950, was accelerating by 1970. However, the normal shrinkage of the agricultural population had not been absorbed, leaving Italy lower than in the seven other countries examined. The movement was from agriculture into inactivity. Fuà estimated concealed employment at an additional 17-18 per cent of the official total, but, even so, Italy showed signs of secular decline and structural limitations to recovery, such as levels of qualification and of fixed capital. (99) International comparisons tell us little about the prospects of national capitalisms, but the experience of 'falling behind' both Northern and Southern models of European development is instructive, as too is the comment that the move to small enterprises, always characteristic of Italian industry, presupposes low productivity. Small means tendentially low productivity and wage levels below the European. With a low effective capacity, Fuà argues, only a few can expect to be paid at European levels. (100)

Policy is thus caught between two conflicting forces. One is the EEC choice, of enforcing acceptable monetary policies, accepting competitive trade and agricultural policies which leave Italy near the bottom of the Community in many, but not all, indicators in this reference group. The second option is that of working out a national form of development within option one, given that at present this is non-reversible and modifiable only from a position of bargaining weakness. Here, however, there are major problems. If indeed the problems of small industry are such that it is condemned to remaining small, it cannot satisfy the aspiration and the activity desired. On the other hand, large-scale industrialization provides too few jobs, too expensively, to justify the risk. It is 'cheaper' to expand the tertiary sector and not face the challenge of finding and implementing management skills. The 1976 survey of workers in twenty large industries, with over half a million employees, shows just under a 5:1 income differential between managers and workers, with white-collar employees about 40 per cent above the workers. (101) The picture is of a small number of not-exceptionally-well-paid managers, but a stratum at the

'European' level, and workers in the more labour-intensive engineering (metal-working) and textile industries which are low paid in comparable European terms.

This does not disqualify the notion of a 'privileged' industrial sector, but it does cast doubts on the belief that workers' wage claims in export industries have been excessive or unusually successful. The tendency is for the 1976 figures to show an impressive clustering of median wages for industrial and non-industrial (excluding commerce) employees at between 4.2 and 4.7m. lire annually. (102) That is, the industrial workers in big industries are roughly at the same level as the employee in the public sector, though not in public industry. The picture is of a sector in relatively stable decline, with the low point in 1975 (from 1969). That low point was indeed so low that it is more realistic to see the 1976 recovery as a return to the late 1974 position. There is little sign that there is a dynamism in the economy capable of reversing this process, or removing structural barriers, even when the labour movement gives its blessing to Southern investment, as with Alfasud.

Another study, for instance, estimates that 69.1 per cent of families earn no more than 6m. lire annually in 1977 (64.1 per cent in 1976 and 78.7 per cent in 1975). (103) Such figures are of limited use because of the distorting effect of inflation, and the difficulty of comparing individual earnings and family incomes. There is, however, a generally stable relation between the major groups of employees - workers in industry and workers in agriculture - the latter two categories being in an income relation of 70 and 47 per cent respectively. These figures seem to cast doubt on the Bank of Italy's claim that incomes are tending to become more equal, at least in the short term. (104)

Pesenti and Vitello said: 'The type of capitalist development which has taken place in our country under the leadership of the monopolies could certainly not resolve the traditional national problems, but only aggravate existing contradictions and develop others.' (105) The question remains, now that the monopolies are no longer a growth area, whether international capitalism will find a new role for Italy, and whether political alternatives to this role exist. One difficulty in the Italian situation is that the failures of the 1960s and 1970s have left little that is positive which can be modified. The weakening and frustration of Catholic socio-economic thought, and the distortion of American neocapitalist doctrine and structures when imported to Italy, were already visible in the early 1960s. Thus, neoliberalism became laissez-faire, and integralism transposed into an 'American' notion of corporate bargaining in a controlled economy.

The PCI's interest in limited intervention in a full-employment economy during the 'miracle' was modified by the failure of monopoly capital to provide the growth base for an ultimately nationally planned and owned economy. The problems of public sector employment showed that its growth was an answer not so much to problems of distribution in an expanding economy as to difficulties in accumulation. Far from being spun-off by monopoly capitalist success, the public sector's combination of low wages and short hours (106) pointed directly to taking a second job. Thus, the inability to impose internal discipline, on absenteeism, for example, created an internal legitimacy problem, underlining the disjuncture between 'state rationality' and 'planning rationality'. Failure to impose internal discipline was politically still more relevant in the case of the 'separate bodies'. The public sector itself encouraged 'private arrangements' to make up incomes, by the incremental tendency to underpaying, underworking and overstaffing. When opportunities outside regular employment become scarce, the economic conflict is already in place within conditions of employment in the public sector.

Lacking a homogeneous, modern-bureaucratic bourgeoisie, as Galli said, state intervention on behalf of rationalization and increased accumulation 'has not succeeded in translating itself into a capacity to rationalize conditions (political, social or of organized and internalized values) which favour the full unfolding of capitalism itself.' (107) However, different strategies prevailed at different times. In the 1950s there was a movement towards state intervention and protection of the bourgeoisie, an attempt to win the confidence of the middle strata now that integralism had been defeated and the working class contained. Galli attributed the failure of the state to retain the confidence of the bourgeoisie to a combination of that class's weakness, and the non-bourgeois character of the Christian Democrats. This, then, rather than the question of when 'lateness' becomes 'backwardness' or 'underdevelopment', accounts for the growth of a 'financial-speculative bourgeoisie', a public as opposed to a private bourgeoisie, with a privileged relation to political power. This state bourgeoisie controls the key positions in the economy, but it is not technocratic, not an administrative, prefectorial stratum. It is concerned not with accumulation but with the construction of zones of power. In that sense it is pre- or non-capitalist, and the dominant alliance is between the 'upper functionary-speculative bourgeoisie and the middle bureaucratic-parasitic bourgeoisie'. (108) Galli argued that despite the precarious and distorted growth of the 1950s and 1960s, a permanent crisis could have been avoided. While it was true that the wage demands of 1963 and 1968-9 put the system in crisis, a stronger and more skilful leadership would have adjusted to this, and capitalized on the post-militant European recoveries in the 1960s and the short, inflationary expansions of the 1970s. However, the overriding interest of the bureaucratic-parasitic stratum was to consolidate power through control of public funds.

The chances of rationalizing capitalist development were present, and missed, in the 1960s. This was due partly to a mis-reading of the 1963-4 recession, and partly to weakness in the centre-Left coalition, leading to its decline and a return to conservative monetary policies in the mid-1960s. Also important was the lack of unequivocal support for industrialization. The Christian Democrats had a strong tradition of rhetorically proposing alternatives to rationalization and to social democracy. (109) Although they accepted the dangers and distortions of uncontrolled economic development and a passive consumer society, they continued to regard that development as self-propelling. On the other hand, when the time came, development would provide conditions for intervention, when growth produced inevitable difficulties for government and society, threatening the quality of life a and of social participation. This was an evangelical version of the 'due tempi'. It was left for the Christian Democrats to subsidize a capitalism whose rationalization was regarded ambiguously, and which in any case had not expanded sufficiently to generate its own resources for rationalization.

This dilemma was paralleled in the PCI, though less directly, and with little influence on the actual course of events. The real competition was that between the Christian Democrats and the PCI in the anti-capitalist appeal to the masses, interwoven with their other appeal on the basis of orderly consumerism (Christian Democrats), and 'rational sociality, with a modernized economy' (PCI). Catholic opinion could attack the ethic of the welfare state and subsidized capitalism along with the consumer society, when the latter had scarcely begun and 'welfare' was primitive. (110) Because of its moralistic attitude to wealth and consumption, praise for 'austerity' and condemnation of absenteeism, 'Catholic capitalism', with all its contradictions, permitted ideological commentary which was both interclassist and reactionary. Interclassist moralism allowed simultaneous attacks on the idle rich from the standpoint of the working masses, and on the consumerist productivist ethic presumed to underlie militant class action. Catholic attitudes were the fuel of populist anti-capitalism, both in the fatalists who accepted the anarchy of self-propelled economic growth as necessary and in the rich who saw 'moral degeneracy' behind workers' militancy.

With industry 50 per cent in state hands, Galli argued that the benefit of intervention went not to the workers or to the public sector as a whole, but to the speculators and the state bourgeoisie. Italy is not backward, but 'it is still valid to apply the analysis for backward countries to certain sectors, as, for example, circulation'. (111) Galli's study is useful, but leaves questions unanswered. First, it would seem that Catholic ideology, always politically weak, has now been replaced by consensus around the pragmatic consideration that without subsidy the precarious economic balance would be lost. This implies that the strength of the state bourgeoisie is really built on structural weakness. Second, how would the state bourgeoisie react to collapse or to accelerated decline? Galli describes a massive concentration of power on a weak economic base. How could that accumulation of power be used in deepening crisis, especially fiscal crisis? It could scarcely be used in a coup against itself, nor by a neoconservative withdrawal from the economy. Could it be used in the overdue rationalization of capitalism, or in reform of the state and public administration? The PCI too tends towards a contradictory attitude to the desirability of capitalist and public economic growth. It also sees the state bourgeoisie as crucially powerful and structurally weak. Yet will it be able to maintain its consensual base when it both places its own representatives in the state bourgeoisie and proposes an alternative capitalist strategy? How real is the power and governing ability of the state bourgeoisie, and how significant is economic power taken over from a weakened private sector?

The argument of 'Il capitalismo assistenziale' ('subsidized capitalism') neatly expresses the dilemma of the PCI and its hopes for transition. To take power from the state bourgeoisie means to some extent returning it to the private sector, on the basis of formalized, consensual, industrial relations. Not to penetrate the state bourgeoisie means exclusion from the use of its capillary power, and possibly from its successful efforts to restructure at some future date. Penetration, however, means the use of that power to 'reform the state', and with it the risk of absorption or co-optation into a strengthened state bourgeoisie. This would be a coherent modernizing strategy, though not if the Italian state bourgeoisie is a local form of the authoritarian-democratic modern state in decline. A modest economic policy of 'rationalization', in short, may commit the PCI not only to further developing capitalism, but, perhaps more significantly, to sharing internally or externally in its political and class management.

This dilemma can be seen in Peggio's remark: 'We have no doubts on the positive functions performed by small and medium industry, and above all those that can be performed, if adequately directed and subsidized, in an advanced capitalist society.' (112) Small industry clearly refers here to private industry. Nor is there a consistency based on the continuity of PCI opposition to monopoly. In 1956, monopoly was regarded as representing the highest form of capitalist growth. Togliatti's insistence on the need to preserve private small and medium industry did not mean he regarded this as the pattern of modern development. (113) It was a means of providing alternatives to monopoly development, encouraging small capitalists to resist the larger, and industrializing to 'catch up' while not alarming the middle strata worried about universal nationalization. Now the future of capitalism in Italy is seen to lie not with monopoly but small and middle industry. Consistent opposition to monopoly development is now irrelevant. Peggio blames the dominant class for failure to intervene in the monopoly sector. Surely what must be criticized instead is the form of that intervention. There is now an economic case for giving priority to small industries doing relatively well, as against faltering large industry. The criterion, however, is economic success in a capitalist society, not the destruction of monopoly. The solution is at once subordinate (assist the periphery), and presupposes a measure of PCI control over public funds. It suggests forms of piecemeal regional development, which sees the future of advanced capitalist development as lying not in tertiarization or rationalization but in small manufacturing. Bets are thus hedged as to whether advanced capitalism is itself de-developing or whether Italian capitalism is still retarded. In either case, small industry seems destined to become part of the 'assisted economy', alongside big industry, under the collective control of the political class.

We must also ask how unions fit into this scenario. If unions returned to their level of strength of 1948-9 only in 1969-70, the 1970s saw a qualitative increase in their economic and political influence. To what extent, though, does the weakening and fragmentation of capitalism tend to weaken trade unions, and in particular the union movement as a whole? Tronti's case was that despite having less 'theory', spontaneous and contract struggles of the USA labour movement had gained more than the more theoretical, more politically determined, European movement, excepting Germany. (114) The economic difficulties of capitalism formed the political terrain of the working class: 'The apparatus of the bourgeois state is today divided up within the capitalist factory.' (115) Italian capitalism was too little advanced to present a reformist option to the PCI. The working class was not to collaborate with capitalism, nor be anarcho-syndicalist, but to perceive the capitalist mode of production as a particular moment of working-class revolution, to be challenged and not regarded as natural or rational. From these early essays Tronti later developed the idea that the Party provided diffuse leadership for the class, not a form of Leninist organization and discipline of the class. (116) In fact the autonomy of the unions and Party was essential: neither must form part of the system of capitalism, and capitalism itself did not determine the success or failure of their strategy.

Sylos Labini attempted a summary of the unions' experience of the 1960s (117) in which we can see in the light of Tronti how their strategy might have weakened or modified capitalism. First, no wages policy as control would succeed: only a planning policy with social guarantees would work. Second, wage rises in 1969-70 did contribute to price rises. Third, there had been a movement in favour of wages and salaries, but these rose less rapidly than profits declined. This shifted the initiative from private to public investment, and to finance capital. Fourth, financial policy became more important, but, despite errors, the real problem was that the government spent too little, not too much. None the less, prospects did not look good, as even agreements over wages and prices would mean that, with less disposable labour as a result of wage increases, the sectors of lowest productivity would be more costly, and increase prices all round. The workers were hurt by inflation mainly by reduced savings. Small industry, in its turn, was put in jeopardy by militancy. Militancy hurt workers as well as entrepreneurs, but in the absence of a state plan the capitalist periphery suffered most.

It would seem that such an economic crisis would more rapidly create a political crisis than in stronger economies. During the 1970s, though, there was a temporizing on that issue. In that decade, the notion of planning and workers' participation, hard to advance when first subordinate and later aggressive oppositional positions were maintained, has had a mixed history. Union organization and readiness to co-operate have increased, but so has employer resistance and the elusiveness of the political class when it comes to compelling negotiations of substance. As Accornero said, union 'productivism' has been unable to avoid presenting plans which do not provide alternatives to exploitation. (118) A feature of the 1970s was a readiness to shift from 'state planning' to 'union planning' and a broader view of 'social productivity' was taken by two of the three union confederations (CGIL) and 'social efficiency' (CISL). (119) However, in the CGIL there is a clear scepticism regarding the possibility of development, and in the CISL a tendency to avoid the issue. Projects have not turned into plans, and planning for growth can no longer command the unthinking cosmopolitan enthusiasm of the 1960s. Stagnation provides the context where the autonomy of the labour movement leads to greater political influence, but not necessarily to clearer objectives. The struggle for autonomy itself marked both greater political maturity and diffuseness. The PCI no longer dictates union policy. On the other hand, unions cannot force political concessions, though the government consults them. Therefore, unions in the Factory Councils must accept the subordinate position which follows from lack of control over national instruments of management. They are thus committed to maintain wage levels despite falling investment, a stalemate reflected in low productivity. The struggle seems stalled, especially as union logic is to support high-wage, high-investment and low-profit industry, as against the marginal small firm with decentralization and low wages. The movement, however, shrinks back from the inconsistency of a class-collaborationist policy based on low wages as a trade-off for employment. (120) Tronti's model does not face the consequences for unions where capitalism declines spontaneously, and unions lack control over investment.

The consequence of stalemate is often described as making Italy both a free and an ungovernable society. Stame, as we shall see later, argues instead that this is only the first phase in the development of a 'modern state'. Social conflict has intensified, the workers will not conduct the struggle as a class, proposing instead national collaboration, while non-institutionalized or unofficial dissent is heavily repressed as deviancy. This is not a freer, higher, form of the state, but 'a necessity born of the problematic of the crisis'. (121) Expansion of the state is a sign of its de-legitimation, and it is the state itself which creates new spheres of conflictuality. No longer does the play of civil society determine class structure, it is determined by the operations of the state itself. Class consciousness is fragmented by horizontal competition between improvised, functional collectivities. This society is highly conflictual, but also closed and authoritarian: 'consensus is the central category through which the democratic-authoritarian state mediates the function of dominance with the needs of stability in the system.' (122)

This notion of the Germanization of the state needs qualifying. It assumes a congruence between public and private capitalism and the political state which in reality is closer to dialogue. The state moves into civil society because the future of capitalism is no longer assured. Repression of the margin is in itself no guarantee that conflict can be put into consensual form. The 'modern state' is not the solution to crisis, but its result. The autonomy of the labour movement did not lead to a lessening of conflictuality followed by a decision to collaborate, but to the stalemate described above, where there was no prospect of victory, or even victory in winning. Stame combines high repression and high consensus. Yet such authoritarian consensus in conflictual societies can surely be maintained only by destroying institutions which are in competition, rather than encouraging their proliferation. Stame's model is that of the beginning of passive revolutions. A revolutionary class movement runs out of momentum. A government of order, repressive and of low legitimacy, establishes a conformist-authoritarian state. The working class accepts, or submits to, this state, as it has hypostasized politics, or in this case democracy, in the state. In order to continue class struggle, the state must guarantee that freely conducted conflictuality will not produce an authoritarian reaction, according to Stame.

This seems a markedly optimistic proposal. A challenge to social authority, when resolved by social conflict, itself tends to produce authoritarianism. If a working class proposes to continue class struggle without a revolutionary assault on the state, it must accept the 'guaranteeing' state which must still retain the capacity of authoritarian response. The alternative to Stame's picture of 'revolution, or guarantees or authoritarianism' has been that of 'democratic planning', the public scrutiny of the economy. (123) This proposal, however, suffers from the consequences of the dual face of the Italian state: its extreme timidity and deference as bestower of privilege and 'privacy' to the economy, and its vigour in penetrating the financial and entrepreneurial system. It is strong in intervention and weak in control. Democratic scrutiny, outside the state system, would be scrutiny both of the state and of its intervention. As Galgano pointed out, the reason for lack of 'confidence in the state' (Cacciari) is the suspicion that 'here, the capitalist class does not need to ask the state for subsidies or infrastructures; it asks it to ensure "public order", or to guarantee by force the persistence of the original conditions of the reproduction of capital.' (124) Again we meet the same dilemma. If the state represents the growth of a bourgeoisie frustrated in the private economic sector because of the narrow foundations of Italian capitalism, surely democratic planning could only be a form of limitation of state power, or follow such limitation. Yet if the narrowness of these foundations is also a limiting condition for political power, how can the working class avoid insertion into the state as a consequence of its economic function, as a subordinate element in economy and state?

Stame may exaggerate the 'modernity' of the state, and separate instead of combine its strengths and weaknesses. He does not exaggerate the difficulty of securing guarantees from it. It is hard to see that there is an easy way out of the stalemate to which class struggle had brought the labour movement by the early 1970s; a situation where, except for armed struggle, the broad vision of social transformation was attached to the problematic notion of large-scale growth, and qualitative demands by organized labour in areas where the Christian Democrats could or would not mobilize the state.

Chapter 7

CRISIS MANAGEMENT OR TRANSFORMATION?: the political system

Change becomes crisis when there is no guarantee that the institutions involved can withstand modification, and when the traditional response to change has been immobilism. In the past, the strength of the parties has seemed to compensate for the 'fragmentary nature' of the state. Now, however, their own structure as an element of this diffuseness must seem suspect, and it is hard to separate them from the crisis of the superstructure itself. The state bourgeoisie does not provide an alternative authority, as it lacks both a political philosophy and an understanding of economic rationality. Nor does it have the consensus-forming capacity to reduce social conflict. The various positions mentioned earlier - the backwardness thesis (Carli), that of the crisis of the Christian Democrats (Galli), the 'advanced crisis' theory of Ingrao and the subsequent search for a third way, and the autonomy of politics (Tronti) - are all in different ways vitiated by the problem of devising and instituting a coherent, and popular, alternative to permanent crisis. Signs of vigour may even be interpreted as signs of further fragmentation, as in the issue-centred Radical revival, or the Socialist Party under Craxi. It may even appear that the PCI strategy of moving into the state at the lowest levels - after the frustrating failure to topple what is commonly, if questionably, held to be a rotten tree, the Christian Democrats - is a sign of weakness rather than ideological bad faith.

The view that the secularization of politics was a healthy sign means, in a declining system, merely a progressive depoliticization. The institutional weakness of the political system, which favoured a weak executive, and coalition politics instead of electoral programmes, is now overtaken by the decline of parties unable to 'programme' capitalism, reverse its crisis or transcend it. These difficulties affect both the historic and the new Left. The latter is dismayed by the war that consensus proposes to wage on dissent, or retreats into the 'dream' as the only dissent possible against capitalism-as-history or system-as-totality (Scalia). The intellectual new Left, having solved neither the problem of organization nor that of violence, finds itself socially and culturally isolated from the 'new barbarians' of the 'marginal Left'. The institutional Left tried to combine traditional destinations with opportunist routes. Overall, however, there was a feeling that the scope for individual and collective action had been greatly reduced, a sentiment on which terrorism tried to capitalize, presenting itself as the only decisive response.

The problem is that the parties must claim to compensate, at least verbally, for the deficiencies of the state, while in fact the parties in different forms operate through it and comprise it. Tendentially, the ability to deploy the coercive power of the state in a consociational system exists. The state is weak in a Weberian-Keynesian sense, but strong in a consensual-coercive one. Constructing the modern, consensual-authoritarian state would not be an impossible task, as it would admit the insolubility of the structural crises and construct a framework for containing social conflict and overseeing the distribution of material and intangible goods to competing corporations. This might be based on a Christian Democratic identification with the state bourgeoisie, though association with the PCI would simplify the process of creating consensus and composing a representative state class. This also involves real risks, both with the PCI left outside (low legitimacy for a Christian Democrat monopoly of the state class) or inside (sacrifice of power by the Christian Democrats). (1) The safest policy is to manoeuvre within institutions, to choose a slow strategy, especially after the 1975 and 1976 electoral 'breakthroughs' which produced much less than anticipated.

Any 'attack on the state' must accelerate authoritarian tendencies, not only because it undermines faith in legal rules, however imperfect and suspect, but because it encourages the state to show its strength. The notion that the Italian or any other advanced industrial state is 'motionless' or immobile is therefore untenable. The political science literature which tends to see the parties as potentially the key, the most dynamic element of the system, formulating universalist values, permitting alternation of governments, parliamentary bipolarization and social reconciliation underestimates the self-propelling power of the Christian Democrat-state connection. (2)

Matteucci identifies this in the 'new political stratum', predominantly Christian Democrat which dominates society by way of clientelism. (3) Put thus simply, this undervalues the dynamics of crisis as changing the function of clientelism. Previously, clientelism might be ascribed to the imperfect assimilation of industrial culture, and the inability to manage technology, seen both as a challenge to traditionalism and a vehicle for socialism. Yet now it is part of the strategy of decline, of pseudo-socialism, where the reduction of available employment is presented and masked as the 'modern', technologically advanced form of labour 'letting machines do the work'. The form taken by clientelism is that of the public institutionalization of semi-autonomous bodies. Fedele additionally notes the capacity of the Christian Democrats to mediate interests and of the PCI to maintain, even increase, its strength despite the general European trend and a seemingly permanent opposition, arguing that this denotes a dynamic, not a static, equilibrium. (4)

The meagre results of the electoral successes of the PCI in 1975 and 1976 show that it is easy to overvalue the effect of electoral politics on the parliamentary division of powers. The insertion of the working class more completely into the state system was both a challenge made by the PCI in the name of the class, and also an offer to the state of the state's own completion, its own representativeness. Intellectuals sympathetic to the Party started to suggest that for them the state was still that of the 'subversive bourgeoisie'. The workers increasingly resisted offers being made in their name when returns were so slight. New Left and autonomous Left also objected so strongly that a return to opposition was a prudent as well as an enforced move. The passive strategy of infiltrating the administrative system and gaining administrative experience at the regional level was less risky than being outmanoeuvred nationally by the Christian Democrats.

The PCI, however, faces a problem deeper than that of oscillating between Right and Left as its own fortunes change and its opponents alter their strategy. For a party of 'efficient administration' has no raison d'être outside the state. On the other hand if it professes no ideology but that of efficiency, it loses its character as the party of the masses, and of the Left electorate. In practice, the PCI's administrative efficiency is limited by a lack of personnel and experience, fields where the Christian Democrats are strong. A party of efficient administration in permanent opposition at the national level is anomalous, and simply gives external support to those who really do have administrative authority (routinized consensus). Yet to acknowledge the exhaustion of its philosophical base would submerge the identity of the Party in the modern state itself.

In the political system, a break appears in the rapid succession of movement transformed into organization. The PCI can no longer expect to win back young 'movement' politicians as steady cadres, nor can it expect a progressively larger share of power if it scores electoral successes. The party's strength is now seen in its relative autonomy from electoral choices, or criteria of competence, in formulating and implementing policy. Ingrao's case, to overcome this, has been to develop the PCI from a party of mass mobilization directed by wise strategists into one of mass participation (and hence of mediation). (5) However, three considerations must be stressed. If the argument is used that the state has a problem of 'immobilism', this means either that it possesses more effective strength than admitted, or that the Left is much weaker than it seems, since it persists and largely excludes the PCI. I have argued elsewhere that the choice of administrative infiltration in fact marks the cultural subordination of the PCI, its lack of a vision of alternative societies and its concern to rationalize existing 'inefficiency'. (6) Second, the rhetoric of 'mass participation' is scarcely applicable now. There are many 'masses', participating as corporate interests. Some masses are more crucial than others, and more homogeneous, as for example the industrial triangle's working class. Others are less easily mobilized, less homogeneous, like the old or the young. Some put forward articulated interests, others are the objects of administration, as the experience of decentralization tends to show. Third, it is not certain that changing the form of the party would alter the national division of power. It is not clear, either, that the connection between decision and power would be more simply established than when decisions are taken authoritatively by the leadership and transmitted through cadres, or that popular participation would relocate decision-making at the grass-roots level. Changing the party form is logical, in view of its social and ideological transformations, but may lead to a dissipation of power in general, especially when ideological intentions are so varied and uncertain. 'Participation' does not resolve the problems raised by turning a party of mass popular propaganda into one of technicians-administrators.

Lucio Magri appears to regard discussion of a suitable party-form as an attempt to rationalize the fragmentation of late capitalist development. He, while arguing that it is pointless to speak of 'resolving' the crisis democratically, describes a state simultaneously strong and weak. It is strong in that it organizes technocracy, manipulates consensus and reconciles the interests of the middle strata, capital, the inter-class parties and the organized employed working class. Its 'waste' is a normal result of growth, as well as of the difficulty of keeping living labour in jobs where production costs are too high to produce a profit. On the other hand, it is weak because of the paralysis of public power and of the mechanism of forming the political will. Technocracy has been unable to solve these structural problems. The structure then disintegrates, and with it the technocratic institutions. This marks the 'ever more difficult survival of a socio-economic formation beyond the rationale which gave it historical legitimacy; this survival is increasingly tied either to instruments of repression or the use of logic and values which deny it; or both things together.' (7)

However, he reverts to a maximalist view. The choice is either capitalist restructuring or revolution. It means either a regulated and subsidized capitalism and a new international division of labour incorporating Eastern Europe and parts of the Third World, or mass confrontation with the logic of capital. Magri demonstrates that the capitalist alternative leads to expanded global contradictions, but does not go beyond the original statement that this is indeed a possible development and basis for survival. Magri criticizes the PCI's defeatism and inconsistency, but the question remains: what if the PCI is correct in implying that the choice for Italy is not transition but remaining an industrial 'European' society? This makes the question of the state's strength or weakness equivocal. Crisis lessens and weakens the possibility of confrontation so long as consensus holds. If consensus (law and order) breaks, then the prospect is of a failed insurrection, defeated by order alone. Modernization thus requires that the state be strengthened on the terrain of consensus.

Asor Rosa's discussion of the relation of intellectuals to the autonomy of the political throws light on the issues involved in consensus formation. The discussion of relations between intellectuals and Party coincided with 'the tension of the latter growing as a party of government, as a party destined for government'. (8) On the one hand, the intellectuals as technicians of culture retained their separateness from the working class, and brought socialist culture to the class via the Party. On the other, the intellectual produced by capitalist society ceases to exist in a socialist one. The future of the socialist intellectual (in capitalism) does not lie with social evolution, proletarianization. He is vital in a 'particularly backward' society like the Italian, where capitalist development is necessary as it gives workers 'time to think'. Industrial progress, or progressiveness, 'is something that should not be rejected, but, rather than being criticized, should be perfected or developed to its limits, freeing it from the negative elements natural to the capitalist direction of the process of production.' (9) In Gramsci's scenario, the workers wait for capitalism to develop, leading to what Asor Rosa sees as a utopian notion of capitalism without capitalists, where workers supervise their own exploitation. Yet, in the last resort, Asor Rosa's 'operaismo' does not solve the paradox of the intellectual, of productivism or of relation of intellectual to state party. He concluded that the intellectual belongs in the superstructure, is already there, in the state to which Party and working class are headed. Thus, 'The problem of the development of a workers' theory of capitalist society sufficient for the historical level ... is not theoretical (even if its substance is): it is political.' (10)

The history of Italian capitalism is thus the history of the state and of intellectuals, the theorist-politicians who are the only alternative cultural agents outside capitalist productivism. Their politics operates whether the state is strong or weak, though the weakness and strength of the state are functions of class struggle. Exhaustion of class struggle would lead to reconciliation in the state.

Tarrow argued that the paralysis of the Christian Democratic power system promotes the spread of other, universalist, values, especially when the economic basis for their power is disappearing. (11) The rapidity of social change produces a dual system of weak advanced sectors and strong disfunctional traditional ones. It would seem, therefore, that a PCI choice of interclassism, of securing representative hegemony which the Christian Democrats, in a fragmented system, never managed, is a coherent one. He assumes that crisis will continue, characterized by a transformation of the political class, modified by the technical weakness and subordinate character of the PCI's power. (12) The late 1970s have seen an institutionalization of the crisis: 'the renewed primacy of politics, as shown by the government agreements of July 1977 and March 1978, has recalled to maximum priority the solution of the economic crisis, subordinating - not for the first time in Italian history - the crisis in civil society to the problems of economic reconstruction ... The Italian crisis is not finished; it has simply returned under the aegis of political direction.' The crisis, though multiform, has the common feature of being determined by political choices dictated by 'relations internal and external to the dominant bloc'. (13)

Farneti and De Felice have discussed the peculiarity of the ruling class and the question of its continuity with the fascist period. In denying continuity between the age of mass electoral parties and those of fascism or pre-1922 politics, they none the less relate the current crisis to one of the whole Republican period. (14) Barbano argues that the propellant of the epoch was the ideology of technical progress and the productivity of labour. Both elements were hurt in the 1960s, as growth slowed, and seemingly were finally disappointed in the 1970s. Change in society centred on these features rather than on a cultural modernization. Barbano characterized the 1950s as years of change, the 1960s as years of 'mutamenti' (mutations) and the 1970s as years of movement. (15) The general picture is one of discontinuity with fascism, and within the Republican period. This casts interesting light on the PCI's struggle to maintain or restore the 1946-7 system and, by inserting itself in government, to give a new cultural sophistication to the ideology of technical progress. These are conservative objectives, which also hinge on the restoration of the state of the first years of the Republic.

This is an attempt to negate the history of Christian Democratic dominance, and to recommence with Togliatti's model whereby the working class is elevated to supremacy by economic growth. It is a sign of the power and traditionalism of the PCI that it should wish to start its grand design again, but also a mark of intellectual conservatism. A break with the old system was made in 1946-7, which implanted in the PCI a belief, fed by exclusion and subordination, that its normal destiny, and the whole of Italian post-war history, had been distorted by its enforced absence from power. Modernization is thus still on the order of the day, and conservation/reform of the Republic the main political aim.

Thus it is hard in that context to agree with Barcellona that 'the tensions, the contradictions and risks *[are]* typical of a phase of transition in which the old society resists and tries to ensure only a space to recover, and a new society has not yet developed to the point of expressing a new "general rationality", a new unitary frame of reference.' (16) The notion of transition as equilibrium, or vacuum, assumes too easily that the second phase of the Republic will be built on the corpse of the Christian Democrats, rather than a PCI return to first principles, or a transformation of the Christian Democrats. The PCI is committed to a version of its original constitutional plan, and the question is whether the Christian Democrats can resist its appeal for re-admission to the state. Barcellona assumes that fragmentation hurts the bureaucracy sufficiently for it to switch loyalties from the Christian Democrats. He argues that crisis lies 'in the system of mediation historically developed between various social relations ... between labour and capital, industrial and finance capital, production and consumption.' (17) Yet the PCI's response to fragmentation is to decentralize, and call for participation. But centralization too is basic to the programme. Making the 1946 constitution operate as a means of social conciliation and transformation requires the party to be in the state. The Christian Democrats cannot give life to the constitution. On the other hand, a 'patto riformistico' to secure national political integration would at this point probably increase social conflict. (18) Institutions must thus be prepared at the grass-roots level to turn mass conflictuality into administrative issues, a demobilized decentralization with a weak state, as against Ingrao's mobilized decentralization.

The PCI case involves seeing social marginality as a sign of backwardness, and the crisis of the state as caused by inability to reconcile traditional and modern. Barcellona characterizes the structural problems of state monopoly capital as that (in Marx's words) of the 'self-valuation of capital [which] becomes more difficult to the extent that it is already valued'. (19) Traditional and modern in the state lead to an uneasy duality. The state is both entrepreneur and subsidizer, both interventionist and the state of law. On the one hand, it guarantees social rules and leaves the private sphere autonomous. On the other, it must guarantee production and economic stability. It is thus mediator and arbitrator in conflicts, and organizer of production in a joint plan with private capital. It is torn between the refereeing function of the liberal-anarchic market society and the operation of a state plan. The Christian Democrats have tried to reconcile this by clientelism, which contradicts the first function and is a 'traditional' response to the 'modern' problem posed by the second. Reform of the state is consequently vital to 'prevent public management helping to bring about the unilateral reversal of the economic cycle'. (20)

The articulation of state and economy in state monopoly capital, in the special circumstances of the Italian 'weak' state and political class, was discussed in the first issues of the PCI's theoretical review, 'Critica marxista'. Ingrao, for example, said 'The liberal "non-interventionist" state has no history in our country and in the political practice of the ruling classes in Italy.' (21) With planning, however, the state has to act as 'regulator and at the same time as competitor of private enterprise'. (22) The interclassist aspect of the plan derives from working-class pressure on the state, not its hegemony. The PCI's proposals in the 1970s, both in their conciliatory (compromise) and 'reasonable militant' (opposition) forms, rest on the analysis that the Christian Democrats have distorted the state of 'state monopoly capital', thus preventing the possibility of transforming the private sector into a subordinate competitor. The state is strong, certainly, but it is weak in the crucial sense that it is not the 'state of monopoly capital', and hence not the state of transition. Pesenti, in the same issue, commented: 'The centralized bureaucratic machine, constructed mainly to confront in police terms the question of social order, is shown to be incapable of responding to the needs which arise from the productive process.' (23) The PCI's answer is to institutionalize social conflict (pluralism), de-legitimating extra-systemic opposition and using the state to solve the problem it had identified in 1964, an earlier crisis of the state, as follows: 'It is the system of accumulation which now seems intolerably costly; the motive centres of industrial development demonstrate insufficient dynamism; the urgent solution of particular bottlenecks, the elimination of backward sectors, demand such a global mass of investment as to require a long-term, rigorous discussion on the formation and distribution of general resources.' (24) The discussion thus concerns priorities and distribution only when the working class has a 'voice' in the state.

This has remained the 'optimistic' view. It has been argued that in general, between 1922 and 1938, Italy stagnated, having experienced rapid 'catching up' before and after. Offe's notion, that intervention is now at an end and only the police function dominates, does not apply to Italy, as intervention has always to date taken on the form of bureaucratic rigidity and authoritarianism. When social consumption increased, it did so without a responsible programme of reform. The crisis of welfare capitalism is one of the Christian Democratic system, not of intervention in general. There is no room for a party 'outside the state'. The Party implies a system of parties, and since they represent masses already 'inside the state', they must operate on the terrain of the state. The PCI must propose 'austerity-planning - development of democracy at all levels - a new model of society - the deployment capable of creating it.' (25) Thus, by extension, the present structure of the Party is still adequate for its historical mission. The 'margins' are results of backwardness and neglect. Healthy intervention does not diminish participation or require repressive consensus, but provides a more solid basis for social co-operation. Thus it is possible to combine the view that monopoly capital declines with the belief that a subordinate working class can transform it into a social, responsible capitalism. For decline is really an aggravated form of stagnation, political and economic. Napolitano argued that Gramsci had foreseen the essentially reactionary or 'qualunquista' nature of catastrophic or decline theorists. Attacks on the idea of progress are 'very self-interested and tendentious'. (26) The catastrophism of the middle strata and popular masses is fuelled by 'huge crises of unemployment in the intermediate intellectual strata'. (27)

Yet the alternative to Gramsci's pre-vision is a situation where Italy remains in crisis. In the late 1950s Italy avoided the repercussions of the USA recessions. It seems unlikely that the country will do the same in the recessions of the 1980s. Whether or not the PCI formally enters the state, recession will tend to fragment the working class further, and to place the initiative firmly on the state bourgeoisie. The corresponding cycle of repression and of intervention to preserve the status hierarchy seems unavoidable. Attachment to Gramsci, and to beliefs in mass participation which do not face the technical problems of administration and planning for decline, has serious implications for the PCI. Application of the 'optimistic' model in times of recession might even have salutary effects. These will probably be slight. Politically, in any case, the PCI's attachment to the juridical forms of the constitution, and the notion that the parliamentary party system is essentially a hierarchical vertical inter-party competition, rather than an alternating or even ideological one, will compel it to act as defender of the state's legitimacy, with or without reform of the state, and with or without its own insertion.

The logic of this position has prompted the Radicals to promote social tolerance as a way of preventing a war between the pluri-party-state and critical sections of civil society. The Socialist Party, or some of its currents, has suggested that the deadlock of the party state is potentially either repressive or chaotic. The characteristic response of the historic Left has been to advocate pluralism or participation. Yet as Bobbio has said of participation, if all participate as equals, 'it is as if no one participates'. (28) Participation in capitalist society cannot in any case be between equals, since the founding principle of society is individual inequality. Participation is meaningful only if it is participation in power: but power requires authority, a hierarchy of 'powers' (consensus), and thus inequality. The pluralist response may be seen as an argument against the bureaucratic-repressive state. It is intended to legitimate and stabilize social conflict, maintain the status quo and mediate conflicts where central authority is unable or unwilling to do so. There seems, none the less, a logical distinction between participation against, or outside, the state, which is a critical and potentially conflictual relation, and participation on the periphery, represented in, say, a pluri-party state which is supportive and confirms power hierarchies. True, participation in the periphery may register shifts in the local balance of power, but that balance itself is soon appropriated and represented in the balance of the powers of central elements of the pluri-party system.

Barbano is probably correctly interpreting the PCI position when he says that taking part is being part. (29) Yet the pluri-party state transfers electoral participation into 'power' by counting votes. Participation implies equality only of access to the institutions of participation. Thus there exists a theoretical option to Rousseau's paradox, that only through individuals' powerlessness, the absence of power and authority, can the common interests of really unequal persons be recognized. There is a concrete probability, too, that participation is really conducted by organized groups which have already articulated interests and already exercise social and political influence.

To many of the non-institutional Left, this talk of participation is a tacit admission of the parties' weakness as interest articulators, of their inability to satisfy their constituents. Sergio Bologna argues that 'inflation and the mechanisms of crisis have seriously weakened the power of the "system of parties" over the process of the reproduction of classes', by reducing distributable resources. (30) The old working class and the old Left are on the defensive, their prospects of power destroyed by its privatization. Togliatti described monopolies as the greatest threat to the subordinate classes and to national independence. Bologna instead places the strategic emphasis on 'marginal capitalism' and the new workers on the margin, the rational use of the irrational. (31) The fact remains that through electoral weight parties do come to dispose of state power. The contest between the parties outside the state is not powerless, and unless the movement becomes a party, electorally competing for state power, the division between institutional and non-institutional Left must deepen. The struggle against capitalism by the margin is a struggle against the state only to the extent that the state is the state of capital. If it is the 'state of the parties', non-institutionalized anti-capitalist militancy cannot justify a declaration of war on the state, as that is to declare civil war within the working class.

Some Communist leaders paint a sombre picture of the necessary insertion into the state. Napolitano said there would be no development 'in a socialist direction ... from the collapse of a capitalist economy, and instead it is a matter of intervening in the crisis so as to affirm the ruling function of the working class, to bind around it a bloc of social forces, a broad system of alliances, and to give the country a new political leadership capable of launching a process of transformation.' (32) In fact, workers' control of the state would not guarantee 'socialism', whatever meaning may be attached to the word, and all depends on the PCI's capacity to run the economy. We see in this a reflection and partial confirmation of Stame's observation that representation is presented in ever-simpler terms, while on the contrary there is a proliferation of interests and subjectivity in civil society. Civil society simply becomes more complex and more difficult to represent in the state.

Now the rhetoric of the past decade is confronted by the bleak moralism of austerity. Scalia's statement: 'we are already living in the integrated apocalypse - the bomb fetish: and in a realized utopia - the industrial city. Terror is normal, constructive' (33) is answered by the PCI's essentially juridical account of the origin of the state. The process of 'the current functionalization of the workers' parties in the system' (34) is not troublesome because the state is not seen as 'the system', but as the institutions which concentrate and express juridically the will of the nation. Therefore, pluralism does not describe a state-form; it is a belief, a tolerance of opposition and corporate competition.

As Guastini suggested, 'For Togliatti, socialism does not require a state different from the "democratic" one.' (35) Legitimation of the state involves legitimation of the Party, and vice versa. In Negri's terms, this institutionalization of the working-class movement makes it 'revisionist in ideology, reformist in objective and technocratic in practice'. (35) Within the PCI there is also awareness that the political rationality of capitalism is more deeply programmed into the existing state than a policy of institutional reform implies, and that the ambiguities of the Hegelo-Gramscian state-spirit allow theoretical discourse to rest on unexamined assumptions about 'democracy', 'strength in the state', rather than the relation of politics to 'socialism'. The process of 'transition towards transition' is sometimes seen to be instead 'integration as synonym for transition'. However, the integration is of two kinds, into the party system and into the political class, and pluralism is vertical, hierarchical.

The PCI's criticism of the centre-Left was that it attempted sectoral reform without popular mobilization. Mobilization is not, of course, to be confused with extremism, which in 1969 was seen as aroused by the Christian Democrats and the traditional power system. (37) Now, it is ascribed to the blocking of the power system, and the decline of rapid social change as a vehicle for mass mobilization. The case now is for the PCI to 'unblock' the political system by entering the state, and replace mobilization by participation. The question brings us back to the analyses of state monopoly capitalism, which justify or condemn entry to the state as an instrument for socializing capitalism. The 10th Party congress revised the position of the 8th, which had been that the state might be used to nationalize sectors of the economy in the interests of reactionary capitalism, and hence clearly did not 'socialize'. It argued that the trend to state monopoly capitalism did not overcome capitalist contradictions nor was it an exclusive factor dominant over society. (38) State intervention exacerbated the conflict between capital and labour, but the state contained non-homogeneous forces, some of which were antagonistic to capital. Intervention was 'a process governed by a supreme effort at political mediation with all the contradictions and tensions that this implies.' (39) Even this was far from suggesting that the presence of the working class in the state decisively shifted the balance in its favour. As the congress stated: (40)

> In reality, mere participation of the working class in planning is not enough to change its character. This is a mistake made also by some spokesmen for the working class and democratic Left, in whose view in order to achieve an anti-monopoly policy, the decisive and pre-eminent element is to be present in the government of this state, even at the risk of splitting asunder the unity of the working class and compromising the autonomy of the unions.

Polemics against the centre-Left cannot simply be turned against the PCI in the emergency of the 1970s. There is, however, a difference between mobilization 'outside' the system and mobilization in its defence. To defend institutions does not compel them to change, rather the reverse. The 1979 Convegno in Bologna (41) went some way to acknowledge that, when the trio of democracy, market and economic growth were split up, a new theory of political action was required, and was absent. Indeed, Asor Rosa said the 'autonomy of the political' was really a weakness, without a theory:

> A contradiction has opened up between the increased potentialities of the political and its real abilities to control power and govern society. This contradiction is the result both of a new and more important dislocation of the social, and a loss of tension and credibility on the part of the political; the economic, in turn, reacts by accentuating the frantic oscillations of its own dynamics, unconnected with any general, strategic vision of the problems.

Tronti was more decisive, arguing that the establishment of the autonomy of the political was unconnected with the achievement of power. There was, moreover, no theoretical grasp of a possible offensive strategy, by making the connection between workers' centrality and organized democracy. Not only had politics stalled in the face of the historic state and the Christian Democratic power system but

> it is necessary to reappraise the concept of labour, together with that of politics. There is now a separation, a schism, between the two terms-realities: the problem is how not to describe this passively ... or reconcile it with an old ideological formula, like producers' self-government ... The relation between class composition in the place of production and the legality and legitimacy of the political system tends to be charged with ever-new mediations: union-political subject and mass parties: political Keynesian and authoritarian state: residues of machine-apparatus and growth of power systems: struggles of strata and anti-institutional struggle: crisis and critique of consciousness, and multiplication of knowledge and languages. In the middle, between labour and the political, there is the complexity of a mature 'social condition'.

To the dilemma of the separation of politics and power Tronti has no answer. Power not only frustrates the political, it conditions and controls it, presenting the temptation to the politician to leave the sphere of politics for that of power. The crisis encourages this on the assumption that the state bureaucracy is backward, a brake on power. The idea of helping the productive system to overcome crisis by modernizing the bureaucracy involves recognizing that this proposes to commit the power of the state bureaucracy to a plan for economic growth. This is not merely a political project, but a view of the state as repository of economic planning power. The aim is not to neutralize the bureaucracy but to use its power. The solution of economic crisis is thus seen as resolving the crisis of legitimacy, and laying the basis for a later re-establishment of a welfare state. But this project is based on a theory not of the state or politics - including workers' centrality - but of power. It acknowledges that the state bureaucracy has power it withholds from the politician, but it sees it as a state class, not an economic class, and one that can be infiltrated by red bureaucrats.

Despite this, it is hard to see towards what model this state bourgeoisie might be pushed or guided. If the future threatens the workers with passive revolution (some form of fascism), it might be defensible to prefer the alternative of integration. Yet the PCI sees no space for the working class outside the state society. There is no alternative to integration; it is not a choice between evils. Its return to opposition did not come out of recognition of the relevance of Stame's argument. This is, that the choice lies no longer between liberalism as limited power and socialism as generalized power, but in the field of new separations between state and civil society, especially between authoritarian states and the natural conflictuality and resistance of civil society, where, by implication, the Left should remain. (42)

> Struggles will explode autonomously from society, and must be seen for what they are, in all their often weighty interference in the interplay of the institutional system, primarily the obvious expression that not everything returns to a prospect of stabilization, and that capitalist society, in the progressive re-absorption of its contradictions, constantly generates new forms of 'otherness', new impossibilities of believing that the process of capitalist totalization has finished.

This re-absorption includes a continuous process of co-option and of excluding what cannot presently be digested, with the aim of consuming it later. The question is how powerful, rather than how free, this excluded sector is. The 'autonomy of the political' is meaningless without power, ideas or a coherent mandate. The 'marginalization' of strata in capitalist societies is a normal, not a pathological, exceptional process. In short, the institutional Left with its idea of 'doing politics in the state' runs a grave risk.

Negri has argued that in this situation, 'insurrection is the order of the day ... Revolution is the process in which the permanence of a violent response, violently organized, against the bosses' state is created.' (43) This statement holds for those states which cannot expand fast enough to smash or absorb violent dissent. Indeed, the operaisti regard the division of power between various corporate forces as an insurance and defence against the state, a tacit dropping of Leninist principles, already abandoned by the PCI 'statists' and the left of assemblyists. (44) The PCI's jettisoning of Leninism is based on the observation that in modern society Leninism as a clandestine movement can operate only in a military form. Leninist organizational forms applied to a mass open party are no threat to the modern state. Indeed, we might add that this organizational form is most easily isolated, or absorbed en bloc. In the modern state, both politics and terror become techniques, functions of a state which offers both 'rational' production and barbarism, not as alternatives but in equilibrium as with administrative efficiency and clientelism. Resistance to the nexus of order-reason unleashes terror and repression, the Weberian state protected by armed men.

If the task of the bureaucracy is control of the labour market and organization of consensus, absorption of the traditional working class would seem a necessary process. The state, and the state petty bourgeoisie, need to control the working class as a means of guaranteeing control of the division of the surplus. (45) In one sense, then, the margin is so defined by the public sphere. This argument implies that the working class would not be integrated as part of the power system, but as objects of administrative control, which would not be counterbalanced by infiltration by the PCI into a subordinate role in the state apparatus. Corporativism springs from the bureaucratic organization of labour. It does not need a strong executive or autonomous politicians. It develops not because of a crisis of parties, but accelerates despite it. It does not overcome the state crisis, but it does allow the political and economic definition of the 'marginal', and organizes the mechanism to maintain and police that frontier and launch offensives from it. The problem is not so much that the PCI has tried to lead the working class into the state as that it presented this unequivocally as a conquest, thereby replacing its theory of the state with a theory of non-ideological, functional systems managed by the intellectual stratum.

One thread in this development leads to Togliatti's reading of Gramsci, and the idea of mass organization which enables the party to enter the state. Another leads to Panzieri's re-examination of the problem of technique and technology. 'Technological progress thus presents itself as the mode of existence of capital, as its development'. (46) 'The automatic factory potentially establishes the domination of the united producers over the labour process', though in practice 'the capitalist use of machines is not ... the simple distortion and deviation from an "objective" development, rational in itself, but itself determines technological development.' Further, 'technological development appears as the development of capitalism ... of the authority of the capitalist.' (47) Hence, only workers' 'insubordination' could confront 'the development of the plan as despotism'. (48) Technological progress, the replacement of living labour, has been developed in its potential, but 'the class level is expressed not as progress but as rupture, not as "revelation" of the secret rationality built in to the modern productive process but as the construction of a radically new rationality, counterposed to the rationality practised by capitalism.' (49) The subversive force of the workers must be used against the despotism-rationality of capital.

Thus gains must be sought outside the economic system and not, as in the PCI case, by administering and improving capitalist rationality. If Italy is backward, then control of the productive process is a political gain. If Italy is in relative and absolute decline, then even if the demise of capitalism is 'premature' in relation to the world-system of capitalism, the destruction of capital and its state are subversive refusals to manage the rationality of capitalism. Thus the operaisti in the PCI must argue that the struggle for control within the state is a contest for political, not economic-rational or administrative-rational, power. (50) Those outside the state must continue to argue that the connection between political and economic systems and rationality is not casual. Panzieri put the position thus, in 1958: 'The claim of the workers for control is by its nature unitary, and is born and grows on the level of struggle. In the concrete situation of our country, control does not present itself as a generic, programmatic claim, and still less as a request for legislative formulas from Parliament.' (51) However, we must ask, at the time the unions developed and when the historic parties of the Left entered the state, how could these struggles remain outside this process of institutionalization, and institutionalized rationality?

Tronti suggested one answer: 'To a particular level of exploitation of labour there corresponds a particular level of capitalist development. Not vice versa. It is not the intensity of capital which is the measure of the exploitation of the workers. On the contrary: it is the specific historical form of surplus labour which reveals the ultimate social determination of surplus value.' (52) Contradictions develop not only in crisis, but in the unself-conscious development of capitalism 'without its being possessed and organized by the classes of capitalists', (53) though the objective is the self-government of capital. Politically, this is expressed by the tendential unity of 'authority and pluralism', democratic planning as 'central management and local autonomies; a political dictatorship and an economic democracy, an authoritarian state and a democratic society'. (54) Capital then becomes the dominant social principle, and labour only partial. Therefore, he concluded, 'the working class must consciously organize itself as an irrational element in the specific rationality of capitalist production ... outside capital, that is, outside its development'. (55)

Does this, however, lead to workers' autonomy, or to institutionalized conflictuality? Is it possible to avoid the cycle irrationality/recomposition of capital/institutionalization? Bruno Trentin, for example, has stressed that the Italian case is special only in one respect, that a late-starting capitalist economy which based its take-off on native rather than immigrant labour has been the first metropolitan country to confront the severity of crisis, and the problems of reorganizing labour and converting productive structures. (56) He sees the causes as backwardness, in a closed labour market where innovation is rigidly superimposed. In this system of accumulation, unions could contribute notably to crisis. Now, there must be a search for a new strategy whereby 'the union will be able to discover a real autonomy, and hence the strength to defeat in practice any form of hierarchical corporativism.' (57) In the earlier phase, capitalism required the separation of unions from politics, and when unions moved into politics they tended to move away, or at least autonomously, from the parties. Where, then, is the location of workers' centrality and 'operaismo'? Is it in issues and organizations or in the extra-institutional struggle in the 'diffused factory'?

Tronti qualifies the idea that operaismo relates to factory and factory struggles. Capital has been diffused, even socialized, and when the centrality of the enterprise disappears, workers' centrality also changes. 'Operaismo and entrepreneurship are two faces of the same position.'

(58) The working class must recover influence lost in its traditional centres by political effort, not rely on its influence spreading in the middle strata and among professionals. Accornero sees operaismo as an importation to the union movement of the view that the unions are closer to workers or class than a party is. This meant 'the relation of factory to society would be equated with an "intra-categorial" affirmation of workers' democracy, and that the Factory Councils came to be seen as a making of the state much more than, and much before, a making of the union.' (59) To say, however, that centrality has moved to the periphery, to the margin, would be to change the class criterion. Centrality must be recomposed as political centrality, not by demands by categories or a moralistic response to exploitation.

Accornero and Tronti argue that workers' centrality moves from the factory and union, wrongly seen as paradigms of the political, state form, to a mature political centrality. This involves revising the notion of enterprise-democracy as central to class struggle. The union is both pluralistic and unitary, but not a society in miniature. Socialization of capital means it must be confronted at the level of the total, class society. The PCI operaisti are trying to move from Panzieri's starting-point of rationality and technology, and despotism in the factory, to the political centrality of labour power. Cacciari describes this as a historical progression not from factory organization to union, but from class to party, and definition of the relativity of autonomy. (60) Autonomia operaia, by this argument, was wrong in failing to see that debate on organizational forms represented a qualitative advance over class movement. There is no longer space for workers' centrality based on the centrality of the enterprise. The enterprise, central to the 1960s discussion of organization, is no longer a focus for class struggle.

PCI operaismo is more concerned with distinguishing itself from syndicalism and 'autonomia' than with specifying the content of its notably abstract politics. The question, as Bobbio asked, is 'Which socialism?' Negri was naive to say that the how and the who of the revolutionary process were the same. (61) Much the same can be said of PCI operaisti. They agree to the Party's emphasis on strong state, strong party, high inter-party competition, non-corporative pluralism, decentralization, popular participation and technical efficiency. As we have seen, however, these are frequently conflicting objectives. The Socialist Party, for its part, proposes more representative institutions (counter-powers) and more individual liberty, but does not explain how these are compatible with abrasive and militant organized social conflict. The distinctions made seem to be not between democracy or liberalism and socialism, but between a definition of democracy as means of self-expression and consultation-participation, and democracy as the consensual-authoritative defence of institutions.

Donolo sees these definitions as referring to a process from first to second, from pluralistic, corporate mediation, through a synthesis of systemic imperatives in the state, to the authoritarian state. In society, the movement is one from mobilization with universalistic values, through social extremism and political marginality, to social mechanics and ghettoes, a social jungle. Such pessimism allows no weight for ideology as traditionally conceived. The political passage could be described as the formation of dominant and authoritative interests from anarchic interest-competition (pluralism), to identification of interests with state institutions, and thence to authoritative enforcement of those interests by the state.

Two criticisms must be made: Donolo is correct in saying that the crisis is not the passive revolution, but his end-state surely is. Second, this formulation underestimates the extent to which the social determines the initial stage of the political. The authoritarian state emerges not from a process starting with mobilization and universal values, but from the corporativism of the first phase. This in turn rests not on sociality or civility, but on the economic principles of universal competition and protection of the 'public' sector. The assumption here is that the existing state, that of the presumed 'mobilized universalism', is weak.

The new Left agreed with Moro, that 'when the state is weak, it is useless for it to pretend it is strong'. (62) Not only is Stame's call to oppose authoritarianism and revive class struggle an evasion of the possibility that the couple are reciprocal functions, but he criticizes the PCI's authoritarianism and its failure to help the middle strata in the same breath. In reality, the authoritarian state is not 'strong' in the sense of satisfying social needs but in containing the social conflict arising from their frustration. In this, the Christian Democrats as conciliators can have only relative success, and their free access to the instruments of repression is vital. In other words, the PCI's subordinate position convinces it of the need for order, rather than increased social subsidy or conflictuality. Insertion into the state is a form of protection for the PCI's constituency. The new Left has no such protection, or rather, it depends on the protection of whatever economic and social prestige its adherents as individuals, as professionals or teachers, for example, have acquired.

The PCI has discussed its view of democracy, as distinct from liberal democracy, in general terms. It has never been discussed with the passion its philosophers brought to the question of Marxism's scientificity. Badaloni's account shows that most discussion of a Marxist theory of politics took place outside, or on the fringes of, the Party, and even then rather rarely. (63) This omission can be explained in terms of the internal politics of the Party, international factors and the commitment to the assumptions of the Constitution. Now, on the other hand, it is significant that discussion is of reform of the state; law and administration take precedence over more generic discussion of politics and political theory.

Emphasis on administrative, rather than political, aspects of reform underlies the concrete experience of policies of decentralization in Bologna, and exemplifies the emphasis at the national level. The second phase of decentralization was intended to accomplish what the first had not, to move from administrative decentralization to a transfer of powers. (64) Yet in many ways, this means simply transferring powers from central to peripheral officials and experts. Different levels of government continue to concentrate power bureaucratically the better to maintain their position in relation to other levels, and to administer the budget as consistently as possible. The political-administrators have both to stimulate participation and then to make judgments on the formulation and formalization of proposals. The quartieri, naturally, reflect the social and political composition of the locality. They do not determine it, and major problems and decisions lie in the competence of the municipality or beyond it. As a means of allotting social services according to different community needs, and giving them an administrative centre, decentralization provides a means of communication to the city bureaucracy, a community centre which is especially significant for new outlying suburbs, and allows administrative and professional services to be organized more flexibly and efficiently. Politically, however, it has little more than the faith that citizens will identify the Party with stable and efficient administration. The Party's real faith is in regionalism and centralization, even on the basis of class alliance and shared power. Decentralization is not a triumph for democracy of a particular kind, but partial success of an administrative procedure; not an end but a beginning. The limits of decentralization are soon found in budgetary questions, the demands of public employees and their recruitment, or changes in overall city policy. Political initiative remains with the Party. Decentralization is not politically an experiment, and ideologically it is of little significance on the general movement to bureaucratization.

Representative democracy in class society seems destined to produce a stalled executive in that the party system attempts to prevent decisive advances by its opponents. One defence, both against opposition and of one's own policies, is to 'politicize' the administration by securing its loyalty and personnel. In this context, mass or base, democracy is indeed only 'a face, a conditioning component of representative democracy'. (65) Without reform of the state, its relative autonomy from the party system, and loyalty to its own, or to a single party's, objectives, prevents the representative element registering in the state changes in the social distribution of power. Mass democracy, like operaismo, is in search of its 'centrality'. In this situation, broad ideological goals and definitions are replaced by a search for alternative centres of power to give decisive weight to the party system, as against the state bureaucracy. This itself is a process of bureaucratization and corporate fragmentation. Disillusion with this party strategy, its 'statism' and the 'common vocation to government at all costs' (66) dates from the early 1960s and was fed by the new, immigrant, Southern workers of that decade. In the 1970s, despite a reflux to the parties, the promise of 'areas of movement' encouraged the new stratum of precarious 'schooled proletarians' to turn away from the parties, encouraged by the sense that they were not only excluded from power, but violently expelled from society by the forces of the state, 'disintegrated and violently expelled from their natural place'. (67) The idealism and voluntarism of the 'autonomy of the political', which subordinates immediate class interests to the game of political manoeuvre, thus has its counterpart in the non-institutionalized Left. As Tronti says, there is economic continuity but political discontinuity, (68) not political lag but political specificity. This autonomy can lead to the point where 'The modern state ... turns out to be no less than the modern form of autonomous organization of the working class', organized not through a party but as a ruling class. (69) Thus the PCI's entry into the state would paradoxically achieve the same goal as that of the non-institutionalized Left, a workers' state.

However, Tronti admitted that he had no easy remedy for operating the political cycle in this direction. Autonomia operaia argued that the productive climate, the new working class and the need for a new theory of organization required the rejection of productivist ethics in the search for autonomy. The aim is to break the continuity of economics, taking to politics in the first person, rejecting capitalist organization of study and culture and proclaiming that liberation comes from discussion, experience, contacts and co-ordination, but not ideas. (70) Tronti's call for continuity of labour as counterpart to the autonomous political cycle contradicts this. Bozzi noted (71) that

> the phases of greater difficulty for the movement had to be paid for by a truce of capital regarding labour power, by an acceptance of the status quo fixed in the preceding phase of conflict. It was this dynamic which prevented the use of proletarian resources towards different modalities of management of a rate of surplus value inversely proportional to the rate of profit, and to make state management by the Christian Democratic regime function as a mechanism itself productive of crisis. Only at this point, in its crisis, was this model of management of command transformed into management of the backwardness and inadequacy of the 'political' as regards the economic (read 'state' and 'workers' and 'proletarian antagonism') and this 'delay' took the form of 'autonomy of the political'.

That is, the economic advance of the working class is slowed by the crisis it has helped to produce. To manage the crisis requires the state to re-take the political initiative. The political backwardness of the working class may lead it to accept a share of state power in managing capitalism in crisis. Yet this wrongly transforms the economic weakness of the working class in a period of economic decline into a necessary strategic political weakness. Here, Tronti argues that economic weakness does not logically lead to political subordination: quite the contrary. Politically, however, Negri's class 'Realpolitik' and Tronti's view that the workers must use crisis and economic decline to master the political cycle, that in crisis the state is like an empty stage to be occupied by rival bands of players, are both superficial. They treat politics as little more than force or manoeuvre. (72) Some have seen in the attenuation of the debate on politics a tendency to irrationalism, to desire and passion, leading Pizzorno to describe the search for autonomy as a social, rather than a political, fact. (73) The movement fails to 'do politics', and this function is usurped by the military, secret, 'armed party'. A pattern is established of a movement towards small groups which either fade away or attempt to hegemonize successive 'movements'.

Negri provides the most forceful analysis of the socio-economic base of the movement of a 'new social worker', really society as worker. This figure replaces the 'mass worker' who was under attack by capital as 'the mass worker of the social wage'. (74) The new struggles, needs and political subject are directed against plans such as Fuà's for an economic revolution from above. Thus, 'New social base, new productive force, new revolutionary organization, dictatorship of the proletariat, extinction of the state, make a sequence which only in that order can we adopt as the basis of our project.' (75) Capital cannot produce a counter-tendency to the falling rate of profit, but does lower the qualitative condition of labour. Capital is forced simultaneously towards socialization, to face growing class struggle and to eliminate more living labour from the productive process. The regression to revisionism in the shape of the 'historic compromise', however, represents the 'political form of the capitalist transcendence of the Italian crisis', (76) just as Tronti's 'autonomy of the political' in that context is mere reformism. The real confrontation is now between worker and state. 'The contemporary state knows no working class struggle which is not a struggle against the state.' (77) Yet Italy itself is still between development and underdevelopment. Possibly this explains the mixture in Negri's work of new theories of needs and his paleo-Leninism.

Negri sees Leninism as a process of destabilization and destructuring, against the capitalist attempt to restructure, using the workers for that purpose if it can. 'The crisis-state has not for a single moment stopped being the planned state. All the elements of destabilization that the workers' and proletarian struggle has used against the state have been gradually taken over by capital and transformed into a weapon of restructuring.' (78) This also involved the 'terroristic' use of savage inflation. 'The opposition can consolidate itself only by practical overthrowing, in subversion', (79) by self-valuation. Thus 'The process of constituting class independence is today first of all a process of separation.' (80) The means for this is a process of 'sabotage' of the history of capital, where the 'crisis-state is a power which lives in the void of meaning, a logic of power-logic, which is itself destructured.' (81) This cataclysmic catastrophism has its own logic: 'Taking the subjective point of view to extremes does not negate its methodical validity.' (82) The greater the sabotage, the more 'fierce, monstrous, and irrational' the state becomes. (83) Reformists then become unable to hold the view that power can be divided between classes. Proletarian dictatorship is achieved through self-valuation, or sabotage, without a programme.

Negri argues that Marx suggests that force decides between two equal rights, and that thus 'violence indeed assumes a fundamental value'. Though he opposes 'Gulags' as well as political parties, he argues that violence is necessary and central to the Communist programme. This is not a codified violence, but 'an element of the rationality of the processes of self-valuation'. (84) 'Sabotage follows the irrationality of capital, imposing rhythms and forms of its further disorganization on it.' Sabotage ultimately organizes 'storming heaven', and finally 'that cursed heaven will be no more'. (85) Despite the analysis of the new social subject of political decline, Negri's is a moralistic appeal to activism, an exhortation rather than a political strategy. There is a recipe for diffuse, unstructured, violence against the organized response of the state, for the implosion of a system which has organized all economic and social life on the basis of its own planned irrationality.

The analysis of decline need not be correct, for the declaration of civil war becomes a self-fulfilling prophecy. It is a war to the death without the prudence typical of other zero-sum theorists of power. The movement recognizes the existence of no mediations of any consequence between itself and the state, whether institutional, ideological or social. The new movement does not organize around new institutions. Reformism and interclassism are swept away by the momentum of the movement. The revolutionary subject organizes itself as dictatorship, as form of assertion, not politics.

The PCI, on the other hand, has argued (86) that the socialist mode of production

> cannot come about inside the bourgeois social formation, in which, however, the objective conditions mature, and in which the new social formation becomes increasingly clear, but only when the capitalist mode of production has been overthrown. The latter does not stop functioning by slow exhaustion like the feudal mode, and does not reduce itself to a shell weakened by the spontaneous growth of new structures. On the contrary, the more the objective conditions of the socialist revolution mature, the more the bourgeois formation, deformed as 'transitional capitalism', strengthens its defences and multiplies its forces of resistance to bar the way to the growth and unfolding of the

new social formation, which still continues to nestle in its heart.

This means that the PCI must argue that the state is really mixed, both state monopoly capitalist and state of law (protector of the new formation). Alternatively, the state may lose its political character by intervention in the economy and become a sphere of 'administered mediation', an apparatus of mediation. The state destroys market mechanisms (politicizes economic questions) but also presides over monopoly 'rationalization', elimination of living labour. These formulations by Barcellona, on the dual character of the state, would contradict Cossutta's version of the inevitable but passive development of socialism to the point where capitalism ruptures. It might explain PCI theory which continues to postulate a socialist, higher alternative, which destroys capitalism, and a constitutional state which manages a non-violent, active politics of transition. (87)

Negri destroys politics, because politics is associated with the state. Along with the state, he proposes the destruction of all public, plural political activity. The PCI, on the other hand, proposed, in the early 1960s, 'participation in political power, together with specific political forces of a capitalist type, to modify some characteristics of the current form of development, and the power itself which directs it, in which they propose to participate.' To Negri, politics implies the state. The PCI separates them, but is ambiguous as regards the process of 'doing politics' in the state. It has suggested participation with capitalist forces, and also expressed faith in the socialist transcendance of capitalism. As we have seen, there are political weaknesses in Tronti as well as Ingrao, though both stress the primacy of politics. Ingrao has defined politics as the area of relations between parliament, parties and regional assemblies. The need to avoid reducing politics to activism, or alternatively to a Hegelo-legal state, prompted his search for a third way. This distinguishes them still from Rodano, who has spoken of the historical re-absorption of Marxist ideology, (88) and Amendola, who in 1965 was speaking of the failure both of communism and of social democracy. (89)

Central to the PCI's difficulty is the problem of reconciling a revolutionary tradition which identified the state with the class enemy with one which sees the state as a sphere of historical necessity, mediation and structural transformation. When capitalism was growing, it seemed acceptable to argue that Italy was relatively backward. Prudence, and a dual strategy of rationalization and reforms, seemed plausible. When growth is no longer assured, it becomes much harder to justify economic optimism, whence arises the discovery of proliferating public and formal terrains in the state in which the Party can 'do politics'. This distinguishes the current debate from that in 1964-5, when the reformists, marginalists and orthodox gradualists discussed the failure of reformism in the context of economic recession. (90)

While the PCI has plausibly argued that the destruction of institutions would now entail the suicide of civil society and of the historical organization of the working class, it has not been so skilful in 'crisis management' and in defining the sensitive areas of political intervention, either in terms of common interest (historic compromise), privileged relations with the working class (austerity) or superior ability in political manoeuvre. Despite the faith in politics, which Negri lacks, the attraction of the historicist state persists in the PCI, and with it the idea of socialism as marking the perfection of the state, a Hegelian realization of the unity of state and civil society. This means that the PCI is vague concerning the content, and not notably successful in its execution, of 'politics'. It also has difficulty in reconciling the Hegelian and the Marxist theories of the state. Exclusion from the state can accelerate the self-managing, self-recomposing process of capital through small surges of recovery at the expense of both institutional and extra-institutional Left. Inclusion in the state, however, is explicitly directed towards facilitating the process of recomposition.

Chapter 8

THE MODERN STATE IN ITALY AND ITS CRITICS

If we abandon essentialist definitions of socialism and ignore the lack or inconsistency of ideological goals, we see more clearly that the central concern is over types of modernization, and the central disagreements over the nature of the state apparatus required to produce economic growth and restrain social conflict. This image is one of socialism as a system of distribution, with transition taking place through plural, or non-monopoly, control of the (arbitrary) system of distribution of material or non-material goods. This involves the distribution of reducing resources using bureaucratic-rational and 'modern' methods, without a zero-sum conquest of the state. The earlier ideological assumptions of the historic Left are of limited use in this kind of 'social distribution'. The issues raised, of the 'rationality' of bureaucracy, the limits of participation, relations between technicians and politicians, and politician and the state, scarcely enter the classical concerns of Marxist politics. Failure of the traditional paradigm, or rhetoric, of socialism, may lead to the danger of following a still simpler solution. In this case, a 'modern state', controlling social conflict by repression and leaving what it cannot control to the 'private' sector, distributing largesse to its supporters and requiring that the mode of distribution leaves the status and command hierarchy in position, might seem the 'easy' solution to the objective, perhaps even universal, social and political difficulties.

The crisis now appears as one of decline, not death, recovery or transcendant socialist transformation. Crisis is endemic in government because of the weakness of the executive and lack of control of state institutions. Crisis in the state is endemic because of the lack or even impossibility of capitalist and bureaucratic modernization, though this permits the state to distribute favours and escape the dead end of fiscal crisis. The crisis of the party system is expressed as separation of the party system from effective power, the separation of politics and economics and the separation of the Christian Democrats as a party of the regime from them as a party of representation. At the same time, the state is capable of organizing and institutionalizing traditional and new forms of exploitation. It defines the frontier between public and private economy, between public and private dissent. There is, in short, no fixed frontier. The private and public economies contain both public and private ownership. The public economy is that directly subsidized by and for the state. The state 'farms' the visible economy to feed itself and its pensioners, and to mediate social conflict, to maintain the balance of forces. The private economy, visible and submerged, shot through with public intervention, open or clandestine, functions as both a reservoir of wealth and a margin for growth.

The state experiments in social conflictuality, trying to reduce it by technique (research on the labour market) or consensus (agreement with the unions). It also defines the area of dissent, by providing a generous area of institutional conflict, and an unpredictable terrain for non-legitimated, subversive activity conducted by, as well as against, the state. This competition is not based on premises that growth will ensue and create social harmony, nor yet that some decisive change will occur in the balance of social forces. There is an attempt to secure the social position of capital primarily by political, and also technocratic, means, as a 'representative state of powerful interests', a competitive, mediating, but non-dialectical state.

The state, that is, lacks any teleology beyond its own existence. It organizes itself as a 'bargaining institution', reflecting the forms of dominance and subordination in civil society, as representative state. The bargaining rules exclude the strategy of 'alternative rationalities'. The bargaining is over power-sharing and patronage (in the 1960s, the bargaining was, for the Left, economic, over wages), and bureaucratic efficiency and institutional reform (productivity in the 1970s). This is a political trade unionization of the Left, entry into a bargaining system, formalized and reciprocal. The PCI now plays the role of a union federation, in the political sphere. It bargains for the interests of its constituents, using militancy or conciliation tactically. 'Participation' by the masses legitimates decisions reached in the system. The rationality of the system is its capacity to produce authoritative decisions, its 'productivity'. It is not a traditional, but a decisional, state. Given the collapse of economic plans, it rests on a master political plan which represents a trend from anarchic corporate bargaining to centralized corporate bargaining. The party system constitutes a threshold to the state, where preliminaries for admission to the bargaining system proper are conducted to determine who shall bargain by proxy, and who in person. This system requires, rather than unwieldy mass parties, a specialized political class of negotiators, with technical and political-managerial capacity.

The modern state prefigures the absorption of Marxism, or the re-entry of Marxism as descriptive of reality, but impotent to change it, since it is a subordinate function thereof. This state is not social democratic, as it divides public and private not on the basis of class (or rather, interclass) ownership but in terms of degree of control and function determined by the state class. The class interest of the bourgeoisie, and hence the dominant state interest, is to institutionalize conflict between the main class alliances so that the rules of conflict maintain a reasonably constant class and status hierarchy. Phases of decline, however, are highly conflictual, especially where class alliances are involved as competing blocs. There is a self-limiting element of conflict in decline, since it is not merely stagnation but recomposition of the conflicting forces. The state is the force organizing irrationality as a means of social survival, and in so doing develops a new political class, with new techniques, representing the social blocs now fragmenting, whose concern lies in the administration of integrated masses interested in remaining within the supported system of labour.

Many commentators have seen the Christian Democrats as inherently vulnerable in this movement towards consociational government because of their traditionalist distribution of patronage, though the same principles would seem to apply in both state-forms. Others argue that the movement towards modernization increases the centrality of the party system, and that stability is maintained by relative stability in electoral choices. None the less, since the decline is not a simple consequence of 'mismanagement', the capacity of the Christian Democrats to preside over the process should not be underestimated. The parties enter the state not as classes, but as negotiators. In a class system the principles of distribution are not rational, they are negotiated. The parties negotiate: the masses are not required to participate. Indeed, in belonging to a negotiating corporation, the exigency of participation is set aside.

This interpretation would imply that the crisis of the 1960s was grave in that it frustrated capitalist rationalization and modernization, and reformism. In itself it was not economically disastrous, but it has meant that there are few instruments for the state save negotiation over the proportions to be distributed. Labour in the 1960s tried to raise the value (the price) of labour by reducing productivity. In the decline of the 1970s, this became self-defeating by cutting the overall supply of wealth produced. The crisis of the 1960s fixed the point at which relative decline began at a fairly low level, and did not provide the political class with institutions and techniques required for crisis-management.

This preparation of the ground has been accompanied in the 1970s by a levelling-off, but still maintained, modern growth. The PCI has separated the economic decline from the general crisis and decline of capitalism. It has stressed the possibility of a technical response, and even a reversal. There is agreement among the constitutional parties that the state must be defended, and that the working class must play a key role in that defence. If the notion of finality is removed from crisis, the link is broken between the crisis of the state in Italy and the state of the crisis of capitalism. The universal power of the state to intervene and mediate gives it a capacity to determine social stratification. From mediating social conflict, it can now shape the bases from which this conflict arises. The state is still searching for techniques of crisis-management, not a 'telos', but all the same it represents an agglomeration of powerful, if competitive, interests.

The PCI is part of a state-centred tradition, and can adopt a liberal defence of the state, given absolute priority by Amendola, as against Berlinguer's notion that entry into the state is an emergency measure. Indeed, by attacking the reactionary class elements of the old state, the PCI is in the forefront of demands for a modern state. However, it is important to consider the effects of what is often described as the de-ideologization and de-theorization of the Party's Marxist orientation. Scalia describes the new situation as follows: (1)

> A political philosopher or a politologue, a journalist or writer in the weeklies, moderate or progressive, 'in the system' or 'extra-parliamentary' ... has to recognize himself as being constantly less dialectical, or even as not being able to be more dialectical. He must abandon dialectics, or pretend (to make us believe, or to believe) to be still dialectical. (Is there no lament on the one hand about the absence of 'dialec-

tics' between opposition and government, between the parties, etc., and on the other about the lack of 'dialectic' between majority-minority, parties-masses, masses-state, in a *common* recognition of the need for 'stability', for the political 'framework', and the 'social pact'? As between various extemporary models, in the common acceptance of the model, of 'consociational democracy' *or* 'conflictual democracy', there is really established what has *[been]* called 'démocratie consentante'.)

To be clear: the so-called debate is only apparent. If in the PCI one can speak of a kind of liberal-Leninism, or democratic Leninism, in the Socialist Party one talks of liberal-socialism. The absence of invention in the historic Left is equivalent to its importance, its incapacity for either self-criticism or transformation. The 'poverty of philosophy' of the Left could not be more evident. The philosophy of the dialectic is at once an alibi, and verbiage, hypocrisy and illusion. 'Dialectics' is supposed to be the potential hegemony of the working class and its 'centrality', the possibility of *[its]* parties being a power of government (given the impracticality of the 'pseudo-strategies' of 'historic compromise' and 'alternative of the Left' ...), or the 'historic bloc' of class alliances, or the 'political framework' of the stabilized emergency or, more theoretically, the integration (the 'third way'?) of 'democratic method' and 'elements of Leninism', or of 'democratic method' and economic-political 'pluralism' or transition to socialism through representative democracy, the combination of existing 'democracy' with the 'method of the political management of the conflictuality of classes' ...

The dialectic, in short, is empty, static, the dialectic of reconciliation. The objective, in Scalia's view, is the perfection of crisis in a social, workers', management of capitalist and bureaucratic rationality, which can be contested only by autonomous dissent, criticism of 'techne', 'ratio', power/state, institutions/ideologies, rejection of dialectics as a positive advocacy of a unitary response to crisis.

Other factors too tend to de-ideologize and secularize party doctrines, and promote social depolarization. One of these is the positivity of technique, and especially administrative technique. Administration respects power, not opinion. An economic pluralism allies without difficulty with a pluralist administration which combines functions of ownership and control. Administrative culture tends to de-ideologize by, e.g., identifying rationality with the exercise of bureaucratic power, rather than with growth and conflict. It destroys or ignores cultural specificity. Once achieved, it has no history in the future. Depolarization is the building of a new consensus based on a public liberalism, a 'political framework' for the anarchy of institutions.

In this context, dissent becomes a form of verbal terrorism, both in the PCI version that terrorism is a reactionary manoeuvre to sabotage working-class penetration of the state, and that of the Socialist Party, that terrorism is an expression of catastrophism to which the best response is reform of the state, not repression. The new Left takes the classical argument that the crisis of the state is part of the general crisis of capitalism, and that the modern state develops its crisis-management in response to a terrorism which is endemic. (2)

The case for the possibility of the state's survival, continuity and recomposition in crisis is thus central to the historic Left's argument. Poulantzas seems to lend support for this view, suggesting that the crisis of the state is one of leadership, not of the state-form. (3) The state is responsible for creating conditions in which capitalist relations of production can be reproduced, and enters crisis when it can no longer maintain the unity of the dominant bloc and organize and control the dominated. Whether this leads to legitimacy crisis or is merely a transient accumulation of political errors, the authoritarian state is a normal response. It is not clear, however, if this recomposed state is an interclassist authoritarian state, or a recomposition of the subjective will of a dominant class, or even of the state bourgeoisie. (4) The historic Left, and Poulantzas, rely heavily on a subjective presence as decisive in determining the outcome of crisis, and the relative independence of political and economic crisis. The crucial choice is in the formula of Hobbes/Cromwell - political force or political skill - not a 'structural' account of crisis at all. (5)

Destabilization tends to reinforce the Hobbesian type of authoritarian response. The choice presented for a recomposed state seems to lie between consensual crisis-management (PCI in the state), conflictual crisis management (Christian Democrats) and reformist crisis-management (Socialist Party, Ingrao). The problem with the new Left case is the unreality of the alternative model offered, literally its 'otherness' regarding the existing world, and its failure to fill the gap in Marx's economic crisis theory with a convincing subjective element which makes authoritarian recomposition impossible. The problem, in short, is that it assumes that the economic configuration of crisis precisely determines, and in the long term decides the outcome of, the political crisis. The new philosophers, in frustration and even in a 'qualunquista' apolitical negativity, have argued that the alternative rationality is either utopian or itself necessarily authoritarian. Thus political utopia is itself authoritarian. In decline, utopia becomes millenarian, produces radical congregationalism like 'Comunione e liberazione'. The choice between elitist terrorism and mass subversion, war on society or class, and war against the state takes for granted the existence and growth of authoritarian response. We see, in short, both regression in the supposed revolutionary subject (Catholic populism) and a strategy of subversion which encourages the use of one or other authoritarian versions as a political response to crisis in the state and economic crisis.

There is common admission in the historic Left that there exists now no sure economic design, and that in economic policy the traditional ideological polarities no longer apply. This leaves space for politics and, given the destruction of the cosmology of divided, or dual-alternative, rationality, capitalist-socialist, scientific/positive-speculative/negative, there is a possibility of reconciling the old polarities within the old institutions. Though this is presented as a 'new politics', it looks like an assertion of the old from what is still essentially a subordinate position. It proposes changes in party structures, a strategy for conciliating state personnel, a change in the independence of the 'separate bodies' (police, army, magistracy) in relation to society, more power to regions and parliament. None the less, these areas of limited innovation, which is scarcely a new politics, remain blocked by the crisis in policy-making and decision-enforcement. To summarize: the historic Left's varieties of new politics are modifications, not alternatives: the non-coincidence of economic collapse with political crisis assists an authoritarian recomposition of the state: the revolutionary subject is subjective and thereby multiform, and it is excluded from the institutional subjectivity of the political process.

Returning to the 'new politics', Marco Cammelli has argued that this model has already been exhausted in the Emilian experience, or at least that the 'exhaustion of every space usable for anticipatory interventions' and lack of national reform leaves 'some foundations of the Emilian philosophy of local government ... profoundly shaken.' (6) From opposition or extraneousness to the state in the 1950s, to the desire for insertion in the mid-1960s and the belated recognition of the need for local government reform there has been a consistent inability to see administration and bureaucracy as self-propelling, rather than 'mere executive instruments of the policies formulated'. (7) Characteristics of the parties themselves are not up for discussion during their frequent complaints at the loss of power by elected bodies to closed 'public' corporations.

Despite the limited usefulness of drawing general conclusions from Emilia, and from the lowest levels of government, there is evidence for the exhaustion of anticipatory measures to overcome the absence of national initiatives for reform. (8) This exhaustion can be seen at the institutional level of conflict between levels of local government, in local autonomous boards and in the social conservatism of the parties when it comes to recognizing new needs and new subjects. In periods of crisis, local power structures tend naturally to become rigid, dependent on moves by the centre. It may also be said that there is now a period of transition from an emphasis on social services and planning to one of economic development and investment policy. It is, however, hard to escape the conclusion that the Emilian way is not, after all, a new way of 'doing politics'.

One key to this exhaustion has been seen as the difficult relation between the professionals and experts and the intellectuals in the Party. Cerroni stressed that, in the 1970s, the attraction for intellectuals of the PCI also presented a challenge. He stressed the need to accommodate intellectuals in the Party, and to intellectuals 'disposed to remain faithful to the mandate of science and reason, we must know how to offer a stable role in the party, in democratic administration, and in mass organizations, in the task of re-thinking and renewing Italian society, so that intellectuals and workers may once and for all stop, as Gramsci said, being "two different races".' (9) However, social conciliation and the offer of organizational and administrative tasks is not enough if intellectuals cannot express new ideas which have some prospect of adoption and application, even at the expense of the leadership's privileged role in policy formation. The autonomy of politics, however, tends to concentrate authority in the professional politicians, and in their technicians.

In 1975 the PCI seemed to offer a prospect of security, but by the end of the decade it provided a support for 'order'. In 1968 (10)

> the PCI entered the scene, succeeding in winning the trust of the young and broad groups of 'dependent, educated workers' on the basis of being able to offer an

> image of itself as both efficient and secure, playing well the 'role of the great church which gives security and protection'. Organizational efficiency, the safety and mastery of a well-tried and refined liturgy after years of experience are at the root of this consensus. But in this attraction there is the danger that the intellectual middle classes may offer in exchange for a little security their own autonomy and self-awareness, their own authentic needs and right.

In practice, the Party can provide at least a partial security for the role played in it, but the role itself is limited by the structure of the Party and the irrelevance of expertly devised policies and programmes to the autonomy of the national leadership.

Ingrao has recently confirmed that reform of the parties forms part of the attempt to make state institutions conform more closely to the changes in Italian society, even if that means relaxing the 'unanimity' of PCI decisions. However, in order to reduce the distance of state and civil society, Ingrao proposed to start by making 'planning the sign of a different quality of the decision-making process'. (11) What then were the parameters of the new 'productive rationality'? The reply was, 'In the reorganization of the relation of school to labour market; in controlled management of the mobility of labour; in a plan for technological renovation which would not only remain within the horizons of the firm; in a rethinking of the whole use and articulation of working hours; and in a wage reform to overcome certain corporative institutions.' (12) This is more a programme than an identification of political parameters, and that returns us to the paradox that exclusion from the state vitiates the PCI's claim that the state is not the instrument or will of a hostile class. Entry into the state, however, without the capacity to reform would prove the whole exercise to be one in futility not only for the working class but perhaps above all for the presumed potential recruits from the middle strata to the political class.

Di Palma indicates how profound a problem reform of the state would be, once initiated. He stresses the 'uncertain compromise' underlying the Constituent Assembly and Constitution. (13) This is effectively a guarantee that no party shall govern by mixing parliamentary with assembly systems. 'Reform' is associated with those unhappy with their share of power. The aim of government has not been greater efficiency or stronger government, but ideological (centralist, jacobin, or consociationalist) and, above all, political objectives. Tamburrano argues that the weakness of the executive and the disincentive to present broad legislative programmes in coalition situations have not substantially changed in the 1970s, save for an increased presence of the PCI. (14) Neither alternative governments nor majority parties have been produced by a system which is intended to immobilize the representative principle and exercise power and influence through groups and institutions outside parliament. The hierarchy of parties represents the social hierarchy in society, and though electoral reform (as Salvatore Sechi has suggested (15)) may not be necessarily a fraud, the parties have presented themselves as bastions against irresponsible functionaries, and their proportions of the suffrage as evidence of popular legitimacy, not the expression of the will of the majority. Weakness in the role of the President of the Chamber, the common weakness of bicameralism where the second chamber is virtually a carbon copy of the first, the slack organization of the parliamentary groups (save for the PCI) and the weak position of the presidents of parliamentary commissions provide a series of structural obstacles made worse by the limited control of parties over other institutions.

In 1979 Enrico Berlinguer reiterated that there would be no recasting of Party organization. Despite muted criticisms from Ingrao, and Sechi's argument that the 'austere charm' (16) of the Party's democratic centralism contributed to authoritarian democracy in a bureaucratic-oligarchic context, the PCI is generally satisfied that its relatively open and informal party style and open, if modest, disagreements among the leadership are adequate for its task. This is a significant, even if not a crucial, attitude. The real question remains: How would the Party reform the state if it were to make a decisive entrance? The PCI is not ready to admit that even if the Christian Democrats were limited, and the Constitution implemented, it might not accomplish what was required; to reverse a secular trend in parliamentary democracies which emphasizes the limitations and inadequacies of legislatures as points of policy formation and policy supervision. On the other hand, if popular participation is an important consideration in legitimating any reform of the state, this leaves aside for the present any discussion of the associated juridical and political principles involved in any transformation of the state. On the one hand the case for reform is conservative, and on the other the case for popular transformation too vague. 'Reform of the state' joins the other non-implemented and amorphous slogans such as historic compromise and 'middle-term' project.

Cacciari has suggested that crisis promoted the erosion

of liberalism's dream of a stable, rational state. Crisis is the opposite of this. However, he does not see this as a fundamental objection to the PCI's project. Crisis can be managed: it enforces choices between different political projects. 'Crisis stops being seen as the arrest of an otherwise "normal" process-progress, or as a functional rupture, just at the moment that a new stability is instituted, and is redefined as a programmatic-productive factor in the context of the new areas of the political and the state.' (17) The state no longer mediates, and is the central terrain on which crisis induces the emergence of the winning political strategy. The emphasis is thus not on first changing institutions, but on political victory. 'The very policies of capitalist recomposition make a logic irreconcilable with its logic appear, multiplying processes of socialization which are contradictory in themselves.' (18) The autonomy of the (proletarian) political rests on the separation of politics from economics, or productivism. The ensuing state is not authoritarian, but the absolutization of the political. Politics runs before economics in founding the new social formation. 'These conflicts are already politically organized, in terms autonomous as regards the given of the social relation.' (19) This 'political' is a specialism, otherwise it would be bureaucratic. Thus Togliatti's view of Italy as backward is transcended, and politics is inserted into technique, rather than vice versa. 'Political organization should "work" within every specialization so that a demand for the transformation of the whole social relation of production can emerge from each one.' (20)

This contrasts with, and ignores, the hierarchy of political powers - legal and institutional - which are already in existence in the political system, including that very legality which 'is an integral part of the workers' movement, and has become its banner'. (21) Does Cacciari's 'autonomy' of politics match the disposable strength of the liberal-Leninist and socialist alternatives? Salvi makes a cogent criticism of currents of thought in the new Left which insist on the class nature and unreformability of the bourgeois democratic state, and simultaneously asks it to give legal guarantees to its militant opposition. The socialist case is open to criticism because of its contradictory elements. Amato, while stressing counter-power, proposed a checks-and-balances presidential system with a strong component of plebiscite, as against the PCI immobilism of consociationism and negotiations. He proposed strengthening both the state and the institutions independent of it. (22) Salvi argued that there could be no useful discussion of reform of the state which did not start out from the given Christian Democratic state. The new Left and the socialist projects imply that 'The state ... does not seem knowable save with the "pure" categories of bourgeois reason, from Weber to Kelsen: and a project with the aim of transforming the mode of production does not seem practicable without the risk of irreparable authoritarian strains.' (23) Salvi's insistence on the need to discuss the transformation process in the state, not outside it, nor in autonomous politics is consistent with acute critiques of the 'counter-power' and maximalist cases. However, he does not go beyond suggestions for transforming the state along the axis of strong executive/closely linked elective assemblies, and of providing guarantees relating constitutional rights to social relations.

The problem with all the formulations discussed is that they mix objectives, problem and reality. Technicians are becoming politicians. Policy is being formulated not ideologically and generically but techno-bureaucratically. In the absence of political initiative, technicians present micro-policies to grateful administrators. Post-Keynesian economics tends to encourage authoritarianism in the state. (24) Changing perceptions also have an influence; the South no longer identifies centralism with 'the policeman, the magistrate, the bureaucrat and the prefect ... today, it is represented by economic holdings, monopolies, state participation; those forces, that is, which accentuate and irritate Southern underdevelopment.' (25) When changes in the state occur, they may be irritant, not palliative, as in the suggestion that the regions have socio-political objectives but no instruments of control, no mandate and no dialogue with elected assemblies. (26)

There are two processes at work here. First, the historic Left is trying to establish continuity with the traditions of the bourgeois state of law and their transformability. Second, in so far as the historic Left occupies institutions, it will defend them to the point of down-playing crisis. The attempt to detach the political crisis of legitimacy and representativeness from the economic crisis is consistent with the view that transition requires transformation of the superstructure prior to change in the economic structure. Transition too excuses the tendency to turn to unitary and absolutist, or authoritarian, solutions. (27) However, the attempt to select from the state in crisis those elements suited to transformation and transition, in preparation for a long historical process of change, exacerbates, not lessens, the crisis of legitimacy and representation. The PCI case requires on the one hand a strong state, but on the other a strong civil society. 'Certainly the autonomous articulation of civil society is recognized as necessary, but considered so charged with corporative potential as to require that political institutions unleash an adequate "counter-power" working through broad assembly groupings as a form of centripetal pluralism.' The PCI position rests on the conviction that 'the only solid anchorage against the dispersive and particularistic forces which fragment our social fabric lies in the centrality of the elective assemblies with a party base.' (28) However, as we have seen, this is essentially a strengthening of the centralist, statist model.

The danger that the state of transition, whose strength lies in consensual or conflictual participation, becomes instead a version of the modern authoritarian state is increased by the context of economic decline, by the condition of subordinate, not hegemonic, insertion of the Left into the state system and problems already mentioned inherent in the limits of participation in centralized systems. The transition state itself runs the risk of merely defending the status quo of existing social relations, permanently frustrating alternatives and becoming a state publicly administering a decaying capitalism. Removing the notion of transition from the Leninist-Stalinist formula of rupture-industrialization-autonomy creates the need for a politics of transition prefigured as one of long duration. The transition from feudalism to capitalism is characterized by a small class struggling for hegemony in a mixed state (land versus capital), sometimes in alliance, sometimes in conflict, with absolutism. The transition to socialism is, in theory, the movement of the largest class to adapt state institutions, as far as materially possible, to a socially equitable system of distributing socially produced goods and, presumably, distributing 'access' to employment so that production itself is no longer distributed on a labour-market basis. The problem is that the conservation and renewal of institutions gives the impression of a new mode of production struggling to adapt itself and be grafted on to the parent mode. (29) In that sense, 'lavoro nero' and 'lavoro doppio' would seem to be a rough pre-vision of rationing-out unpleasant or precarious labour and breaking up the division of labour, not simply forcing it upon the weak and de-qualified.

The PCI's strategy is tacitly consistent with this 'assisted and compliant' form of transition. Yet any analogy with the rise of capitalism rests on the rising class possessing a superior means of production. The classical transition to socialism is propelled by the contradictory productivity of capital, which cannot maintain its class dominance, increase its fixed capital and its profits without over-producing for the living labour it has forced out of the production process. At this point, the proletariat uses its (still intact) political power. When the new mode rests on declining economic prospects - albeit distributed with equity - and when the state has been reinforced by renewal-conservation, certain linkages become crucial. For example, the relation between assemblies, parties and decision-making raises the problem that pluralistic-corporative participation is a barrier to a strong decision-making apparatus and encourages the blurring of distinctions between the parties, to create a generalized party-system-state.

The Socialist Party has frequently drawn attention to inconsistencies of this type. True, corporativism is not representative of general, but only of particular, interests. Are arbitrary decisions by parliament preferable? Institutional pluralism may sound sweeter than 'consociational democracy with latent authoritarian tendencies', (30) but it does not resolve the question of alternation of governments, of equality of competitive access to power, or compromise which is not merely weaker elements submitting to others' dominance. The existing agreement that Italy's problem is backwardness, even though that allows the country to undercut - in theory - the international market, makes the very process of transition ambiguous, a process of technical 'catching up' in the public sphere. Indeed, discussion seems at the pre-transitional phase concerning the merits of parliament versus assemblies, politics versus the state system and unitary parties versus volatile movements, even though transition-recomposition is actually occurring. As Cacciari has recognized, 'it is we who are speaking Latin'. (31) Crisis as transition requires the devising of new categories, but he proposes not a theory, but a common language, an everyday speech, 'democracy' not philosophy or speculation on the closure of rationally-designed systems.

From this perspective, exclusion from a Christian Democratic government is secondary to the ability to manoeuvre with an eye on the everyday language of potential majorities. It is partly a movement towards syncretism, partly an admission that strong state and representative participation are not alternative models, but co-present and conflicting principles. They cannot, however, be the only principles of transition, containing as they do such paradoxes as that in the democratic-authoritarian state: the greater the consensus, the smaller the power of individuals and the less the incentive for participation. The PCI can back the strong state and participation simply as the programme of those who do not fear institutions to which the mass has access, as against the conservative-Catholic view that institutions are fragile and artificial, and that pastoral care, rather than, for example, economic motivation, is suitable for the masses. In this anti-conservative perspective, the PCI can simply wait for the Christian Democrats' conservatism to make mistakes. The PCI could thus appear as a 'modern' party which accepts the autonomy (and dominance) of the technical, a centrist acceptance of the primacy of technique and expertise. The modern, like democracy, is always changing, and should be left to its autonomy by the parties. At present, the initiative lies with the Christian Democrats to innovate, and the PCI gains nothing by proposing precise institutional reforms. It accepts transition, without having the power to guide it.

Yet, beyond a certain point, decline weakens and damages everyone, as Tronti pointed out. (32) The conditions of the formation of a class, and its development, become a part of its genetic structure. The future of a class is what its past has made it. A working class which becomes a function of capitalist development or decline may indeed encourage its party to propose 'autonomy' for its politics. However, what does that signify? It is not possible for a party to make transition in the form of a party-church, independent of civil society. A party may resist crisis, closed in the immobilism of its own structure, but it may also atrophy or be absorbed. This idea lay behind Colajanni's insistence that the ideological vagueness of the PCI's Left be replaced by a pragmatic view of how the economy might function and how it might be controlled, as against Ingrao, as well as against Rodano's integralism. (33) The essentialist argument about socialism was worthless unless real aims and functions were defined.

Such a non- or less ideological formulation might, indeed, accomplish little. The appeal of direct action is easily explained: (34)

> Social disruption indeed remains the only certain reality inculcated by the struggle. Once the model of the factory was extended to the whole society, control over workers' lives was broken up against complex, subversive, daily life; the struggle rebounded on the social fabric, disrupting it through the reproductive separation of the class from the places of production of the capital-factory, the capital-district, the capital-man and the capital-sex.

Hastening decline also accelerates the political process

of the ultra-Left. It leads in directions not to be channelled and restored to 'the fixed schemes round which a generation of neo-officials of the mini-parties has crystallized'. (35) There is a cataclysmic optimism in the notion that 'the workers' interest ... is the disruption of the apparatus of control over the machine, and the enforcement of dislocation elsewhere, as self-transformation of the figure itself, by the masses.' (36) By analogy with the Giolittian era, rhetoric of this kind encloses and smothers the PCI rather as its rhetorical exhaustion prepared Turati's Socialist Party for the passive revolution. Within the ultra-Left, too, Marazzi observed, 'the provincialism of operaismo becomes ... an elegant way of speaking in the abstract of concrete things', or, as Cacciari put it, the diffused factory is in fact an immense spread of division within the class. (37)

We may say that the administrative solution of the PCI is technical and subordinate. The second step to the economy and the institutions has yet to be taken, or planned. Initiative still lies with the traditional political class and the state bourgeoisie. Ingrao's notion of an equilibrium between decisive government and assemblies seems to lead to authoritarianism or immobilism. Amato's proposal of counter-powers sounds like the existing tendency to insert mixed public-private bodies into the state without defining functions. (38) More fruitful, perhaps, is Barcellona's idea of re-ranking the powers and institutions of the public sphere in a more rational and orderly manner. The functional, and moral, decay of the state was not in his view because of the Christian Democrats, but of the mixture of pre-capitalist and productive elements pressing for political representation. (39) These conflicting elements, intervening in the material basis of society through the mediating state, have led to an overcrowded and contradictory institutionalization of society. The mixed political motives of the state, that is, lead to compromise, immobilism and competing rationalities. Representative democracy and the creation of parallel administrations destroy the liberal element of the state. A new democracy would build on the broken alliance between the speculative bourgeoisie and the disappointed sectors of the middle strata which had hoped for social unification. The aim must be to transfer to public control the centres of private power, on principles of elected assemblies, parliamentary control and pluralism - an advanced mass democracy. (40) However, like all such schemes already referred to, this rests on two assumptions: first, that political unity can be constructed in such a way that all parties involved will enforce the rules equally, and second, that the establishment of the principles and order proposed will provide means of crisis management. In fact, unless there is agreement on the causes and nature of the crisis, and its desirable solution, 'resolution', 'transformation' or 'transition' from it, there can be neither agreement to reform nor a coherent response of democratic policy to a class society in crisis. Until then, reformism, like Turati's or Togliatti's, will exist either in theory alone, or be applied in the area of common-sense gradualism.

In the foregoing work of Barcellona and others there are elements of a reformism the PCI might adopt, and might put 'politics in command'. This might also attract the new 'Left' members of technical elites and the old bourgeois-professional strata. Marazzi has pointed to the provincialism of the 'new politics', still concerned with a dialogue between Americanism and maximalism, (41) and Meriggi to the fact that the centrality of politics, or rather the working class, indicates a failure to produce a central, efficient, political subject. (42) It is also reasonable to complain of 'Weberian' and 'Paretan' elements in the notion of a new political class, a state bourgeoisie attempting to consolidate a class alliance including entrepreneurs, state employees, organized workers and the tertiary-commercial middle strata. This is an attempt to overcome the basic problem of shifting distribution from private to public spheres.

At the same time, there is a minimal consensus about Weberian objectives, and views of systemic rationality, which require substantial modifications to the political roles of the state bourgeoisie's traditional constituencies. There is increasing agreement that productive labour, and labour (unproductive) consuming value, are not substantially different and thus not politically contradictory. Technology and administrative technique tend to increase the input of technicians and undervalue, or devalue, the cultural-political presence of the proletariat. The tendency of capital to homogenize, or level, the condition of living labour makes control and leadership of this homogeneous labour increasingly a 'technical', not a class, question. (43) Rather, the dominant class itself is composed of layers of technicians, specialists in the problems of their constituents, a 'state-party'. The PCI, and to a lesser extent the Socialist Party, remains separate from this process as a mass organization, but is increasingly dependent on, and a source of, the public administrative technician. As regards social goals and needs, the Left is a subordinate element. The political class, or quasi-class, is essentially articulating an interclassist administration of post-Keynesian crisis based not on alternative methods of distributing resources but on a new equilibrium and hierarchy of the 'productive'. This recognizes the end of the spontaneous political subject and announces the beginning of the administratively stimulated economic subject.

To what extent, then, can we describe the state bourgeoisie as an administrative class, or an identified embourgeoisement of the 'red experts', implied by the insertion of the PCI as a subordinate element in the administrative stratum? In so far as this relates to the class origin of the professional/expert, though professionals are largely drawn from the old dominant classes and appear to be independent of material production, they are really increasingly ancillary to it. True, some PCI technicians and experts make a Fabian-type analysis of the transformation of an extensive, unregulated, private sphere. Yet theirs is also a project for insertion and technicization clearly revealed in a project outlined by the PCI in Emilia-Romagna in 1977.

> In a phase of transition like that now developed in the country, in the midst of a fall of values and a confrontation from which the new emerges with difficulty, and as elements of a new hegemony take shape, it is not only opportune but vital to assert the need to put to the test all the capacities we have to compete for the leadership of the country; to put forward the need for a general, mass raising of levels of consciousness; to follow the labyrinth of the crisis and leave it behind through stronger social and political knowledge.

On the one hand this mass acquires knowledge and consciousness: on the other, 'we intend to set forth the need that the new protagonistic forces of national renewal and national leadership should acquire, as rapidly as the increase in the task dictates, all the abilities which allow for the operation of political and economic syntheses to assume leadership of great social advances.'(44)

In theory, this is not a role for 'functionaries of humanity', 'critical consciousnesses', or for (45)

> 'suggesters' of any desired political line, or for those wishing to exercise vicarious functions as regards the organs responsible for bringing about the great synthesis of the global responsibilities of government. It involves leaving these shoals to reconsider, in the light of new tasks and new commitments no one can evade, the critical and organic level of the relation with the forces of transformation, with the projects being drawn up and also with the obstacles ...

posed by the old which slowly decline, and the new which emerges with its characteristics still uncertain. Now, the 'critical' and 'organic' in synthesis is generally the technical, at the level of the project. The state bourgeoisie is also technically involved in crisis-management. It is thus hard to distinguish participation in crisis-management from general control of the public sphere, in which the classes appear as subordinate functions. The Christian Democrats re-emerge as broadly representative.

At present, the PCI is precariously inserted as a technical-populist sub-stratum of the state bourgeoisie. This interpretation is supported by Fausto Anderlini's model of local administration as a sub-system of the political-administrative system, communicating with the sub-system of unions, co-operatives and middle-stratum associations (the sub-system of the socio-economic system) through disrupted relations (increased autonomy, broken 'transmission belts') and the new social bloc alliance. (46) This is a picture of the subordinate insertion of the PCI into the administrative-political system and the establishment of new means of sub-system communication. It is inserted not as a representative of a class, but in its aspect of administrative unit.

This analysis is not confined to Emilia. The technician is a national, not a regional, figure. A typical, limited figure as both subject and object of administrative integration, he is not simply, and not only, the key to the PCI's strategy. The PCI is not the autonomous subject of this process. The mass worker too is part of the process of insertion as object, not subject, and also as object of the administration designed to organize reduced social conflict. That is why administrative options do not absorb all reality, or totally camouflage social conflictuality. However, as strategy of transition, this connects the proletariat with capitalist decline under the banner of Weber, but without his self-criticism. In the end this is not betrayal or PCI reformism but a search for raison d'état in its administrative strategy and in its re-absorption by the very institutions it had attempted to hegemonize. The important thing now is to recognize the limits and needs of a condition in which to modernize means also to 'anticipate the decline'. The reverse has normally been the case, to anticipate growth, to regard the mission of the proletariat as the alternative to the decline of the old order, to see the growth of the class in the inability to administer it within capitalist rationality. Now, however, in decline, the working class becomes the prime object of administration.

It would be oversimplified to see the influx of new technicians and recruits from the old dominant classes to the PCI as a fusion of the historic Left and an administrative-authoritarian-corporative state bourgeoisie engaged in subsidizing private industry and diverting resources to the public sphere. We may, though, discount the inflated claims for intra-systemic transformation, as in the case of law no.382 (for administrative decentralization), (47) without assuming that such a composite political class would necessarily be unitary. It would be created as a direct consequence of the fragmented nature of the Italian dominant economic class. In this regard, recent changes in the social composition of the PCI should not be underestimated. They mark its electoral success, the growing representativeness of the middle strata, the 'normal' path of a successful party developing its technical intelligentsia, and as a party on the threshold of government, the encouragement of a 'skill reservoir'. However, while we should expect the latest wave of recruits to support the immediate strategic aims of the Party, the figures for the 1979 federation delegates to pre-congressional discussion are significant. The delegates included 60 per cent who had joined the Party since 1970, 9.8 per cent of the total in 1975 alone. Full-time Party functionaries comprised 9 per cent, and 9.6 per cent were functionaries in unions or other mass organizations. Two-thirds of the Party functionaries were appointed in the 1970s, four out of ten since 1975. 48.6 per cent were members of some elected body. Of the total, 14 per cent were councillors of municipalities, provinces or regions, and 13 per cent of lower representative bodies (quartieri, health and school councils). Of the total delegates completing the questionnaire, 3.2 per cent were full-time administrators out of the approximately 9 per cent with administrative responsibilities, and 15 per cent were graduates. (48)

If the Party is becoming an administrative one, this does not necessarily mean it is becoming an authoritarian one. However, an administratively closed system in decline imposes certain constraints. True, Barbagli and Corbetta point to areas of ideological difference between leadership and base which do not allow us to assume that federation delegates are representative of leadership positions in the 1970s. In part, this is obvious: new members generally join a party because they agree, or do not violently disagree, with current leadership policies. In turn, the PCI involves new militants in pre-congressional activity as it wants to involve and retain them in the Party. New recruits will also reflect the trend to higher levels of qualification in the population overall. Yet a trivial feature speaks for the Party's sense of civic order, in that the highest number 'always against' certain forms of struggle, 67 per cent, should be opposed to painting slogans on walls, followed by 57 per cent against attacking police in demonstrations and 55 per cent against wildcat strikes: the last two categories had the lowest number in favour: 3 and 4 per cent respectively. (49)

We are witnessing a gradual movement from a 'backward' missionary party to an administrative one. In the Togliatti era, the policy was to try to establish, on the basis of a new democracy, closer ties between literary intellectuals and the masses, and to broaden the basis of support of the literary intellectuals by associating, albeit in a subordinate and non-leadership role, intellectual sympathizers with the propaganda of the Party. In the 1960s, when the movement from mass to representative party began, this archaic relation was superseded and simplified by the mass production of intellectual labour, and the attempt to find a basis of unity between the fragmentary character of mass intellectual labour and the new dependency of 'traditional' intellectuals on monopoly capital and the cultural industry. (50)

In the 1970s, when the era of 'easy Marxism' is long past, the emphasis is more on the political skills of experts than on expert advice itself, which is always procurable through consultants, through public channels or on a voluntary basis. There is less concern to recruit ideologues, whose original function was to convert the masses. This tends to accentuate the traditional slowness of the PCI in responding to challenges to its Marxist legitimacy, and to attract those less interested in theoretical speculation and doctrine. The Party, in short, is continuing to speak of transition to an ideological, if vague, socialism, while slowly coming to terms with political problems of large-scale administration and economic decline which have played no part in its former ideological paradigm. It has increasingly moved towards a generalized conviction that government and administrative reforms secured by the Party could allow a period of rapid cultural modernization, against both the reactionary terrorism of Right and Left and the inefficiency of a 'blocked' society. To that end, it recognizes Marx's dictum that 'Every new class, therefore, achieves its hegemony only on a broader base than that of the class ruling previously, whereas the opposition of the non-ruling class develops all the more sharply and profoundly.' (51) In this situation, customary definitions of the traditional working class, and of the class loyalty of the state petty bourgeoisie, no longer hold. We may still ask whether the movement in Italy is towards the hegemony of a new class or of a new representative movement, replacing organic working class leadership as a possible objective and substituting a technical-administrative intelligentsia as its leading stratum, not as a consequence of revolution by the subaltern classes but as a substitute for it. The goal of this stratum is to 'manage transition', and its ideological objective is primarily to manage consensus in an efficiently ruled, stratified, society.

There is thus a wide range of public and elected institutions which may be much more easily controlled than enterprises under private ownership. Where 'participation' in the public sphere rapidly exhausts itself in efforts to modify the dominant property relations, emphasis - irrespective of doctrine - is more easily placed on pushing decision-making up the power hierarchy in the public, especially the state, sector than in the private. Yet this process, whereby any popular modification of property relations is mediated, and generally annulled, by political forces at a higher level (eviction of squatters, for example), adds increasingly to the weight and initiative of the administrator-politician. (52) One might argue that this mediation, while it excludes militant participation, wears down the ideological polarization of administrators and assists in the creation of more tolerant attitudes towards social change. On the other hand, it creates increased intolerance towards those who reject this gradualist approach. The change from ideology to technique, to administrative participation from revolutionary subjectivism, is a transition which prefers the administrator to the militant; hard for a subordinate class, but natural for administrators of the status hierarchy.

In the short term, the PCI has been developing its expertise to insert into the power structure competent administrators drawn largely from party cadres and professionals. For the most part, the conflict between career bureaucrats and political administrators has yet to be resolved. To the margin, this conflict appears irrelevant. The margin in transition becomes not revolutionary subject but victim ('sturdy beggars'), and is betrayed by both its lack of historical sense and its flawed recognition of, as well as by, society (the 'petty-bourgeois insurrection').

The key relation in Italy now seems not so much that between classes, though the classes remain in conflict, as between socially determined corporate interests and the administrative state. Increasingly, the state organizes production, dominates the service sector, determines the character of the labour market and wage levels and provides an extensive market for services and goods through taxation and investment policies and by the legal recognition of corporate interests. The state appears as the national representation of social interest. Yet the Italian state is a relatively backward example of the type, and therefore, though relations between state and corporations are mutually supportive, they are also conflictual. Such a state requires a representative political class as management of consociational, distributive or authoritarian democracy. In so far as the state class itself is a corporation, it naturally resists attempts to redistribute or dilute its power. All these types of democracy exclude from the political system demands which are not organized in corporate forms, and the 'margin', which makes the greatest claims but has least weight to back them. All modify the notion of alternative governments, the social-democratic model, and all modify the Marxist model of historical alternation of dominant classes until politics itself is universalized and eliminated in a society of equals.

The 1970s have seen the modification of the idea of society-as-enterprise and the emergence of one of 'society of societies' in need of administrative co-ordination. The paradox of this was noted by Nicola Licciardello: 'If we are all integrated workers, what can save humanity? On the other hand, if we are not, then any possible synthesis is broken a priori, it gives no one any serious ideological security.' The 'general proletariat' is the 'last great sub-stratum of the unitary appearance of the human condition'. (53) Now, not only does the process of homogeneous proletarianization seem at an end, at least unless the economic decline accelerates, but the tendency to generalize the condition of subordination is modified by the distinction between the subordinate class and its administrators. This feature has been discussed for some years: in 1968 Asor Rosa and Cacciari were suggesting in 'Contropiano' that the mass production of the proletariat produced a vanguard which could resolve the problem of the 'externality' of the working class, its autonomy, by establishing a closer relation to the base, a duality (between leaders and led) the PCI seemed unable to overcome. Thus, the distinction 'between bureaucracy and factory work is thus nothing more than the distinction between two different levels of capitalist appearance ... In a word, it is philosophy which stands at the head of the revolutionary process and directs it.' (54)

The limited attempts at capitalist rationalization and 'homogenization' have, however, led not to continued tension between fragmentation and mass production in the subordinate class but to the primacy of fragmentation and administration of bureaucracy over the corporate fragments. Capitalist homogenization has failed, not as a tendential movement towards society-as-worker, but as a strategy for development. Its legacy is the major (administrative) difficulty of distributing resources between corporate structures and 'valorizing' the contributions made by corporations. The fragmented masses need administrative articulation, but no longer have the imminent vision of the totality of the 'general proletariat'. This is the culmination of the process of the integration of intellectual-labour into the political organs of the proletariat, not, as for Togliatti, as an autonomous grouping prompted by subjective choice, but as a 'public class' of administrators and mediators. This professionalization of the political process and integration of its constituencies ends, or at least suspends, the philosophical vision of the new Left of the 1960s. The administrative model does not so much contradict classical class theory as substitute a diadic, public, clientelist one (55) as the bridge between traditional, individualist, exchange politics (market individualism), and corporate exchange (market collectivism). In this, as has been noted, 'participation helps the planner'. The planner also 'helps'. The planner is given social or political mandates for specific objectives, but institutional restraints remain. 'The aim of a public department is to defend itself collectively against criticism, rather than to clarify the responsibilities of individual officials.' (56) This does not exclude ideology, but it is a specific way of 'doing politics'. As Peter Self said: 'Political activity is like lightning, in that it may strike into any corner of the administrative system, but only rarely does so. The great bulk of administrative operations continues in political obscurity, and the main interactions between politics and administration occur at the top levels of government.' (57) This process of 'routinizing and stabilizing' politics is a normal feature of the modern state, without requiring the existence of a 'state plan'. It challenges the historic Left's notion of 'open politics', mass or participatory politics, and it is also a result of the Left's emphasis on the state in the process of modernization. Participation is an input of the administrative system, not a transfer of power to the periphery.

Discussion of this issue has centred on the relation between professionalization and politicization of the public service, unless indeed professionalization is the form of its politicization. In addition, it is important to note that the administrative system is a closed, conflictual arena, multiform in terms of policies, and class or stratum interests. Though it is multiform it may be interclassist (low politicization with respect to social ideology, high bureaucratic politicization as 'state class') or conservative (politicized alignment with a dominant, or formerly dominant, class). Politicized bureaucracies aligned with dominant classes easily make efficiency synonymous with political order. But what the PCI is proposing is a mixed, politicized, bureaucracy in the name of representative political order. This is either contradictory, in that it proposes importing conflict into administration, dis-order into the state or, as is more likely, the fusion of plural interests in a consensual, universalistic political class. A politicized bureaucracy which represents class and ideological division in civil society is a recipe for chaos. The PCI, if it proposes to occupy part of the state and its administration, must really be suggesting doing so on the basis of a consensual political order or a political order based on consensus within the administrative-political class. (58)

Sechi has attempted to demonstrate a relation in Emilia between the PCI's administrative policies and areas of neglect and rejection (particularly 'autonomia'). His proposal is a party-centred alternative: (59)

> a conception of Marxism which will not be a theory of compromise ('to resolve peacefully the contradictions existing in history and society'), but a theory of the contradictions of the subaltern classes, a theory of the transformation of the very principle of hegemony. This leads to the establishment of a relation of necessary correspondence between the democratic conception of the state and the internal democracy of the party.

However, the administrative aspect is not confronted by appeals to party or state democracy. Nor, indeed, does it refer to the question of leadership renewal or intra-party conflict between leaders, cadres, administrators and base. Sechi proposes to revive the centrality of the party (as opposed to the centralism of the party), when the institutionalization of the existing participation has already led to immobilism and distance between leaders and base. The Party, in short, becomes a function of part of the system of contradictory subordination: in order to institutionalize itself it must either reconcile contradictions or exclude those it cannot.

The PCI was quick to reject suggestions that the party form and state plan were in crisis, and that a modern,

'Germanized', authoritarian consensual state was at hand. Germanization implied a collaboration between state, employers and working class to permit a declaration of war on the so-called 'enemies of freedom'. To Angelo Bolaffi, for example, the German case had 'Nothing, or almost nothing' to do with political dissent and political violence in Italy. (60) The margin in Italy was isolated and precarious, and in any case Italian development was unlike the German. The PCI emphasized productivism and attacked parasitism and waste. The margin's slogan, 'History is killing us', (61) was the authentic voice of the 'right to hatred'. Where there was collaboration, it was essentially local, between small entrepreneurs and workers' organizations, not big capital. The 'modern state' is not Germanized, but concerned with problems common to many advanced capitalist societies, such as those of distinguishing between subversion and dissent, reducing social conflict by administrative selection of just claims and a retreat from (verbal) commitment to the equal distribution of resources in the public sector.

This argument has been extended to suggest that, whatever the immediate tactical influences, the historic compromise was an appeal to intellectuals to put their expertise at the service of 'depoliticized', or non-regime, administration. The 'autonomy of the political' can be presented as a definition of an effective but limited terrain of politics. The slogan of austerity was a call to productivism. (62) The alternative case, made by critics of the 'German' modern state, would argue that historic compromise means collaboration, the autonomy of the political an authoritarian distance from civil society, and austerity a direct attack on the working class, calling for more work and less reward. The PCI argued that an appeal to the intellectuals to gather around or penetrate a new, composite, ruling class was also necessarily a consolidation of intellectuality in the state, and a necessary integration of intellectuals, as critics as well as experts. Political autonomy at the level of the state allows objective and rational decisions and a real critical function, unlike the mystified, abstract, autonomy of the sphere of 'culture'. Austerity is not only an appeal for discipline and conciliation but a recognition that Italy is a fragile society which needs peaceful transition to socialism, and whose working class is strong enough to resist violent reaction. Transition needs an alliance with the middle strata to preserve the productive base. Political order and social stability are not only enjoined by Italy's position in international capitalism, but necessary in themselves and for transition. Gramsci's 'demographic rationalization' (63) for class alliance - too few workers - and his fear of a spread of parasitism mean that a recent development of a 'modern state', or at least its idea, is not the adoption of the German model but of a conciliatory, pluralistic, state, repressive only to guarantee its survival, conciliatory to secure national continuity and the maintenance of a social dynamic.

This, however, has analogies with Poulantzas's account of the difference between German and Italian fascism. The Italian case was a reaction to crises of imperialism, of the petty bourgeoisie and the dominant ideology, and also the exacerbation of contradictions within the dominant bloc. (64) This does not mean that the modern state is a return to fascism, and at least one champion, big capital, seems to play a lesser role. The modern state in Italy would be a 'social state' in that it would represent corporate social interests. It would be arbitrary-consociational rather than authoritarian-democratic. Its basic plan would be that of preventing claims breaking out of, and modifying, the institutional framework. Its assumptions might be that the working class has exchanged its extra-institutional challenge for a share of power, a partial victory and a partial defeat, as well as a surrender of the idea that it might constitute a state and society alone. Its second assumption is that the petty bourgeoisie is in crisis, and that this prevents a stable alliance with the proletariat or traditional working class as well as with the more normal partner, the dominant class. Though it tends to share the general economic condition of the working class, it sees itself as lacking the negotiating power to maintain its privilege in the status hierarchy. Though it is not as a whole attracted to ideological extremism, it is directly involved in fiscal crisis and the legitimacy crisis of the state. It is thus peculiarly dependent on, and sceptical of, the political and economic skills of the dominant class (a sign and cause of whose weak hegemony is its inability to gain the support of the petty bourgeoisie). Though increasingly organized in the public sphere, the petty bourgeoisie still sees itself as insufficiently protected as both victim and subordinate advocate of administrative crisis - for example, in terms of inflation, inefficiency or terrorism. The dependent petty bourgeois thus wants stability, growth and guarantees of financial and status stability. For this reason, it is prepared for the curtailment of the liberty of the 'destabilizers', and for reasons different from those of the organized working class which, according to the PCI, is pursuing a strategy of acquiring power in which instability aids its opponents.

In this scenario, the insertion of the working class into the negotiating system is a guarantee against extremism. Conflict would continue, but as managed, intercategorial, conflict. A hierarchy emerges from this institutionalized conflict, and is one whose maintenance requires a private productive sector from which a surplus can be extracted to maintain the public sphere. The hierarchy in the last resort depends on the skill of the administrators in collecting and distributing revenue to the public sphere. Corporativism means that the more important problem is to ensure that adequate revenue is available for the self-regulating competition between corporations. Such a system lacks the dynamic goals of fascism, but is constructed around 'permanence'. Its interest lies in satisfying claims of the institutionalized bargaining units so far as possible, and within the limits of the status hierarchy. Quantitative demands by the various sectors and lowering productivity to raise the price of labour de-stabilize the social, but not necessarily the state, system. Qualitative demands become acceptable, especially when they call on public services like the 150 hours, as they make the state's role as mediator and satisfier more salient. On the other hand, the state is not committed to the principle of expansion as supplier and producer, as legitimacy and consensus suffer if it shows that it lacks that capacity. Indeed, it is likely to recognize its areas of lack of competence, and draw back from direct involvement in them.

In this system, private capitalism is guaranteed but precarious, in that its services to the public sector place it under threat from labour and the state bourgeoisie. However, small industry is especially favoured, being both subsidized and ignored when it operates irregularly. It is in that area that the historic Left begins organizing the state-project. This stimulation of small industry is neither the distance between parties and class, proposed by Asor Rosa on the grounds that politics is governing, nor Ingrao's suggestion that the crisis of the welfare state opens the state to democratic control. Indeed, the system sketched above allows the state to overcome fiscal crisis by managing the process of distribution, and legitimacy crisis by managing the status hierarchy. It does not solve the problem of capitalism, but gives order to the decline.

The parties increasingly become outputs, as well as inputs, of the administrative system. They produce consensus, and traditional ideology increasingly becomes an embarrassment, as is shown both by the 'autonomy of the political' and by Luigi Berlinguer's notion of 'organized democracy'. The insertion of classes and parties into the politico-administrative system changes their functions, and links their future to that of the state. In what sense, then, are the relations reproducing those of capitalism, and is this an authoritarian state?

On the one hand, as Zolo admits, there exists a high degree of consensus, the 'democratic integralism' of 90 per cent of the population. (65) It is authoritarian in that no place is allotted to organized opposition or individual dissent. In this, it is not liberal, neither does it take the optimistic Marxist view that dissent is not a problem in consensual systems. It is statist, in that neo-Gramscians and operaisti see the state as the terrain on which the working class matures, overcoming its own, and the state's backwardness simultaneously. It does appear to modify the system of reproduction of capitalist relations, already in trouble vis-à-vis the social margin. It does not need to suggest that capitalism, especially in its post-welfare stage, is benevolent, or yet that socialism grows from it. Yet the tendentially two-class model it presents is a model of collaboration between private capital and public administration in which capitalist relations of production are reproduced in the division between accumulation-distribution and production. The new model rests on failures in alternatives to resolve the problem of authority and command in socialist societies, and the failure of individual capitalists to constitute the basis for economic growth and unified political direction. It is the distributive-accumulative sector of the public sphere organized as collective capitalist, in alliance with the subordinate private sector capitalists. As yet, it is only a tendency, not programmatic, and of course the PCI is still formally excluded.

This marks the failure of the philosophical, libertarian, aspects of Marxism to be reconciled with a 'democratic state'. As Scalia has suggested, Marxism is a two-headed beast, negative and positive. A negative dialectic destroys Marxism, a positive one is either pragmatic (historical) or stands for order-in-the-state, or philosophical raison d'état. Liberalism cannot admit the possibility of socialism, since this involves the very transcendence of liberalism and legitimates social conflict destructive of the state of law. Stame attempts to evade this by requesting that the state of law guarantee intensified class struggle. Luigi Berlinguer's is a degenerated, late-Hegelian, account of corporate-democratic representation in the techno-bureaucratic state, where all distinctions have been blurred between public and private spheres, hence all distinction between liberalism and socialism. As Zolo points out, these unsatisfactory formulations can be traced to Marx's unsatisfactory theory for a revolutionary transformation of representative institutions, the transcendence of 'Bourgeois political autonomization, which operates through bureaucratic-representative mediation, as the criterion of alienation and the division of power, and as the norm of authoritative hierarchization of social roles.' (66)

Marx's scenario, through its gaps, turns out to be one of a non-transcendable capitalist crisis. In Lenin, Marx's suppressed philosophical content becomes little more than a quasi-Hegelian state-party dirigisme, in which a political class puts itself forward as the representative of the interests of a one-class society. This vindicates Marx's economics, as central and elaborated, and qualifies the politics and sociology as less objectively worked out. As Zolo neatly puts it, the problem with Marx's theory of the state is whether the state disappears or everything becomes the state, whether dissent is rooted in civil society or in a project to reform the state from within. (67)

The assumption behind the foregoing is that the modern state is a particular long-term response to economic decline and the fading confidence in or abandonment of ideological alternatives. This leads to new forms of intervention in the mechanism of distribution and accumulation, and in repressive consensus by a representative ruling class. Preuss, however, (68) speaks of the precarious balance between democracy and dictatorship in capitalist states, and thus apparently the potential of oscillation between these, less as forms than as practices. Offe sees the capitalist state as a state form, but with a dual function, that of protecting capitalism, but also that of exercising the universalist 'state functions' of maintaining the state and the social order. (69) This view of the state sees it as both interventionist and autonomous. Offe's notion of universalist functions implies a post-ideological framework for the state, or rather a state ideology not susceptible to ideological presences in civil society. Foucault expresses this generically, in his attack on the nexus of (intellectuals') knowledge and power. (70)

> There does exist a system of power which blocks, prevents and invalidates this discourse, and this power *[that is, of the masses who do not require intellectuals; J.F.]* is not simply the upper levels of censorship, but is based deep and very subtly in all networks of society. Intellectuals themselves are part of this system of power, and the idea that they are the agents

> of 'knowledge' and discussion is part of this system. The role of the intellectual is no longer to put oneself a little 'on one side' to tell everyone's silent truth; it is rather to struggle against the forms of power where it is at once the object and the instrument, in the order of 'knowledge', of 'truth', of 'consciousness', of 'discussion'.

Yet Foucault, in identifying the pursuit of knowledge with the pursuit of power (or self-satisfaction), not only eliminates ideology, but intellectuals themselves. For the pursuit of power is the pursuit of gratification, not merely of knowledge. His is a disillusion not only with intellectuals, their 'selflessness' and claim to wisdom, but with society itself and the masses' desire for democracy. This is a desire for power in itself, and its frustration leads to masochism or passivity. (71) We might say that there is a disappointment that the demise of open, contractual 'Gesellschaft' society does not tend to a return to 'Gemeinschaft', which is a precondition for, and primary stage of, 'Gesellschaft' and is destroyed by it once and for all. The disillusion is rooted in the fact that the modern state reasserts the classical division between rulers and ruled: it is not the 'beginning of the end of the state', or the transfer of power to all so that none may exercise power over others.

This is a version of moral catastrophism, the collapse of the contractual and traditional forms of society, and the supposed loss or absorption of individuals and classes in the social power. Ruffilli argues that such theories of the state are not only disappointed rationalism but ignore the force of ideology and intent which make the modern state a historical, not a permanent, form. For example, 'coexistence at the super-structural and substructural level of unstable equilibria between system and counter-powers' (72) is essentially a dynamic element. We might argue, however, that the experience of the project for a modern state in Italy is characterized as follows. First, it is a design for a long, seemingly irreversible, process of decline and resulting conflict. Second, it assumes that corporate competition can be organized with a consensual basis for the use of repression of non-legitimated opposition. Third, it assumes that the state will supervise negotiations between class organizations and represent all classes and interests engaged in production. Finally, it assumes that the class hierarchy will be represented in the state by an integrated but hierarchical state class, or political class. One key question is the extent to which the Christian Democrats will use their modern and traditional expertise either to delay the formation of such a class or to maintain their hegemonic position over it, when formed. There has been a collapse of traditional ideological polarities and proposals, though not a disappearance of them. 'Administration' is a mark of the replacement of traditional ideology as a dynamic for change by the insertion of 'Left technicians' into a piecemeal planning process. The signs of mass depoliticization are as yet inconclusive. There is no definitive sign that consensus politics is a reacculturation on the basis of indifference to politics. But the technocratic emphasis on institutions and enterprises, the acceptance of 'rational repression' and the failure of liberal-democratic institutions to provide a decisive response to the crisis are indicative of two developments. First, there is a failure to extend the liberal-democratic theory of continuity and universal values in the state (and its counterpart, the Leninist theories of the destruction of the liberal system and replacement by mass dictatorship) to the actual development of capitalist and socialist states. This is a failure to identify and debate the values of the two systems, reflected in general ideological disillusion and disorientation. The problem is compounded in Italy, as the search for 'national interest' is not accompanied by a strong conviction in the political class that 'national objectives' exist and are attainable. Luigi Berlinguer's 'organized democracy' negates both the subjective political and the moral responsibilities of individual and class.

Second, an analysis of the state by a variety of structuralist, functional, instrumental and neo-Hegelian interpretations is based on the composite notion of the state as synthesis of generalized, but not universalized, interest. The state is organized according to the disposition of power in society, and in turn organizes the terms of conflicts of interest. It does not see itself as universal, nor does it rest on universal rights and interests of citizens. The middle strata, and the intelligentsia as their sub-stratum, have already produced a range of alternative planning rationales in supposedly different modes of production, the capitalist 'state plan', the DDR's 'socialist mode of production', the Czech 'scientific-technical revolution'. It fulfils a traditional Mannheimian role of governing in the interests of other classes, as well as in its own as state class. It thus promoted itself from the middle ranks by means of political expertise, maintaining the status hierarchy but also directing it and thus dominating it. As distinct from the Weberian bureaucracy whose rationality is essentially hollow and objective-less, the technical intelligentsia has a monopoly of knowledge and rationality criteria. Crisis and crisis management is the rationale for its position in the state. As a state class it can, of course, satisfy its own interests by constructing 'finite provinces of rationality' without a commitment to change based on the liberal ethic of the person or a Marxist commitment to specific sublations. It should also be added that in the Italian context there has been a massive overproduction of an intelligentsia which is neither inserted into the 'modern' state nor likely to overcome rapidly its often marginal and parasitic conditions.

Nineteenth-century ideology is pitted against a state whose effectiveness lies in ignoring liberal responsibility, conservative community and Marxist species-history. Ideologies have not always been the reverse of the modern state, but have been used to legitimate it. In the administrative state, however, they are absorbed into a general theory of interest, as for example in 'participation helps the planner and the planner helps the poor.' This state would by no means be a guarantee of crisis-management, but it is efficient in incorporating or de-activating alternative critical theories. As Negri said: 'The historical picture introduces us thus to the heart of the institutions of that democratic state in which the system of parties is dominant: it shows us, that is ... the model of modern representation ... the relation between state sovereignty and popular sovereignty is wholly formed by the parties which, through their system, take on all the mechanisms of integration and subordination, of representation and mediation', until 'the parties seem in short to constitute a useless and harmful diaphragm to the development of democratic integration into the plan', so that the 'democratic processuality of the state thus requires, for its full realization, the transcendence of the system of parties.' (73)

Parties, that is, represent interests which can either be included and mediated within the state, de-ideologized and represented in the state without active participation, or must be excluded from the state because they are ideological contributions to conflict. Marxists have perhaps failed to consider that a theory of the mortality of capitalism may also be a pre-vision of its own, within the same system. This does not mean, of course, that 'socialism' as a form of more equitable distribution of resources and production, even within an older or broader system of national objectives, does not exist. Negri's analysis of the party system is not negated by the alternation of parties in the state. Alternation is the formal recognition of the temporary dominance of particular interests, but not the exclusion of others. Capital, in short, has identified its survival with the maintenance of the public sphere, and hence it must eliminate the main conflicting ideological forces, responsibility (liberalism), custom (conservatism) and history - the theory of the mortality of capitalism (Marxism). This is a project which seeks to contain the irrationality of capitalist distribution within a framework of administrative efficiency.

Negri points to the paradox: the only response to 'democratic integration' is a democratic resistance. This is possible on the basis of the socialization of the productive forces, and of the non-neutrality of the state as the 'internal regulator of the relations of capital'. (74) If the state were really relatively autonomous, there could be no struggle against it. However, civil society no longer retains control of ideologies and institutions, which pass into the state sphere. The essence of the state and state plan for Negri is the need to ensure the automatism of capital within the state, and thus contain the basic contradiction of capital within the state itself. This is plannable, or containable, even though we have witnessed the 'crisis of the Keynesian state, as a project of state intervention for capitalist development, based on a policy of regulation of the major proportions of income, an essentially financial instrumentation, and on a socializing ideology.' (75)

That state plan failed because it did not establish automatism and was insufficiently extensive. It was artificial and restrictive. The only way to achieve the dominance of capital is by manoeuvres such as historic compromise, which sustain the essentially short-term destructiveness of capital, its inefficiency and battle-ready condition. Class war is now between state (capital) and the new proletarian subject and the 'permanent illegality of his daily activity'. (76) Negri's conclusions are well known. The proletariat needs 'to resume the offensive on the basis of a Communist programme of appropriation and armed struggle, to give an organizational reply to the mass demand for counter-attack, following a line which runs from workers' autonomy to the political organization of the proletariat.' (77) The 'catastrophe' of capitalism is the working class itself, while even planned capital cannot overcome the problem of the falling rate of profit, despite devaluing and expelling living labour from the productive process. The permanence of the horizon of profit is only the permanence of the power of capitalism, the exaltation 'of its irrational face of command'. (78) The refusal to work, to accept the rationality behind capitalist power, leaves the workers in large factories as the vanguard. However, 'the infinite fantasy of liberated productive labour is revealed in struggle, from sabotage to the mass strike, confrontation in the piazza to armed struggle.' (79) This is a movement outside any party in which 'the concept of appropriation must include that of insurrection'. (80) Strategy is determined not 'by the errors of the bosses' but by the power of the workers' own organization. 'Only armed struggle is potent in the relation of forces between the two classes.' (81)

Thus expressed, Negri's position sounds like the end of 'doing politics', or of elaborating ideology. Constant, destabilizing assaults on the destructive state-class enemy is seen as the only possible response. There is no need of politics for, we have seen, the 'who' or the 'how' of 'the revolutionary transformation constitutes a single process. There is no need for a theory of the state in socialism, as there is no need for 'prefigurations and/or mystifications'. (82) With this verbal declaration of war, Negri sees more fluid organization outside parties and Constitution as leading to a centralized recomposition of the class.

As we have seen, the critique of the state implies an alternative conception of values and institutions, and to deny this is a mark of poverty. The decline of capitalism does not lead directly and logically to armed struggle and the end of politics. Stame has attempted to fill these gaps: 'the automatic character of the market leads to the formation of needs which the political system is constitutionally unable to satisfy.' (83) Liberalism's optimism rested in the last resort on the antagonism of the marketplace. At the other extreme, the bourgeois state's alternative form was natural law absolutism. Even if the new authoritarian state were managed by the working class, it would not be able to satisfy these needs. The authoritarian, post-liberal state faces the problem of 'how to govern in an authoritarian way with the consent of the governed'. (84) This, however, promises a future of the 'authoritarian regulation of social conflicts which are not rationally resolvable, and the recognition that only the foundation of the state outside the subjects can permit the necessary autonomy, or legitimation, to the social compact.' (85) That is, the state is not simply the state of the capitalist class, with an integrated working class. It is not so much relatively autonomous as necessarily distant from civil society and its real needs, so as to suppress conflictuality arising from them. For Stame, then, the key terms are 'distance' and the production of consensus/manipulation, an essentially political project. The post-liberal state may thus be vulnerable both to a legal challenge from liberalism, the older form of consensus, as well as to conflictuality arising from unsatisfied needs. Liberalism in this context is not seen as authoritarian, but a satisfier of needs.

Stame also comments on the 'impotence of political theory and of the conception of the state as regards any long-term political proposal'. (86) The essential point is the restoration of the subject, an idea derived from Adorno's view that the elimination or weakening of the subject is the 'theoretical origin of false conciliation'. Stame's view of the 'coincidence of freedom and necessity, identification of freedom and reason, freedom as dominance of rationality' (87) is closer to the Anglo-Saxon liberal tradition than the Marxist. So, for that matter, is the call for a 'heteronomous political system legitimated by the masses'. (88)

To Stame, the PCI's view of pluralism is one of organized interests, not a subjective, collective liberty. This notion of representative democracy is functional not for freedom, but for late capitalism. The spaces of representative democracy 'are filled by parties whose capacity to centralize and homogenize consensus is very functional to control of the (capitalist) cycle.' (89) The PCI has reduced its programme to 'a project of integration into capitalist rationality' in which there is a major difference between 'respect for legality as external behaviour and arguing that this state is the model of legality'. (90) There is thus a lack of congruence between the PCI's historical mission and its insertion into the late capitalist, authoritarian-democratic, state. It may have misread or underestimated the significance of a movement to the left in a non-revolutionary situation, the meaning of increased conflictuality in late capitalist society or the disequilibrium between the concrete situation of a class and its representation. At all events, the insertion of the working class into the late capitalist state would involve a serious miscalculation by the PCI, as it inhibits both class struggle and the liberty of the subject. 'Awareness of the possibility of such regressive processes in the development of capitalism, not to mention the problems of the phase of transition from capitalism to socialism, is deficient in the Marxist tradition.' (91)

Stame's formulation, however, is not wholly consistent. Class struggle and the freedom of the subject are both, after all, concerned with power. It is not enough to say that socialism has made the mistake of 'dissolving the problem of freedom in that of power, arguing that freedom is the self-government of the masses', (92) since the two aspects cannot be separated. Indeed, it is clear that

Stame approaches the question of freedom and power from the centrality of dissent: 'the problem of dissent and its existence no longer presents itself to socialist thought as a residue of forms of organization now obsolete.' (93) For freedom of dissent, though it forms part of a freedom and power of the masses, does not play a role only in socialism and in socialist thought. Where Scalia had rejected 'doing politics', Stame argues that the insertion of the PCI into the late capitalist state freezes the passage to socialism by immobilizing dissent, including the dissent of class struggle. Class struggle is not the only form of dissent, though Stame proposes to include it in dissent. However, class struggle is about freedom-as-power, not the right to protection following a challenge to power.

Stame ultimately proposes no alternative strategy against the state, save to request from it the legal right to dissent. All hangs on the sensitivity of the authoritarian state to legal forms. Negri's call to subversion, on the other hand, is pointless unless it leads to revolution. Negri and Stame represent the opposite poles of opposition to authoritarianism, subversion and guarantees. Neither believes in 'doing politics through the state', and transition is seen as a process taking place outside, and against, the state. The historic Left's 'autonomy of politics' is seen as a limitation imposed on the transitional process, an attempt to rationalize the irrational and manoeuvre on the terrain of the bosses'/authoritarian state.

Stame does remain within the legal rationality of the liberal state, suggesting that Marxism and socialism have made mistakes and omissions in their account of freedom, but that the apparatus exists for rectifying this. Negri scarcely troubles to indicate a new rationality, arguing that subversion against the irrational is the only rational response available. Organizing a new rationality, in short, seems as tentative as the attempts to discuss a new 'order', a new raison d'état, from within the state system itself. The state of transition, caught in decline of the economy and lacking an optimistic vision of the future, is concerned primarily with 'stabilizing crisis'. Transition seems less likely than a long struggle by administrators and technicians to maintain the controls which limit conflictuality and protect the state form and productive core, a struggle for survival which in the long term may come to resemble a transformation of society, even if not to a higher form.

At one extreme of this model of a society of imperfectly repressed conflictuality there is a drive for administered consensus; at the other, an arbitrary authoritarianism. The dynamics of the system lie in the degree of conflict in the composite state class, and the success or failure in locating a strategy of economic renovation.

CONCLUSION

If we avoid the predictive (Marxist) and moralistic notions attached to crisis, it is clear that attempts to devise a strategy both for limited 'catching up' and for secular decline will be presented as 'social transformation' and successful crisis management. In the absence of a decisive transitional alternative, the 'philosophy of decline' may well be represented in a strategy of cutting social costs and using repression and consensus to manage ensuing conflict, and of defining more closely the function and improving the performance of state, corporate responsibilities - the inexpensive function of mediation (political management) and the more risky one of economic intervention - in the context of an enlarged public sphere of state and corporate para-state enterprises.

Crisis theory in its classical form rests too heavily on the assumption of an optimistic political resolution to the crisis, a post-modern socialism, which minimizes the effect of protracted, managed, decline on social integration, ideology and organization. The discussion of modernity in Italy conflated the criteria of political modernity, mass plural democracy, with those of uniform, co-ordinated, modern industrialization. The PCI never fully came to terms with the implications of the bureaucratic organization of modern society, nor with the conflictuality of a transition period accompanying 'pluralism' (corporate competition) and 'counter-powers' (the non-centrality of the state). This conflictuality could be contained neither by 'mass' pressure nor by a statist solution without authoritarianism.

Italy now seems in a phase typical of de-development and the growth of a marginal economy. The Italian Left is now divided between those considering the terms for promoting the counter-tendency to further development and survival, and those looking for an ideological resolution of the problematic of capitalism. In terms of the literature of the mode of production, (1) the PCI seems to be abandoning the catastrophic scenario of rapid collapse and rapid transition, and accepting that of assisted transition, where the dominant mode supports the weaker replacement, while itself declining. This strategy risks being too economic in the notion of mode of production, and excessively political in its insistence that both modes of production be represented and conciliated in the state. The alternative ideological project, however, rests on an optimistic and often old-fashioned conception of the total dispossession of the propertied class, the exploiters of the private sphere, and the political class, exploiters of the public sphere. It is unrealistic in terms both of assessing its own strength, and of the local character of economic decline in the world system.

Paradoxically, new forms of organized democracy find accommodation within the traditional ruling class, or as Mosca calls it, properly, the political class. As Michels said, 'Organization is, in fact, the source from which the conservative currents flow over the plains of democracy, occasioning there disastrous floods and rendering the plain unrecognizable.' (2) Half-consciously, the PCI has been carrying on a discussion about trying to deal with the problems of a developing country in terms of an ideological assumption about Italy's frustrated modernity. It has thus seen, as pathological, phenomena which are 'normal' in developing capitalist economies. It has acted as though it could produce a socialized version of Americanism, at once productivist, bureaucratic-rational and democratic. At the same time it has been forced to realize that the process of growth in advanced, let alone developing, societies does not have a 'normal' progression compatible with predetermined ideological objectives.

A strategy for declining, or at least contradictorily-developing, economies in 'Italian' situations, from a Third World perspective, would challenge the 'modern' ideology of the PCI. Thus it should consider forming part of a national political class only if the class is committed and electorally answerable to a strategic economic policy. A second imperative is alliance with weaker, as well as with stronger, countries. Third, it should face the reality that Italy, unlike Third, as against Fourth, World countries, has no major resource but labour. It must therefore rely on an artificial socio-political stability provided by the whole working class, employed and unemployed, in or involuntarily outside the labour market, as bearers of all economic burdens and success.

It must therefore expound its criteria for encouraging

market, as against welfare, capitalism. It must come to terms with the fact that the working class in this scenario is not the subject of transition, but the motor which sustains its forward momentum as directed by the state class. The state cannot be a working-class state; it can only mediate between classes, become corporate and interclassist, or both. The working class is thus better served if the political class is not highly integrated and articulated, but internally competitive, even plural.

Italy has certain advantages, such as privileged links with the advanced capitalist world and successful experience of partial industrialization. It has expertise, and a climate of potentially informed and open debate. In this perspective it has the advantage of a working-class movement which is non-revolutionary and not easily instrumentalized. Even though the goal of modernity needs revision, it is still committed to civility and the progressive satisfaction of needs.

Italy has disadvantages, too, in addition to resource poverty. One is the openness of the economy, a result in part of that poverty. Ideological objectives conflict with the material possibilities of realizing them. Its dominant political class has not only been corrupt, it has been incapable of devising any strategy for economic development which made sense in market terms. Marxism points to a transition period with rising expectations. In reality, however, periods of transition may tend to lower them or make them more precarious, and for that reason the memory of the last capitalist boom is of exceptional importance for the Left. Transition too tends to rely on authoritarian, not spontaneous or ideological, optimism: Gramsci noted the American, Soviet and fascist responses to transition, the first no less authoritarian in its techniques of Taylorism than the latter two. Italy also forms part of the advanced industrial world, and this deep conviction is as true for the messianic marginals as for the liberal pluralists of the Socialist Party. It is therefore not psychologically prepared for a strategy to confront de-development, or of re-development from a restricted potential.

It would be easy to argue that the Italian case is of little significance to the debate on the collapse of capitalism, and that Italy has simply reached the limits of her resource base and become part of the capitalist periphery. Yet it is the inability to utilize the human resource base which is indeed typical of capitalism. Partial equilibrium may be re-established. Decline may be slowed, transition long. Yet it is possible to hope that the partial-equilibrium-decline phase will not be protracted past the historical objective of a more equitable system of distribution of resources.

The institutional Left has abandoned its messianic approach, but has not articulated a strategy which both envisages continued economic activity and presents social objectives and means of recasting or restoring social relations. Without this, it seems unlikely to develop an autonomous model of transition (productivism plus satisfaction of needs), a process of rapid economic recovery on the narrow basis of capitalist development, or even the possibility of autonomous political objectives. It is committed to maintaining a polity characterized by legal order, and a society committed to social equity. These principles are threatened not only by subjective political terrorism and objective marginal anomie, but by the competitive, corporate interest groups which increasingly make up the central social fabric. The barbarous alternative to socialism is no longer simply a rhetorical slogan, and its objectives of 'efficiency' and rationality can be pursued even by an ideologically 'mixed' political class. If the visionary goals of Marxism remain visions, the prospect of an administered barbarism must still appear a drastic alternative.

Marx managed to unite two scenarios of socialism which now, in conditions of decline, appear to be contradictory, or at least temporarily in conflict. One view is that the 'telos' of socialism is human liberation, and revolutionary mobilization through some such nexus as class-party-movement. The other postulates a socialism which is a system of equitable (that is, arbitrarily and bureaucratically determined) distribution of resources by the monopolists of political and planning resources. The 'telos' of this system may be surplus maximization, pre-'socialist' cultural or ideological goals (Soviet geopolitical aims, for example) or economic growth with reduced social conflictuality. Marx resolved the contrast between these two visions, the revolutionary-subversive and the bureaucratic-organized one in which the nexus is class-party-state, by having the workers freed from enforced capitalist labour first by their exploiters (maximum alienation, class war aimed at the elimination of living labour from the productive process), and then reconquering this alienated 'liberty' by expelling the capitalists and taking command of the robots the workers created and which had replaced them. Negri, of course, represents the subversive-revolutionary strand, and the PCI the bureaucratic-organized one, though both would claim 'in the last resort' that the two are not incompatible. However, it is hard to see that at this point Marxism still supplies a unitary theoretical case, or the possibility of political compromise between movement and party-state politics in which entry to the hierarchy of state institutions, not revolution from outside them, is the objective. That is why the success of either of these currents, or their relative degrees of success, is so important for the study of the varieties of socialism, and for the new composite, corporatist, state form.

NOTES

INTRODUCTION

1 For example, J.O'Connor, 'The Fiscal Crisis of the State', 1973; J.Habermas, 'Legitimation Crisis', 1975; K.Offe, 'Strukturprobleme des kapitalistischen Staats', 1972.
2 E.Mandel, 'The Second Slump: a Marxist Analysis of the Recession in the Seventies', London, NLB, 1978.
3 See C.Meillassoux, 'Anthropologie économique des Gouro de Côte d'Ivoire', Paris, Mouton, 1964; P.-P.Rey, 'Les Alliances de classes: sur l'articulation des modes de production', Paris, Maspero, 1973; B.Hindess and P.Hirst, 'Pre-capitalist Modes of Production', London, Routledge & Kegan Paul, 1975 (also their 'Modes of Production: an Auto-critique of Precapitalist Modes of Production', London, Macmillan, 1977).
4 Some would argue that the real problem in the Italian case is the immobility of the South, its dependency and rigidity when confronted with modernity, and with crisis.
5 See Giuseppe Vacca, Introduction to N.Poulantzas, ed., 'La crisi dello Stato', on the crisis as simultaneously present in ruling and ruled classes.
6 On marginality, see A.Bianchi, F.Granato and D.Zingarelli, eds, 'Marginalità e lotte dei marginali', Milan, F.Angeli, 1979.
7 Cf. Carlo Tullio-Altan and Roberto Cartocci, 'Modi di produzione e lotta di classe in Italia', Milan, ISEDI/ Mondadori, 1979.
8 For example, Antonio Negri, 'Marx oltre Marx', 1979.
9 Cf. John Low-Beer, 'Protest and Participation: the New Working Class in Italy', Cambridge University Press, 1978.

CHAPTER 1 CRISIS THEORY

1 See H.Grossmann, 'Saggi sulla teoria delle crisi: Dialettica e metodica nel "Capitale"', ed. Gabriella M.Bonacchi, Bari, De Donato, 1975; 'Il crollo del capitalismo: La legge dell'accumulazione e del crollo del sistema capitalista'; and his 'Marx: l'economia politica classica e il problema della dinamica' ('Marx: die klassische Nationalökonomie und das Problem der Dynamik' (1940)), Bari, Laterza, 1971. See too Roman Rozdolski, 'The Making of Marx's "Capital"' (note the comments on Rozdolski by Rafael Echeverria, Critique of Marx's 1957 'Introduction', 'Economy and Society', 7(4), November 1978). On rationality, see M.Godelier, 'Rationality and Irrationality in Economics', London, NLB, 1977, especially p.51. Note too Makoto Itoh, Production of Marx's Theory of Crisis, 'Science and Society', 42(2), summer 1978.

2 S.Amin, 'La crisi dell'imperialismo'.

3 See G.Vacca's Introduction to N.Poulantzas, ed., 'La crisi dello Stato'.

4 Rozdolski, op.cit., p.488.

5 Ibid., pp.521-2.

6 Ibid., pp.527 ff.

7 Ibid., pp.578-9. See too the articles by Marco Lippi and Guido Carandini, in Crisi della teoria economica e crisi del capitalismo, 'Quaderni di Problemi del socialismo', Milan, Angeli, 1976.

8 E.Mandel, 'Late Capitalism', London, NLB, 1975, p.155.

9 Ibid., p.571.

10 Ibid., p.575.

11 Amin, op.cit., p.41, and cf. E.Mandel, 'La crisi: Una risposta marxista alle congiunture attuali', Milan, La Salamandra, 1978, and his La natura della crisi economica attuale, in 'La crisi contemporanea' (Annual Register of Political Economy, ed. G.Folloni and Paolo Parra), Milan, Jaca Book, 1978.

12 Michio Moroshima, 'Marx's Economics: a Dual Theory of Value and Growth', Cambridge University Press (1978 edn), p.2.

13 Ibid., p.39.

14 Ibid., p.187.

15 See Bonacchi's introduction to Grossmann, 'Saggi', and Grossmann, 'Il crollo', p.558 ff.; Grossmann, 'Marx: l'economia politica', esp. pp.18-20.

16 Roberto Racinaro, 'La crisi del marxismo nella revisione di fine secolo', Bari, De Donato, 1978, p. 26. Cf. too Tito Perlini, Il ruolo della cosidetta

'teoria del crollo' nel pensiero di Rosa Luxemburg, 'Aut Aut', no.126, November-December, 1971, and Massimo Cacciari, Lavoro, valorizzazione, 'cervello sociale', 'Aut Aut', nos 145-6, January-April 1975.

17 P.Sweezy et al., 'The Theory of Capitalist Development', pp.190 ff.

18 E.g., the indices in Michael Kalecki, 'The Last Phase in the Transformation of Capitalism', New York, Monthly Review Press, 1972, pp.87,91.

19 See Sweezy, op.cit., and also 'La crisi degli anni '70 nel dibattito marxista', ed. Liliana Bàculo, Bari, De Donato, 1976. On the overproduction theory of crisis, see Paul Mattick, 'Marx and Keynes: the Limits of the Mixed Economy', pp.66-8,73-5. See also Karl Kautsky's 'Teoria della crisi', ed. Gianni Celato and Bruno Liverani, Florence, Guaraldi, 1976, and Alessandro Casiccia, Ideologia dei limiti dello sviluppo e ristrutturazione, 'Aut Aut', no.147, May 1975. Note too that it is less the rising proportion of fixed capital in relation to (falling) profits which hurts capital than its desire to eliminate living labour, especially the traditional working class, from production.

20 His edition of Friedrich Pollock, writing on tendencies to surmount the crisis and their political limits, has a useful introduction: Giacomo Marramao, ed., Friedrich Pollock, 'Teoria e prassi dell'economia di piano: Antologia degli scritti 1928-41', Bari, De Donato, 1973, and his 'Il politico e le trasformazioni: Critica del capitalismo e ideologie della crisi tra anni Venti e anni Trenta', Bari, De Donato, 1979. Notice too the introductions by L.Colletti and C.Napoleoni in 'Il futuro del capitalismo: Crollo o sviluppo?', Bari, Laterza, 1970.

21 Joseph M.Gillman, 'The Falling Rate of Profit', London, Dennis Dobson, 1957, e.g., chs 6 and 7. Note too the discussion of technological innovation in Ladislaus von Bortkiewicz, 'La teoria economica di Marx e altri saggi su Böhm-Bawerk, Walras e Pareto', ed. Luca Meldolesi, Turin, Einaudi, 1971.

22 C.Bettelheim, 'The Transition to Socialist Economy', p.16.

23 S.Amin, 'Sulla transizione', Milan, Jaca Book, 1978 edn. Note too his 'Unequal Development'.

24 M.Salvati, 'Note sulla analisi marxiana della crisi e del crollo', Milan, Giuffrè, 1977, p.176 ff.

25 A comprehensive statement of the PCI's new economic line of the late 1970s is in Carlo Guelfi, Caratteri generali della crisi: egemonia o cooperazione, and

G.C.Olmeda, Caratteri generali della crisi: i principali indicatori, 'Politica ed economia', no.5, September-October 1978.

26 Ibid., pp.9-11.

27 Nicos Poulantzas, 'L'Etat, le pouvoir, le socialisme', Paris, PUF, 1978, p.225 ff., and for his account of class composition, see his 'Political Power and Social Classes', London, NLB and Sheed & Ward, 1973.

28 Massimo Cacciari, 'Krisis: Saggio sulla crisi del pensiero negativo da Nietzsche a Wittgenstein', pp.25, 41.

29 Ibid., pp.32-53 and ch.2.

30 H.Lefebvre, 'The Survival of Capitalism', London, Allison & Busby, 1976, p.39.

31 J.Habermas, 'La crisi della razionalità nel capitalismo maturo', Bari Laterza, 1975, and especially in 'Legitimation Crisis'.

32 On leaving the review 'Il cerchio di gesso' in 1978.

33 Karl Polanyi, 'The Great Transformation', New York, Farrar & Rinehart, 1941, p.249, ff.

34 See Pier Aldo Rovatti, Irrazionalismo è una categoria politica, 'Aut Aut', no.161, September-October 1977, pp.3-9.

35 V.I.Lenin, 'Selected Works', vol.9, London, Lawrence & Wishart, 1938, p.447.

36 Karl Marx, 'Capital', vol.3, Moscow, Foreign Languages Publishing House, 1967, p.245.

37 A.Negri, in 'Manufattura, società borghese, ideologia' (with F.Borkenau and H.Grossmann, ed. P.Schiera), Rome, Savelli, 1978, p.138. The distinction here is actually made between bourgeois and capitalist revolution.

38 See Nicos Poulantzas's critique of the 'nouveaux philosophes' in 'L'Etat, le pouvoir, le socialisme'.

39 Reinhart Koselleck, 'Critica illuminista e crisi della società borghese', Bologna, Il Mulino, 1972 edn, p. 171.

40 See this notion in Gramsci, expanded in F.Bon and M.-A.Burnier, 'Les Nouveaux Intellectuels', Paris, Cujas & Seuil, 1971, pp.15 ff.

41 C.Lasch, 'The Culture of Narcissism', New York, Norton, 1978; Burton J.Bledstein, 'The Culture of Professionalism', New York, Norton, 1976.

42 A.Giddens, 'The Class Structure of the Advanced Societies', London, Hutchinson, 1973, pp.236,285. See too P.-R.Rey, 'Les Alliances de classes', Paris, Maspero, 1973.

43 See Mario Tronti, and the remarks made at the Bologna conference 'Politica e potere nella crisi italiana'

(February 1979). Tronti criticized the Left for retaining views of the economic crisis as spontaneous, and mistakenly responding with a (utopian) neo-liberal response - i.e., trying to return to a pre-crisis economy.

44 G.Cardechi, Reproduction of Social Classes at the Level of Production Relations, 'Economy and Society', 4(4), November 1975, p.404.

45 See Palmiro Togliatti, 'La politica culturale', ed. Luciano Gruppi, Rome, Editori Riuniti, 1974.

46 Bon and Burnier, op.cit., p.193.

47 Michel Foucault, 'Microfisica del potere', Turin, Einaudi, 1977, p.109.

48 Jean Baudrillard, 'Dimenticare Foucault', Bologna, Cappelli, 1977, p.84 ff.

49 Gianni Scalia, Al di là del 'politico', 'L'Arma Propria', 1, no.0, 1979, p.10.

50 Scalia, La cosa più importante, in 'Filosofi senza contratto', p.163 ff. See too André Glucksmann, 'Les Maîtres Penseurs', Paris, Grasset & Fasquelle, 1977.

CHAPTER 2 MODERNISM, TRADITIONALISM AND REFORMISM

1 See the discussion of David Beetham's articles ('Political Studies', 25, 1977) in R.J.Bennett, The Elite Theory as Fascist Ideology: a Reply to Beetham's Critique of Robert Michels, 'Political Studies', 26(4), December 1978, and Beetham's response in ibid.

2 Enrico Berlinguer, Il compromesso nella fase attuale, 'Rinascita', 24 August 1979. Note Leonardo Paggi's comments in Comunismo e riformismo, in ibid.

3 On social image, see F.G.Castles, 'The Social Democratic Image of Society', London, Routledge & Kegan Paul, 1978, though it emphasizes mainly policy and ideology.

4 See E.Ripepe, 'Gli elitisti italiani', vol.1: 'Mosca - Pareto - Michels', especially p.103.

5 Ibid., p.446.

6 Ibid., vol.2: 'Gobetti - Burzio - Dorso', p.564. See Gordon J. Di Renzo's study of 'traditional' political leadership, 'Personality, Power and Politics: a Social Psychological Analysis of the Italian Deputy and his Party System', Notre Dame University Press, 1967.

7 E.C.Banfield, 'Le basi morali di una società arretrata', ed. D. De Masi, Bologna, Il Mulino, 1976, reprinting critical comments on the original 'The Moral Basis of a Backward Society' (1958). The comment here is by Alessandro Pizzorno, p.243.

8 G.Mosca, 'Elementi di scienza politica', p.7 ('The Ruling Class' ('RC'), p.1).
9 Ibid., p.62 ('RC', p.40).
10 Ibid., p.78 ('RC', p.50).
11 Ibid., p.99 ('RC', p.64).
12 Ibid., p.154 ('RC', p.118).
13 Robert Michels, 'Political Parties', p.65.
14 Ibid., p.299. Cf. too, his 'power is always conservative', p.33.
15 Ibid., p.335. 'The struggle carried on by the socialists against the parties of the dominant classes is no longer one of principle, but simply one of competition', p.339.
16 Vilfredo Pareto, 'Trattato di sociologia generale', vol.2, p.623 (no.2178) ('The Mind and Society' ('MS'), vol.4, p.1515).
17 Ibid., pp.891-2 (no.2480) ('MS', pp.1791-4).
18 Ibid., p.1 (no.1397) ('MS', vol.3, p.885).
19 Ibid., p.530 (no.2029) ('MS', vol.3, p.1423).
20 Ibid., p.277 (no.1714) ('MS', vol.3, p.1164). See too Bobbio's introduction to the Italian edition.
21 Ibid., vol.1, p.691 (no.1152) ('MS', vol.3, p.685).
22 Maurice Halbwachs, 'Les Cadres sociaux de la mémoire', Paris, PUF, 1952, p.296.
23 Santino Caramella, 'Senso comune' and 'Teoria e pratica', Bari, Laterza, 1933, pp.3-4.
24 See my 'Introduction to the Thought of Galvano della Volpe', London, Lawrence & Wishart, 1977, and Lisa Mangoni, 'L'interventismo nella cultura', Bari, Laterza, 1974, p.339.
25 A point expressed vigorously by Gianni Scalia in J.Fraser and Franco Ferrarotti, 'PCI e intellettuali a Bologna', Naples, Liguori, forthcoming.
26 P.L.Berger and T.Luckmann, 'The Social Construction of Reality', New York, Anchor Books, 1967, p.1 and passim, esp. pp.24-7.
27 Werner Stark, 'The Sociology of Knowledge', London, Routledge & Kegan Paul, 1958, p.48.
28 Ibid., p.181.
29 The distinction is made by Clifford Geertz, Ideology as a Cultural System, in David Apter, ed., 'Ideology and Discontent', New York, Free Press, 1964, p.72.
30 Georges Gurvitch, 'The Social Frameworks of Knowledge', Oxford, Blackwell, 1971, pp.114 ff.
31 J.-P.Sartre, 'Search for a Method', New York, Knopf, 1963, p.6 ff.
32 Marvin Farber, 'Phenomenology and Existence: Toward a Philosophy within Nature', New York, Harper, 1967, p.27.

33 Alfred Schutz, On Multiple Realities, 'Philosophy and Phenomenological Research', 5(4), June 1945, p.543.
34 Ibid., pp.550-1.
35 Alfred Schutz, Tiresias, or our Knowledge of Future Events, in A.Brodersen, ed., 'Collected Papers', The Hague, Nijhoff, 1964, p.291.
36 Ibid., p.278. See too Florian Znaniecki, 'The Social Role of the Man of Knowledge', New York, Octagon, 1965, and Jacques Maquet, 'Sociologie de la connaissance', Louvain, E. Nauwelaerts, 1949.
37 See the discussion in Laura Balbo, Giuliana Chiaretti and Gianni Massironi, 'L'inferma scienza: Tre saggi sull'istituzionalizzazione della sociologia in Italia', Bologna, Il Mulino, 1975.
38 See Max Horkheimer's discussion of Vico and Machiavelli in 'Gli inizi della filosofia borghese della storia', Turin, Einaudi, 1978, esp. p.73.
39 In 1961-2.
40 Mario Tronti, in 'Operai e capitale', and Gramsci in 'Quaderni del carcere', p.2159.
41 Luigi Masella, 'Passato e presente nel dibattito storiografico: Storici marxisti e mutamento della società italiana', Bari, De Donato, 1979, Introduction.
42 C.Buci-Glucksmann, 'Gramsci et l'état', Paris, Fayard, 1975, pp.363-6.
43 It has also been suggested that his early productivism was seen by the Turin workers as contrary to their interests.
44 Lucio Magri, What is a Revolutionary Party, 'New Left Review', no.60, March-April 1970, p.114.
45 Mario Telò, Strategia consiliare e sviluppo capitalistico in Gramsci, 'Problemi del socialismo', no.2, 1976; Luis Razeto Migliaro and Pasquale Misuraca, 'Sociologia e marxismo nella critica di Gramsci'. On the Gramsci-Togliatti continuity, see Robert Paris's criticisms in 'A.Gramsci, Ecrits politiques', ed. R.Paris, Paris, Gallimard, 2 vols, 1974, 1975.
46 Op.cit., pp.232-3 ('Ordine nuovo', 21 February 1920).
47 Ibid., p.233.
48 Ibid., p.237 ff.
49 Ibid.
50 Migliaro and Misuraca, op.cit., p.104.
51 Ibid., p.107. Earlier in the 'Notebooks' Gramsci refers to a bureaucracy which becomes a caste, leading to popular demands for election of officials, which is 'extreme liberalism, and at the same time its dissolution', ibid., p.105. The end of a technical bureau-

cracy would mark the end of the state as an organization coercively determining the disposition of class forces at the political level. It remains ambiguous whether entry of the masses into the state is the Hegelian prelude to its dissolution, or the conquest of technique over the whole of civil society. The tying of bureaucratic to productive rationality links the proletariat of the modern state indissolubly to technical competence.

52 Ibid., p.107.
53 Ibid., pp.108,116.
54 Ibid., p.123.
55 A.Gramsci, 'Note sul Machiavelli', Turin, Einaudi, 1966, p.188.
56 A.Gramsci, 'Quaderni', pp.1171,1384.
57 Ibid., p.2139.
58 Ibid., p.2141.
59 Ibid., p.2146.
60 Ibid., pp.2146,1516,2171.
61 Ibid., pp.2158-80. He does wonder, however, if high wages are counterbalanced by poor conditions, pp. 2172-3.
62 Ibid., p.2157.
63 Ibid., pp.1312-3.
64 Ibid., pp.1281-2.
65 Ibid., pp.2141,2142-4.
66 Ibid., p.2179.
67 Ibid., p.388.
68 Ibid., p.1407. In this connection, he noted that 'the state is the instrument to adjust civil society to the economic structure, but the state must "want" to do that, that is, those leading the state should be representatives of the change which has occurred in the economic structure', p.1254. The notion of the *azienda-nazione* (enterprise-nation) appears on p.1259.
69 Ibid., p.956.
70 Ibid., pp.761-2.
71 Ibid., p.439.
72 Ibid.: 'Progress is an ideology, becoming is a philosophical conception.'
73 Ibid., p.1335.
74 Ibid., p.1348.
75 Ibid., pp.2010-34.
76 Ibid., pp.2038-9.
77 Ibid., p.1004.
78 Ibid., p.1604.
79 Ibid., p.2170.
80 Ibid., pp.1994-5,1757 ff., on the relation between stationary and progressive industries.

81 Ibid., pp.1519-21,2267.
82 Ibid., p.1521.
83 Ibid., p.1522.
84 Ibid., p.1532.
85 Ibid., p.1755.
86 Ibid., p.1756.
87 Ibid., pp.757-8.
88 Gerardo Chiaromente, La trama teorica di Togliatti, 'Rinascita', 6 February 1976, reviewing G.Vacca, 'Saggio su Togliatti e la tradizione comunista', Bari, De Donato, 1974.
89 Vacca, op.cit., p.393.
90 Ibid., p.395.
91 Ibid., p.396.
92 Ibid., pp.513-14.
93 Giorgio Bocca, 'Palmiro Togliatti', Bari, Laterza, 1973, pp.411-21.
94 P.Togliatti, 'Opere scelte', pp.112-55.
95 Ibid., pp.296-355.
96 Jon Halliday, Structural Reform in Italy: Theory and Practice, 'New Left Review', no.50, July-August 1968, esp. p.85 on Togliatti's scepticism regarding the capacity of the system to withstand the strain of reform.
97 Togliatti, op.cit., p.464.
98 Ibid., p.761.
99 Ibid., p.1162.
100 E.g., in Gianfranco Polillo, Sul 'modello di sviluppo' dell'economia italiana, 'Critica marxista', no.5, September-October 1975, p.71.
101 See for example A.Asor Rosa, 'Intellettuali e classe operaia', pp.581 ff., on Agnelli's paternalism. Note Giuseppe Berta, Olivetti e il movimento di Comunità: fra centrismo e centro-sinistra, 'Studi Storici', no.3, 1978, and Ettore Masucci, Imprenditore e operai in una grande industria moderna: la 'Olivetti di Ivrea', 'Quaderni di sociologia', no.38, 1960.
102 Umberto Cerroni, 'Crisi ideale e transizione al socialismo', Rome, Editori Riuniti, 1977, p.60.
103 Max Weber, 'Economia e società', vol.2, p.260 ('Economy and Society' ('E&S'), New York, Bedminster Press, 1968, vol.3, p.956).
104 Ibid., p.303 ('E&S', pp.990-1).
105 Ibid., p.698 ('E&S', p.1394).
106 Ibid., p.712.
107 Ibid., p.739.

CHAPTER 3 THE ITALIAN CRISIS

1 Carlo Donolo, 'Mutamento o transizione? Politica e società nella crisi italiana'; see too his Per l'analisi della crisi attuale, in 'Crisi economica e crisi delle istituzioni', Palermo, Edizioni Praxis, 1974.
2 Donolo, 'Mutamento', p.27 and passim.
3 Ibid., p.20.
4 Ibid., p.23.
5 Ibid., p.47.
6 Norberto Bobbio, Le radici della crisi italiana, 'Mondoperaio', no.4, April 1979, pp.5,9-10.
7 Gerardo Chiaromonte, La crisi italiana, 'Critica marxista', nos 3-4, May-August 1973, p.4.
8 Chiaromonte was commenting on P.Sylos Labini, Sviluppo economico e classi sociali in Italia, 'Quaderni di sociologia', no.4, March 1973.
9 Chiaromonte, op.cit., pp.5-7.
10 Ibid., p.14.
11 Alfredo Reichlin, Centralità della questione meridionale, 'Critica marxista', no.2, March-April 1973, p.3.
12 Ibid.
13 Chiaromonte, op.cit., p.23.
14 Giorgio Napolitano, Pericolo di destra e svolta democratica: Considerazioni sulla crisi italiana, dopo il 'golpe' cileno, 'Critica marxista', no.5, September-October 1973; Giorgio Amendola, La classe operaia nel decennio 1961-71, 'Critica marxista', no.6, November-December 1973.
15 See the comments of the experience of the centre-Left in relation to the PCI in the 1970s, in Giuliano Amato, Quella cosa che il PCI non vuol capire, 'L'Espresso', 22 July 1979.
16 Danilo Zolo, Democrazia corporativa, produzione del consenso, socialismo, 'Problemi del socialismo', 19(9), January-March 1978, pp.117-19, now in Luigi Ferrajoli and Danilo Zolo, 'Democrazia autoritaria e capitalismo maturo', Milan, Feltrinelli, 1978.
17 Zolo, op.cit., commenting on the PCI operaisti, p.120.
18 Ibid., pp.121-2.
19 Ibid., pp.126-9.
20 Ibid., pp.129-31.
21 Ibid. For example, see the criticism by Vacca that the movement from 'organized democracy' to the autonomy of the political was essentially a concentration of decision-making power, ibid., pp.134-5.
22 Ibid., p.135.

23 Ibid., pp.136-47.
24 Ibid., p.150.
25 Michele Salvati, L'origine della crisi in corso, 'Aut Aut', no.46, March 1972; Carlo Donolo, Sviluppo ineguale e disgregazione sociale: Note per l'analisi delle classi nel Meridione, 'Aut Aut', no.47, July 1972.
26 Donolo, Sviluppo, p.102.
27 Ibid., p.104.
28 The process of growth and autonomous adaptation is described in the collective volume 'Gli anni della conflittualità permanente'.

CHAPTER 4 SOCIAL 'DISINTEGRATION' AND ADAPTATION

1 Francesco Ciafaloni, Il movimento operaio e la crisi economica, 'Quaderni piacentini', no.55, May 1975, p.3.
2 Paolo Sylos Labini, 'Saggio sulle classi sociali'. The argument was first aired in 1972.
3 Ibid., p.xii.
4 Ibid., pp.38-9.
5 For example, N.Gallo, Solo il reddito definisce le classi?, 'Rinascita', 3 January 1975. The 'Saggio' was discussed for six months in 'Rinascita', starting with G.Chiaromonte's Una 'quasi-classe' tra borghesi e proletari, 'Rinascita', 27 December 1974.
6 Sylos Labini, op.cit., pp.44,50-5.
7 Ibid., pp.66-89.
8 Ibid., p.83 ff., 121-2.
9 G.Chiaromonte, I ceti medi possono contribuire al rinnovamento, 'Rinascita', 27 June 1976.
10 Aris Accornero and Fabrizio Carmignani, La composizione della classe operaia italiana, 'Critica marxista', no.2, 1978, p.130.
11 Ibid., pp.92-5,126-8.
12 Fabrizio Carmignani, La classe operaia anni '70 nelle principali ricerche, 'Congiuntura sociale' (Cespe/PCI), no.1, January 1978.
13 Ibid., p.9.
14 Aris Accornero and Chiara Sebastiani, Mutamenti nella struttura sociale italiana 1968-1978, 'Congiuntura sociale', no.10, October 1978, pp.7 ff. This speaks of the tendency to a non-antagonistic relation between the workers' bloc and the 'public bloc', p.11. See their Le principali trasformazioni sociali, 'Politica ed economia', no.6, December 1978, p.18.
15 See Mario Dal Co et al., Rivelazione Istat sulle forze

di lavoro, 'Congiuntura sociale', nos 5-6, May-June 1977.

16 Franco Cassano, Teoria del blocco storico e ricomposizione del lavoro nel capitalismo maturo, in 'Marxismo e filosofia in Italia, 1958-1971', Bari, De Donato, 1973, p.75. See too the discussion in 'Aut Aut' in 1976 on productive and unproductive labour, manual and intellectual labour, and Maria Grazia Meriggi, Le classi sociali nello sviluppo e nella crisi capitalistica: Terziarizzazione e ricomposizione di classe: Una proposta di discussione, 'Aut Aut', no.151, January-February 1976.

17 C.Donolo, Oltre il '68: La società italiana tra mutamento e transizione, 'Quaderni piacentini', nos 60-1, October 1976, for the critique of Stame. Notice too his Istituzioni, società e movimento sindacale dentro la crisi italiana, 'Quaderni' of 'Rassegna sindacale', no.58, January-February 1976, and his important article Struttura sociale, disgregazione e istituzioni nel Mezzogiorno, 'Rassegna sindacale', no.71, March-April 1978, from which the quotation is taken, pp.106-7. Note too the contribution of A. Bagnasco, 'Tre Italie', and Ermanno Gorrieri's pioneering 'La giungla retributiva', to which passing reference has been made. An interesting study of the use and misuse of data by Istat is Enrica Guglielmotto's and Antonella Martina's 'I conti non tornano', Turin, Einaudi, 1979.

18 There are many empirical studies on social structure, regional (especially Southern) development, and interpretation of the relation between social stratification and politics, the submerged economy and the pathology of the labour market. Intervention, however, seems to have no alternatives between an intolerable interference with civil and corporate liberties, or risk of further legitimacy crisis if it fails. Cf. M.D'Antonio's discussion of schools of thought and policy implications in 'Sviluppo e crisi del capitalismo italiano, 1951-1972'.

19 Carlo Trigilia, Sviluppi della ricerca sulla struttura di classe italiana e prospettive, Rome, Cespe, April 1977. See too Francesco Apergi, Per una riconstruzione critica della sociologia italiana: il caso di 'La critica sociologica', in 'La critica sociologica di Franco Ferrarotti', ed. M.Lelli, Rome, Savelli, 1976, and Sulle origini di una sociologia marxista in Italia: il caso dei 'Quaderni rossi', 'Critica marxista', no.1, 1978.

20 Alberto Asor Rosa, 'Le due società: Ipotesi sulla crisi italiana'.

21 Ibid., Introduction, p.viii.
22 Ibid., Gli intellettuali e la Repubblica, p.81.
23 Ibid., Le due società, p.64.
24 Ibid., pp.65-6.
25 Terrorismo e stato della crisi, 'La questione criminale', no.1, 1979.
26 Camillo Pellizzi, La cosidetta crisi, 'Rassegna italiana di sociologia', no.3, July-September 1978, p.369.
27 Note too its project reports and publications, such as the 'Quindicinale di note e commenti'.
28 'Rapporto sulla situazione del paese', vol.1: 'Rapporto generale', Rome, CNEL/Censis, 1968, p.iii.
29 Ibid., p.xii ff.
30 'Rapporto sulla situazione sociale del paese', Milan, Censis/Angeli, 1970: 'Considerazioni generali', pp. 9-10 (on 1968).
31 Ibid., p.10.
32 Ibid., pp.11-3.
33 Ibid., p.15.
34 Ibid., p.21.
35 'Rapporto sulla situazione sociale del paese', vol.1: 'Considerazioni generali', Rome, CNEL/Censis, 1970, p.12 (on 1969).
36 See for example, the disjuncture between 'social reality and the current political debate' and 'the consequent profound difficulty in bringing a new collective consciousness to maturity', and 'the continuing practical impossibility of a rational, long-term solution to the more or less explicit tensions' in the present situation. Ibid., p.15.
37 Ibid., p.13.
38 'Rapporto sulla situazione sociale del paese: Considerazioni generali', Rome CNEL/Censis, 1971, pp.15-16 (on 1970).
39 'Rapporto sulla situazione sociale del paese: Considerazioni generali', Rome, CNEL/Censis, 1972, p.11 (on 1971). However, despite 'open pessimism', there are curious phenomena such as the hidden pressure of economic growth and a rise in personal savings, pp. 7-8.
40 Ibid., p.15.
41 'Rapporto sulla situazione sociale del paese: Considerazioni generali', Rome, CNEL/Censis, 1973, p.9 (on 1972).
42 Ibid., pp.16 ff.
43 Ibid., p.24.
44 'Rapporto sulla situazione sociale del paese', vol.1, Rome, CNEL/Censis, 1975, pp.1-3 (on 1974).

45 Ibid., p.10.
46 Ibid., p.12.
47 Ibid., p.15.
48 Ibid., pp.18 ff.
49 Ibid., p.24.
50 'Rapporto sulla situazione sociale del paese 1975-6', vol.1, Rome, CNEL/Censis, 1976, p.4.
51 Ibid., p.16.
52 Ibid., p.20.
53 'Rapporto sulla situazione sociale del paese', Rome, CNEL/Censis, 1977, pp.13-14 (on 1976).
54 Ibid., pp.14-15.
55 Ibid., p.16.
56 Ibid., p.18.
57 Ibid., pp.19-20.
58 Ibid., p.31.
59 'Rapporto sulla situazione sociale del paese', Rome, CNEL/Censis, 1978, p.11 (on 1977).
60 Ibid., pp.13-16.
61 Ibid., p.24.
62 Ibid., pp.32-5.
63 Ibid., p.68. The report for 1978 seemed to accept the end of the effectiveness of the state and of politics as establishing a stable condition of 'neither calm nor anxiety', a 'molecular stabilization'; 'Rapporto sulla situazione sociale del paese', Rome, Censis, 1979, p.15.
64 Max Horkheimer, Lo Stato autoritario, in 'La società di transizione', Turin, Einaudi, 1979, p.23.
65 Luigi Berlinguer, Democrazia ed efficienza, unità e autonomia nello sviluppo istituzionale del paese, 'Critica marxista', nos 4-5, 1977, p.30.
66 Umberto Minopoli, A proposito del nuovo estremismo: autonomia, bisogni e individualismo radicale, 'Critica marxista', no.2, 1977, pp.67-9. Minopoli links his analysis to the work of Heller, Tronti and Negri. Luigi Berlinguer's analysis of 'extremism' concentrates on the journal 'Critica del diritto' (he edits the PCI's legal-political review, 'Democrazia e diritto').
67 Berlinguer, op.cit. This article is an important statement on the nature of the change in the nature of the state in relation to the working class, and the possibility of starting to plan by means of the state, given a new articulation between workers' organizations and the state.
68 Ibid., pp.64-5.
69 Cf. Vittorio de Matteis, L'ideologia di Comunione e Liberazione, 'Critica marxista', nos 5-6, 1977. The

1977 issues of 'Critica marxista' are an impressive attempt to provide theoretical justification and a basis for a social explanation of the policy of the insertion or association of the working class in the state.

70 Marco Eller Vainicher, La questione del terziario e la crisi italiana, 'Critica marxista', no.1, 1977.

71 Franco Cassano, Il caso italiano: patologia del 'ritardo' o 'anticipazione'? Riflessioni su 'Masse e potere' di Pietro Ingrao, 'Critica marxista', no.2, 1977.

72 Vainicher, op.cit., p.60.

73 Cassano, op.cit., p.37.

74 Biagio de Giovanni, Intellettuali e potere, 'Critica marxista', no.6, 1977, p.25.

75 Mario Tronti, Politica e potere, 'Critica marxista', no.3, 1978, p.32.

76 Ibid., pp.33-4.

77 P.Bassi and A.Pilati, 'I giovani e la crisi degli anni settanta', p.82 and passim.

78 For example in the round table on La questione giovanile, in 'Rinascita', 30 May 1975.

79 Cf. Romano Luperini, 'Il PCI e il movimento studentesco', Milan, Jaca Book, 1969, p.17. See too G. Chiarante, 'La rivolta degli studenti', Rome, Editori Riuniti, 1968.

80 See 'Riforma e democrazia nella scuola', Rome, Editori Riuniti, 1973.

81 Gianfranco Borghini, in 'Scuola e socialismo', Rome, Editori Riuniti, 1971, p.109 (proceedings of the Conferenza nazionale del PCI per la scuola, Bologna, February 1971). See too Rossana Rossanda, 'L'anno degli studenti', Bari, De Donato, 1968; Alberto Asor Rosa, 'Intellettuali e classe operaia'.

82 Cf. Giuseppe Vacca, ed., 'PCI, Mezzogiorno e intellettuali dalle alleanze all'organizzazione', Bari, De Donato, 1973.

83 Among the many books and reports issued by the PCI on education after 1968, note Giovanni Berlinguer, Per la ripresa del movimento nelle università, speech to the PCI-FGCI Convegno, Ariccia, 14-16 November 1969, and Giorgio Napolitano, Iniziativa del PCI e confronto aperto per la riforma della scuola e dell'Università (for the PCI Central Committee, April 1969).

84 Per la ripresa, p.7.

85 School of Barbiana, 'Letter to a Teacher', Penguin Books, 1970, p.46.

86 See Giovanni Berlinguer, I comunisti per l'università, 'Critica marxista', no.1, 1971.

87 The realization that democratization of the educational system was not preventing its structural decay is clear in Crisi politica e riforma dell'università (regional conference for Lazio, 1974), published by Editori Riuniti, Rome, 1975. See too the FGCI journal, 'Nuova generazione'.
88 Editorial, 'Angelus novus', no.11, spring 1968.
89 See J.Fraser and F.Ferrarotti, 'PCI e intellettuali a Bologna', Naples, Liguori, forthcoming.
90 See my 'L'intellettuale amministrativo nella politica del PCI', Naples, Liguori, 1977.
91 On the recasting of the PCI's cultural policy in 1965-6. see 'Il contemporaneo/Rinascita' for those years. See too Valerio Castronovo and Nicola Tranfaglia, eds, 'La stampa italiana del neo-capitalismo', Bari, Laterza, 1976, on one aspect of the growth of the cultural industry.
92 Furio Cerutti, Lavoro produttivo e improduttivo, 'Quaderni piacentini', no.43, April 1971.
93 See Scuola, qualificazione, qualifiche e ciclo produttivo (Centro Carlo Marx di Torino), 'Nuovo impegno', no.31, autumn-winter 1970-1.
94 The phrase was Giovanni Berlinguer's.
95 See Gian Paolo Prandstraller, Il potere degli intellettuali, 'Rinascita', 16 May 1964.
96 See Franco Fortini, 'Dieci inverni', Bari, De Donato, 1973 (first published 1957). The notion of the 'autonomy' of culture becomes that of its 'separateness-isolation'. For Fortini, reconnection with society is not through a technical, productive process, but through politics. See too Gian Paolo Prandstraller, 'Intellettuali e democrazia', Rome, Edizione dell'Ateneo, 1963.
97 Note the change in Gianni Scalia's views, discussed in the previous chapter, as compared with his identification of the revolutionary subject in intellectual labour power, in La forza-lavoro intellettuale, 'Classe e stato', no.1, autumn 1965.
98 Marzio Barbagli, 'Disoccupazione intellettuale e sistema scolastico in Italia', Bologna, Il Mulino, 1974, p.323.
99 Mario Sentorrino and Simonetta Piccone-Stella, 'Laurea e sottosviluppo: Il mercato del lavoro intellettuale nel Mezzogiorno', Bari, De Donato, 1974, p.15. See too Simonetta Piccone-Stella, 'Intellettuali e capitale nella società italiana del dopoguerra', Bari, De Donato, 1972.
100 A.Asor Rosa, 'Scrittori e popolo: Saggio sulla letteratura populista in Italia', Rome, Samonà e Savelli, 1965.

101 Historically, literary intellectuals were both attracted and repelled by the idea that the cultural industry would make them 'technicians', and that they would thus enter the vanguard of the new working class both as communications experts and dependent workers. See Pio Baldelli, 'Politica culturale e comunicazioni di massa', Pisa, Nistri-Lischi, 1968; Romano Luperini, 'Marxismo e intellettuali', Padua, Marsilio, 1974; Franco Fortini, 'Verifica dei poteri', Milan, Il Saggiatore, 1965.

102 For example in Rossana Rossanda, Politica e cultura, 'Rinascita', 30 January 1965, and also her Le Ragioni della cultura, 'Il contemporaneo/Rinascita', 27 February 1965, and Unità politica e scelte culturali, 'Il contemporaneo/Rinascita', 28 August 1965.

103 In estimating the size of the margin, Istat's method of analysing data becomes crucial. See Margherita Totaro and Ottavio Andolina, L'andamento dell'occupazione in Italia 1970-77: un'analisi per settori, and the conclusion, Nota del Cespe sulla maggiorazione Istat ai conti economici nazionali, 'Congiuntura sociale', no.4, April 1979.

104 I.e., the consequences of neglecting science, or the difficulty of appropriating it for the working class, in Giovanni Berlinguer, 'Politica della scienza: Il movimento operaio e la rivoluzione scientifico-tecnologica', Rome, Editori Riuniti, 1970.

105 E.Scalfari and G.Turani, 'Razza padrona: Storia della borghesia di stato'.

106 Franco Cerase and Fiamma Calvosa, 'La nuova piccola borghesia', Venice, Marsilio, 1976, p.151.

107 Antonio Mutti and Paolo Segatti, 'La borghesia di Stato', Milan, Mazzotta, 1977, p.21 ff. See too G. Galli and A.Nannei, 'Il capitalismo assistenziale'.

108 See Luciano Barca, in Silvano Andriani and Luciano Violante, eds, 'Le evasioni fiscali', Bari, De Donato, 1979, on tax evasion as the most glaring aspect of state welfare capitalism, p.5.

109 Arcangelo Leone De Castris, Intellettuali e Stato: profilo di una crisi, 'Rinascita', 27 December 1976.

110 For example, in a 1975 PCI document, Note e dati statistici sui ceti intellettuali, intellectuals were described as 'in formation', 'employed' and 'unemployed'.

111 Norberto Bobbio, 'Politica e cultura', Turin, Einaudi, 1955.

112 G.Napolitano, Gli intellettuali comunisti nell' attuale scontro politico e di classe, 'Rinascita', 16 January 1970.

113 A.W.Gouldner, Prologue to a Theory of Revolutionary Intellectuals, 'Telos', no.26, winter 1975-6. This argues that intellectuals assume leadership of popular revolutions in the interests of the masses and 'rationality' because of their 'greater speech repertoire'.
114 See Pier Aldo Rovatti, Intellettuali e compromesso storico, 'Aut Aut', no.147, May-June 1975, and on this theme in general, Gian Carlo Ferretti, 'L'autocritica dell'intellettuale', Padua, Marsilio, 1970.
115 See the argument of Marcello Lelli, 'Tecnici e lotta di classe', Bari, De Donato, 1971.
116 See Antonio Giolitti, Riforme e sviluppo: per superare la crisi in una prospettiva di progresso sociale e civile, in a Socialist Party Convegno, Rome, 17-19 May 1973, commenting on Federico Caffè.
117 Giolitti, in ibid. Other contributors to the Convegno were Luigi Spaventa, Paolo Sylos Labini, Lucio Izzo, Francesco Forte, Nino Andreatta and Giorgio Ruffolo.
118 See Bassi and Pilati, op.cit.

CHAPTER 5 THE 'ARMED PARTY'

1 The latter case is made by Sabino S.Acquaviva, 'Guerriglia e guerra rivoluzionaria in Italia', Milan, Rizzoli, 1979, and Franco Ferrarotti, 'Le radici della violenza', Milan, Rizzoli, 1978.
2 Cf. the editorial committee's conclusion to Oreste Scalzone's Lotta armata, movimento e dibattito nella sinistra, 'Pre-print', no. 2(i), June 1979.
3 See A.Negri, 'Marx oltre Marx'.
4 See 'La Repubblica', 25 July 1979. The authorship and authenticity of the document were not established.
5 Giorgio Bocca, 'Il terrorismo italiano 1970-78', Milan, Rizzoli, 1978, p.16.
6 Ibid., p.21.
7 'Paese Sera', 24 February 1979.
8 Ottavio Cecchi, I piccoli titani della spranga facile, 'Rinascita', 30 March 1979.
9 For example, Roberto Fabiani, Quondo la mala si allea coi terroristi, 'L'Espresso', 4 March 1979.
10 See Giorgio Bocca's comment that terrorism in Genoa was widely believed to be financed by the Right, 'La Repubblica', 6 April 1979.
11 Mario Tronti, Il maggio 9 fu una svolta: come rispondere, 'Paese Sera', 9 May 1979.

12 See Paolo Franchi, Queste le tesi dei capi di Autonomia, 'Paese Sera', 9 April 1979.
13 Fabio Mussi, Una generazione che deve battersi per neutralizzare i suoi fanatici, 'Rinascita', 30 March 1979.
14 Note Lidia Menapace's argument that 'Autonomia operaia' chose to initiate violence at a level much lower than that suggested by the analysis of its problems, and Stame's remarks that opportunism and maximalism are always signs of a 'pessimistic and fatalistic conception of man', both in 'Sulla violenza', Rome, Savelli, 1978, pp.xvii,85. A useful discussion of the varieties of 'autonomia' is contained in Gabriele Martignoni and Sergio Morandini, 'Il diritto all'odio - Dentro: fuori: ai bordi dell'area dell' autonomia', Verona, Bertani, 1977.
15 Angelo Bolaffi, Le varianti del partito armato, 'Rinascita', 20 April 1979. See too Massimo Cacciari, Negri, un compagno perduto nel '68, 'La Repubblica', 10 April 1979.

CHAPTER 6 STRATEGY FOR DECLINE

1 Note the paradox of Michael A.Ledeen's observation, 'The Italians do not believe their country is in crisis', 'Italy in Crisis', Sage, Beverly Hills, 1977, p.71. There are many reasons for denying the existence of crisis.
2 Un bilancio dell'economia italiana negli ultimi cinque anni, 'Bollettino Cespe', no.15, February 1968, pp. 4-5.
3 Ibid., p.6.
4 Ibid., p.7, 'Only in a phase of strong dynamism is it possible to carry out the necessary modifications to the economic mechanism without meeting with too-high costs.'
5 Ibid., p.9.
6 Luciano Barca, Franco Botta and Alberto Zevi, 'I comunisti e l'economia italiana 1944-1974', Bari, De Donato, 1975, pp.14-16. Note too the various periodizations, economic and political, in Barca's contribution.
7 Ibid., p.25.
8 Ibid., pp.25-8.
9 Barca mentions 1970 as the crucial year in the PCI's 'organic design'.
10 See Francesco Forte, ed., 'Dibattito: il progetto '80', Naples, Guida, 1970, pp.27 ff.

11 See Giorgio Napolitano, A che punto è la crisi, 'Rinascita', 9 May 1975, which sees no end to the crisis, but views it as composed of a series of minor recoveries and sectoral difficulties. See too Paolo Forcellini, Crisi e ripresa produttiva, 'Politica ed economia', nos 1-2, January-April, 1979.
12 Franco Ferrarotti criticized the non-Marxist categories used by two of Cespe's investigators of class structure in 'Rinascita', 12 January 1979.
13 Gerardo Chiaromonte, Note sulla linea di politica economica del PCI, 'Politica ed economia', no.3, November-December 1970, p.8.
14 Ibid., p.16.
15 Giorgio Amendola, Crisi economica e crisi politica, 'Politica ed economia', no.4, July-August 1971, p.3.
16 Antonio Pesenti tried to maintain continuity of analysis with the 1960s, for example in Crisi monetaria e crisi del capitalismo, 'Politica ed economia', no.5, September-October 1971, p.16.
17 Eugenio Peggio, Tassi di sviluppo, produttività, programmazione democratica, 'Politica ed economia', no.1, January-February 1971, p.3.
18 Peggio's case, expressed in 'Politica ed economia', may be found in the articles and contributions: Crisi economica: dove porta la svolta a destra?, no.4, July-August 1972; Come uscire dalla crisi (a round table discussion with Barca, Sylos Labini, Antonio Giolitti and G.Bodrato), nos 1-2, January-April 1973; Come fronteggiare la crisi economica (a discussion with Barca, Ugo La Malfa, Giorgio Amendola, Andreatta and Lombardini), no.1, January-February 1974, and La crisi economica al punto cruciale, nos 2-3, June 1974.
19 Giorgio Amendola, Elezioni politiche e crisi economica, 'Politica ed economia', nos 1-2, January-April 1972, pp.6-7.
20 Gerardo Chiaromonte, Questioni della crisi nel mondo e nell'Italia, 'Politica ed economia', no.6, December 1974, p.10. See in the same issue Eugenio Peggio, La piccola e media industria nella crisi italiana.
21 Peggio, in Come fronteggiare la crisi, pp.14-15.
22 Ibid., p.15.
23 Eugenio Peggio, Per salvare il paese: governo di unità nazionale e democratica, 'Politica ed economia', nos 2-3, March-June 1976, p.7.
24 Giorgio Amendola, La crisi economica mondiale e l'Italia, 'Politica ed economia', no.5, September-October 1974, pp.7-9.
25 Luciano Soriente, Crisi generale del capitalismo e crisi ciclica, 'Politica ed economia', nos 1-2, January-April 1975.

26 Giorgio Amendola, Stato di allarme per la crisi economica, 'Politica ed economia', no.4, July-August 1975, p.7.
27 Eugenio Peggio, 'La crisi economica italiana', Milan, Rizzoli, 1976, p.10. Note the Convegni Crisi economica e condizionamenti internazionali dell'economia italiana (Cespe, 1976) and Il capitalismo italiano e l'economia internazionale (Cespe and Istituto Gramsci, 1970) and Peggio's 'Capitalismo italiano anni '70', Rome, Editori Riuniti, 1970.
28 Peggio, 'La crisi', pp.101-2.
29 'Proposta di progetto a medio termine', Rome, Editori Riuniti, 1977, p.19.
30 Ibid., p.54.
31 'I problemi dell'economia italiana: Superamento della crisi e nuove prospettive di sviluppo sociale', Rome, ed. Cinque Lune, 1973 (Christian Democratic Convegno, December 1972): Siro Lombardini, I problemi dell' economia italiana: Superamento della crisi, p.29.
32 Ibid., p.30.
33 Ibid., p.34.
34 Ibid., pp.46 ff. Lombardini argues that the failure was due to wrong policies, not structural weakness. He saw the Christian Democrats as divided between the De Gasperi and Dossetti approaches, with the latter ultimately the weaker.
35 Pasquale Saraceno, Le radici della crisi, 'Il Mulino', 25, no.243, January-February 1976, p.12.
36 Ibid., pp.16-17.
37 Ibid., p.23. On points of similarity between Christian Democratic and PCI positions, see G.Galli and A.Nannei, 'Il capitalismo assistenziale'.
38 Carlo Donolo, Per l'analisi politica della crisi attuale, in 'Crisi economica e crisi delle istituzioni', Palermo, Praxis, 1974, p.140.
39 Cesare Donnhauser-Florio, in ibid., p.8. See in the same volume Giuseppe Ugo Rescigno, Nascita e morte della programmazione in Italia.
40 Cf. Ricciotti Antinolfi, 'La crisi economica italiana 1969-73', Bari, De Donato, 1973. See too the supplement to 'Inchiesta', no.6, July-August 1979, criticizing the utopianism of Baffi's neo-liberalism.
41 Gisele Podbielski, 'Italy: Development and Crisis in the Post-war Economy', Oxford University Press, 1974, pp.21-2.
42 Guido Carli, 'Intervista sul capitalismo italiano', ed. Eugenio Scalfari, Bari, Laterza, 1977, passim and pp.11-13.
43 Cf. A.Graziani, Aspetti strutturali dell'economia

italiana nell'ultimo decennio, in Graziani, ed., 'Crisi e ristrutturazione nell'economia italiana'.

44 M.D'Antonio, 'Sviluppo e crisi del capitalismo italiano 1951-1972', p.11.

45 Ibid., pp.127 ff., and pp.152 ff. D'Antonio argues: 'Italian development is characterized by a relative underaccumulation of capital, which is a constant feature of the last twenty years and has taken on more marked characteristics in comparison with the other two countries with high rates of development (West Germany and Japan), especially in the 1960s', p.38.

46 Criticized by Chiara Sebastiani, in Gabriella Pinnarò, ed., 'L'Italia socio-economica 1976-7', Rome, Editori Riuniti, 1978, pp.40 ff.

47 P.Forcellini, 'Rapporto sull'industria italiana', p.36. This emphasizes the undercurrent of restructuring despite, for example, the fall in investment.

48 M.Salvati, 'Il sistema economico italiano: analisi di una crisi', pp.56-7 ff.

49 P.Sylos Labini, Prezzi e distribuzione del reddito nell'industria manufatturiera (1977), from 'Dispense Integrative' (Facoltà di scienze statistiche, demografiche e attuariali, Rome), pp.53-4. See too G.Fuà, ed., 'Il "Modellaccio": Modello dell'economia italiana elaborato dal gruppo di Ancona', vol.1: 'Il quadro generale', Milan, Angeli, 1976.

50 Augusto Graziani, La teoria della distribuzione del reddito (September, 1978), paper prepared for a University of Pavia conference on 'Economisti e politici: scelte politiche e teoria politica in Italia, 1945-1978'.

51 Eugenio Peggio, Bilancio di un decennio: la crisi italiana 1968-1978, 'Politica ed economia', no.6, December 1978. Recovery was predominantly in external demand.

52 Ibid., p.8.

53 Cf. estimates prepared by Censis (50-60 billion lire, half exported), by Frey of Ceres (about 27 billion lire, 3m. people involved) and Alvaro of Rome University (5-6m. people in second or 'black' jobs). Istat made no estimate. 'Il Messaggero', 10 February 1979.

54 Augusto Graziani, Le tre Italie, 'Quaderni piacentini', nos 65-6, February 1978. Graziani did not suggest this would necessarily be effective.

55 Napoleone Colajanni, 'Programmare in Italia', Bari, De Donato, 1979, p.8.

56 Ibid,m p.75 and passim.

57 Ibid., p.180.

58 Pietro Alessandrini, ed., 'Retribuzioni, produttività e prezzi', Bologna, Il Mulino, 1979: this refers to the possibility of replacing the pre-modern units with those of a higher technological level. However, the submerged economy in the South is largely commercial, and would require complete transformation. See too Augusto Graziani and Enrico Pugliese, eds, 'Investimenti e disoccupazione nel Mezzogiorno', Bologna, Il Mulino, 1979, and the volume 'La piccola impresa nell'economia italiana', Bari, De Donato, 1978.
59 'Proposta di progetto a medio termine', p.55.
60 Ermanno Gorrieri, 'La giungla retributiva'. The late 1978 upturn was discovered early in 1979.
61 They are confusing because, though they show the rates of growth, they do not show the relative sizes of local economies: Aris Accornero, La mappa dello sviluppo, 'Rinascita', 23 March 1979.
62 Cf. G.Chiaromonte, 'Un piano per il Mezzogiorno', Rome, Editori Riuniti, 1971; Silvano Andriani, Il Mezzogiorno nell'economia italiana: analisi e tendenze, in 'Il Mezzogiorno nell'economia italiana', Rome, Cespe, 1979, and Giovanni Papapietro, Il Mezzogiorno nella crisi italiana, 'Critica marxista', nos 3-4, May-August 1974.
63 Ministero del Bilancio e della Programmazione economica, 'Documento programmatico preliminare per l'impostazione del programma 1971-1975, obiettivi e risultati del programma 1966-1970', discussed in Gianfranco Polillo, Sul 'modello di sviluppo' dell'economia italiana, 'Critica marxista', no.5, September-October 1975, p.49.
64 Banca d'Italia, Assemblea generale ordinaria dei partecipanti, Rome, 1962, on the previous year, p.384.
65 Ibid., pp.388,412.
66 Ibid., Rome, 1963, p.469.
67 Ibid., Rome, 1964, p.475.
68 Ibid., Rome, 1965, p.467.
69 Ibid., Rome, 1966, p.430.
70 Ibid., p.435.
71 Ibid., Rome, 1967, p.371.
72 Ibid., Rome, 1968, passim.
73 Ibid., Rome, 1969, p.367.
74 Ibid., Rome, 1970, p.405.
75 Ibid., Rome, 1971, passim.
76 Ibid., Rome, 1972, p.7.
77 Ibid., pp.77-8.
78 Ibid., p.366.
79 Ibid., p.378.
80 Ibid., Rome, 1973, p.379.

81 Ibid., p.381.
82 Ibid., Rome, 1974, pp.413 and passim. On the relations between balance of payments, borrowing, lira devaluation and the second oil crisis, see pp.209 ff.
83 Ibid., p.415.
84 Ibid., Rome, 1975, p.437.
85 Ibid., p.439.
86 Ibid., Rome, 1976, pp.428-9.
87 Ibid., Rome, 1978, p.391.
88 Ibid., p.395.
89 On the balance of payments, see G.Basevi and A.Soci, 'La bilancia dei pagamenti italiani', Bologna, Il Mulino, 1978. On the differential effects of inflation and price reduction, see Giorgio Rota, 'L'inflazione in Italia', Turin, Valentino, 1975, and A che punto è la lotta all'inflazione, 'Quaderni di politica ed economia', no.3, January 1977. On the role of the bank, see Giuliano Amato, 'Economia, politica e istituzioni in Italia', Bologna, Il Mulino, 1976, p.143 ff.
90 G.Mottura and E.Pugliese, 'Agricultura, Mezzogiorno e mercato del lavoro', Bologna, Il Mulino, 1974.
91 Ibid., pp.73-4.
92 Ibid., pp.162 ff.
93 See N.Zitara, 'Il proletariato esterno', Milan, Jaca Book, 1972, discussed in Mottura and Pugliese, op. cit., p.178.
94 Luca Meldolesi, 'Disoccupazione ed esercito industriale di riserva in Italia', Bari, Laterza, 1972.
95 L'economia italiana nel 1978, Ceres, 'Notiziario di economia del lavoro', 16 April 1979, and Il lavoro minorile in Italia, Ceres, 'Tendenze della occupazione', 4(4), April 1979.
96 'L'occupazione occulta: Caratteristiche della partecipazione al lavoro in Italia', Rome, Censis, 1976, p.41.
97 M.Paci, 'Mercato del lavoro e classi sociali in Italia'.
98 G.Fuà, 'Occupazione e capacità produttiva: la realtà italiana', p.13.
99 Ibid., p.33.
100 Ibid., pp.51 ff.
101 Aris Accornero and Fabrizio Carmignani, Uno spaccato della realtà retributiva italiana, 'Politica ed economia', no.5, September-October 1977, p.53.
102 Ibid., passim.
103 Carmela D'Apice, La distribuzione del reddito nelle indagini della Banca d'Italia, 'Congiuntura sociale', no.8, August 1978.

104 Ibid., pp.11,17.
105 Antonio Pesenti and Vincenzo Vitello, Tendenze attuali del capitalismo italiano, in 'Tendenze attuali del capitalismo italiano' (Istituto Gramsci, 1962), Rome, Editori Riuniti, 1962, p.46.
106 Aris Accornero and Vincenzo Visco, 'La selva degli stipendi: Politica e sindacato nel settore pubblico', Bologna, Il Mulino, 1978, p.106.
107 Galli and Nannei, op.cit., pp.12,18.
108 Ibid., p.22. Welfare capitalism 'organizes consensus on the basis of populist reaction to industrial rationalization', p.65.
109 Ibid., for example pp.61 ff.
110 Ibid., p.65.
111 Ibid., p.196. See too Alberto Mortara, ed., 'Il settore pubblico 1970-4', Milan, Angeli, 1976.
112 Eugenio Peggio, La piccola e la media industria nella crisi dell'economia italiana, in the volume of the same name, Rome, Editori Riuniti, Istituto Gramsci, 1975 (2 vols), p.10.
113 Ibid., pp.13,25.
114 M.Tronti, 'Operai e capitale', 1971 (rev.edn); see esp. Le lotte di classe in America.
115 Ibid., La fabbrica e la società (first published 1962), p.59.
116 'Operai e capitale', provided much of the continuity between the pre-1969 and later 'operaismo' inside and outside the PCI.
117 Paolo Sylos Labini, 'Sindacati, inflazione e produttività', Bari, Laterza, 1972, pp.5 ff.
118 Aris Accornero, ed., 'Problemi del movimento sindacale in Italia 1943-1973' ('Annali Feltrinelli', 16, 1974-5), Milan, Feltrinelli, 1976, especially his Per una nuova fase di studi sul movimento sindacale, p.55.
119 Ibid., p.57.
120 Ibid., p.73 ff.
121 F.Stame, I processi di socializzazione nello Stato moderno e la funzione politica e sociale del rapporto di autorità, in Tendenze autoritarie del capitalismo sviluppato, 'Problemi del socialismo', nos 10-11, April-September 1978, p.28. The effect is accelerated as the function of the Italian state has always appeared political and social, not 'welfare economic' in the social democratic sense.
122 Ibid., p.40.
123 Cf. Francesco Galgano, La riforma dell'impresa: società per azioni ė impresa pubblica, in 'Il governo democratico dell'economia', Bari, De Donato, 1976, pp.164-5.

124 Francesco Galgano, 'Le istituzioni dell'economia capitalistica', Bologna, Zanichelli, 1974, p.19. See too his interesting 'Le istituzioni dell'economia di transizione', Rome, Editori Riuniti, 1978. Many of these problems were anticipated in Charles S.Maier, 'Recasting Bourgeois Europe', Princeton University Press, 1975, and the still inchoate discussion of pluralism, corporatism and consociationalism in the modern state owes much to this book, as also to Philippe C.Schmitter's celebrated article, Still the Century of Corporatism?, 'Review of Politics', 36(1), January 1974.

CHAPTER 7 CRISIS MANAGEMENT OR TRANSFORMATION?

1 This would not be so if the state were regarded as synonymous with power and politics and with the whole sphere of public activity, not only as 'various' activity, but the crucial arena of the political. On the alternation between movement and institution, see Francesco Alberoni, 'Movimento e instituzione', Bologna, Il Mulino, 1977. See too Massimo Ilardi, La crisi di potere del partito politico, 'Democrazia e diritto', 19, March-April 1979.
2 Cf. M.Fedele, 'Classi e partiti negli anni '70', Rome, Editori Riuniti, 1979, pp.32 ff.
3 N.Matteucci, 'Un compromesso storico, perchè?', Bologna, Il Mulino, 1974. See too G.Galli's 'Il bipartismo imperfetto', Bologna, Il Mulino, 1966 and his 'Dal bipartismo imperfetto alla possibile alternativa', Bologna, Il Mulino, 1975.
4 Op.cit., p.44.
5 Ingrao, 'Masse e potere'.
6 J.Fraser, Il tecnico e la tecnica, 'La Società', no.20, January 1979.
7 Lucio Magri, Qualità e dinamica della crisi, in 'Uscire dalla crisi o dal capitalismo in crisi?', Rome, Alfani, 1975, p.15.
8 A.Asor Rosa, 'Intellettuali e classe operaia', Florence, La Nuova Italia, 1973, p.24.
9 Ibid., p.580 ('Un "Ordine nuovo"').
10 Ibid., p.596. Asor Rosa argued that Italy had passed the stage of the progressive, productive, bourgeois development seen by Gramsci as the remedy for backwardness.
11 In Luigi Graziano and Sidney Tarrow, eds, 'La crisi italiana', Turin, Einaudi, 1978, vol.1, p.11 and passim.

12 Ibid., pp.19 ff.
13 Ibid., p.36.
14 Franco De Felice, La formazione del regime repubblicano, in ibid.; Paolo Farneti, Partito, stato e mercato: appunti per un'analisi comparata, in ibid.
15 Filippo Barbano, Mutamenti nella struttura di classe e crisi, 1950-75, in ibid. See too his 'Classi e struttura sociale in Italia', Turin, Valentino, 1976, and Paolo Ammassari, 'Classi e ceti nella società italiana: Studi e ricerche', Turin, Valentino, 1977.
16 Pietro Barcellona, 'La repubblica in trasformazione', p.8.
17 Ibid., p.181.
18 Cf. Michele Salvati, L'origine della crisi in corso, 'Quaderni piacentini', no.46, March 1972, p.18.
19 Pietro Barcellona, Appunti per una discussion sullo stato delle istituzioni e il ruolo della DC, 'Democrazia e diritto', 14(1), 1974, p.69.
20 Ibid., p.82.
21 Ingrao, La crisi degli istituti rappresentativi e la lotta per una nuova democrazia, 'Critica marxista', no.3, May-June 1963, p.13.
22 Ibid., p.15.
23 Antonio Pesenti, Sul capitale finanziario, ibid., p.17.
24 Editorial, Crisi di governo o crisi di regime?, 'Critica marxista', no.2, March-April 1964, p.7.
25 Giuseppe Chiarante, Crisi dello Stato assistenziale e cultura politica della sinistra, 'Critica marxista', no.6, November-December 1978, p.12.
26 Giorgio Napolitano, 'I comunisti nella battaglia delle idee', Rome, Editori Riuniti, 1975, p.28.
27 Ibid., p.14.
28 Quoted in Leonardo Tomasetta, 'Partecipazione e autogestione: Dentro e contro il sistema', Milan, Il Saggiatore, 1972, p.14.
29 Discussed in ibid., p.30.
30 La tribù delle talpe, in the volume of that name, ed. Sergio Bologna, Milan, Feltrinelli, 1978, p.19.
31 Ibid., p.34. Togliatti's position is stated in the collection 'Teoria e politica della via italiana al socialismo' (Introduction Luciano Gruppi), Rome, Editori Riuniti, 1979 (report to 8th congress).
32 Giorgio Napolitano, 'Intervista sul PCI', ed. E.J. Hobsbawm, Bari, Laterza, 1976, p.61.
33 Gianni Scalia, Presso Marx, 'Che fare', no.1, May 1967, p.31.
34 In Materiali del Movimento Studentesco italiano, 'Che fare', no.4, winter 1968-9, p.208.

35 Riccardo Guastini, Guerra di posizione e 'via italiana al socialismo', 'Critica del diritto', nos 5-6, May-December 1975, pp.21-2.
36 A.Negri, Stato, spesa pubblica e fatiscenza del compromesso storico, ibid., p.56.
37 Giorgio Amendola, La crisi della società italiana e il Partito comunista, 'Critica marxista', no.2, March-April 1969, pp.48 ff.
38 Luciano Barca, Per lo sviluppo dell'analisi teorica sul capitalismo monopolistico di Stato, 'Critica marxista', nos 5-6, September-December 1966, pp.58 ff.
39 Ibid., pp.62-3.
40 Ibid., p.64.
41 'Politica e potere nella crisi italiana', Abstracts, Seminario di studi, Bologna, Istituto Gramsci/Fondazione G.G.Feltrinelli, 9-10 February 1979.
42 Federico Stame, PCI e autonomia della sinistra, 'Quaderni piacentini', no.57, autumn 1975, p.87.
43 A.Negri, 'La crisi dello Stato-piano', p.56.
44 See the classification in the 'Premessa' to 'Quaderni di fabbrica e Stato', December 1977, pp.6 ff. See too Giuseppe Chiarante, Crisi dello Stato assistenziale e cultura politica della sinistra, 'Critica marxista', no.6, November-December 1978; Vittorio Dini, A proposito di Toni Negri, and Costanzo Preve, L'ideologia italiana: A proposito di Cacciari, Tronti, Asor Rosa e altri, both in 'Ombre rosse', no.24, 1978.
45 See the argument in Saverio Caruso, 'Burocrazia e capitale in Italia: Struttura e ideologia', Verona, Bertani, 1974.
46 Raniero Panzieri, Sull'uso capitalistico delle macchine nel neocapitalismo, 'Quaderni rossi', no.1, September 1961, p.54.
47 Ibid., p.55.
48 Ibid., p.56.
49 Ibid., p.60.
50 Michele Salvati, La crisi internazionale e il movimento operaio italiano, 'Quaderni piacentini', nos 53-4, December 1974, p.136, and his Paura dell' industrializzazione o paure delle riforme?, 'Quaderni piacentini', no.57, November 1975.
51 Raniero Panzieri, 'La crisi del movimento operaio', ed. Dario Lanzardo and Giovanni Pirelli, Milan, Lampugnani Nigri, 1973 (from 'Mondo Operaio', no.2, February 1958), p.116.
52 Mario Tronti, Il piano del capitale, 'Quaderni rossi', no.3, June 1963, p.50.
53 Ibid., p.51.
54 Ibid., p.58.

55 Ibid., p.70. Note too his La fabbrica e la società, 'Quaderni rossi', no.2, June 1962. This presupposes workers' self-government within the economic system of capital (p.29).
56 B.Trentin, 'Da sfruttati a produttori: Lotte operaie e sviluppo capitalistico dal miracolo economico alla crisi', Bari, De Donato, 1977, pp.xxxv-xl, liii.
57 Ibid., p.cxxix.
58 Mario Tronti, Operaismo e centralità operaia, in the volume of that title, with Giorgio Napolitano, Aris Accornero and Massimo Cacciari, Rome, Editori Riuniti, 1978, p.22.
59 Aris Accornero, Operaismo e sindacato, in ibid., pp. 38-9.
60 Massimo Cacciari, Problemi teorici e politici dell' operaismo nei nuovi gruppi dal 1960 ad oggi, in ibid., p.55.
61 Cf. Norberto Bobbio, 'Quale socialismo? Discussione di un'alternativa', Turin, Einaudi, 1976, pp.xii-xiii.
62 Federico Stame, Oltre il bolscevismo per un'etica di liberazione, 'Quaderni piacentini', nos 66-7, June 1978, p.5, and note his judgment that the Christian Democrats' revitalized image as a moderate party was based on its proposal to recompose in unity the absence of unity, p.8. See too 'Libertà e socialismo: Momenti storici del dissenso', Milan, Sugar, 1977, and Domenico Porzio, ed., 'Corraggio e viltà degli intellettuali', Milan, Mondadori, 1977.
63 See Nicola Badaloni, 'Il marxismo italiano degli anni sessanta', Rome, Editori Riuniti/Istituto Gramsci, 1972; Giuseppe Vacca, 'Politica e teoria nel marxismo italiano 1959-1969', Bari, De Donato, 1972; Franco Cassano, ed., 'Marxismo e filosofia in Italia (1959-1971): I dibattiti e le inchieste su "Rinascita" e "Il Contemporaneo"', Bari, De Donato, 1973.
64 See 'Secondo tempo del decentramento: Orientamenti ed attuazione', Comune di Bologna, 1969. See too 'Per un ulteriore sviluppo del decentramento e della partecipazione democratica', Documenti del comune, Bologna, February 1974; F.Bondioli, I quartieri a Bologna: Elementi per l'analisi di un caso di decentramento comunale, 'Centro sociale', nos 118-20, December 1974; Armando Cossutta, Marcello Stefanini and Renato Zangheri, 'Decentramento e partecipazione', Rome, Editori Riuniti, 1977, Bruna Zacchini, ed., 'Dieci anni di decentramento a Bologna', Bologna, Luigi Parma, 1976; 'La partecipazione dei cittadini al governo della città', special number of 'Il comune democratico', no.5, May 1977; Max Jäggi, Roger Müller

and Sil Schmid, 'Bologna rossa: i comunisti al governo di una città', Milan, Feltrinelli, 1977.

65 Ingrao, 'Masse e potere', p.233.

66 Cesare Pianciola, Attualità di Panzieri, 'Ombre rosse', no.5, March 1974, p.96, quoting a letter by Panzieri. See too A.Negri, Ambiguità di Panzieri?, 'Aut Aut', nos 149-50, September-December 1975, and articles by Edoardo Masi and Massimo Cacciari in ibid.

67 Luigi Manconi and Mario Sinibaldi, Uno strano movimento di strani studenti, 'Ombre rosse', no.20, March 1977, pp.13,26.

68 Mario Tronti, 'Sull'autonomia del politico', p.11.

69 Ibid., p.20.

70 'Autonomia operaia' (Comitati autonomi operai di Roma), Rome, Savelli, 1976, pp.53-5.

71 G.Bozzi, Note su bisogni operai e 'autonomia del politico', 'Aut Aut', nos 159-60, May-August 1977, p.59.

72 L.Berti, L'idea del potere, 'Aut Aut', no.169, January-February 1979, pp.53-4,64, on Tronti's notion of the blockage of the working class on the road to power, despite the ruling class's break in continuity. See too D.Degli Incerti, ed., 'La sinistra rivoluzionaria in Italia', Rome, Savelli, 1976.

73 Quoted in Nino Monicelli, 'L'ultrasinistra in Italia 1968-1978', Bari, Laterza, 1978, p.134.

74 A.Negri, 'Proletari e Stato: Per una discussione su autonomia operaia e compromesso storico', Milan, Feltrinelli, 1976, p.19.

75 Ibid., p.9.

76 Ibid., p.27.

77 Ibid., p.31.

78 A.Negri, 'Il dominio e il sabotaggio', p.13. An early volume in the series was 'La crisi dello Stato-piano' (1974), Partito operaio contro il lavoro (in S. Bologna, P.Carpignano and A.Negri, 'Crisi e organizzazione operaia' (1974)), 'Proletari e Stato' (1976), and Autovalorizzazione operaia e ipotesi di partito (in 'La forma stato', 1977), all published by Feltrinelli, Milan.

79 'Il dominio', p.14.

80 Ibid., p.17.

81 Ibid., p.19.

82 Ibid., p.20.

83 Ibid., p.23.

84 Ibid., pp.86-7.

85 Ibid., p.71.

86 Armando Cossutta, Sovversivismo delle classi dominanti ed estremismo, 'Critica marxista', no.1, January-February 1972, p.71.

87 Pietro Barcellona, 'Stato e mercato fra monopolio e democrazia', Bari, De Donato, 1976, pp.45 ff.; Vittorio Rieser, Sviluppo e congiuntura nel capitalismo italiano, 'Quaderni rossi', no.4, 1964, pp. 164-5. See too Togliatti's remark at the 10th congress of the PCI: 'We are introducing the concept of gradual development.'

88 Franco Rodano, 'Sulla politica dei comunisti', Turin, Boringhieri, 1975, pp.93-4. Rodano's notion of reconciliation and centrism was supported by a quotation from pope John 23rd on the transitoriness of Marxism as ideology.

89 Francesco Ciafaloni, L'ideologia della sinistra cattolica in Italia (La Rivista Trimestrale), 'Quaderni piacentini', no.43, April 1971, p.24.

90 Cf. Eugenio Peggio, Aspetti della politica economica italiana dal 1961 ad oggi, 'Critica marxista', nos 4-5, July-October 1964, and Sei domande su riforme e riformismo, ibid., nos 5-6, September-December 1965. See too Francesco Ciafaloni, L'ideologia della sinistra cattolica in Italia, 'Quaderni piacentini', no.43, April 1971.

CHAPTER 8 THE MODERN STATE IN ITALY AND ITS CRITICS

1 Gianni Scalia, interview with the author, December 1978, to appear in John Fraser and Franco Ferrarotti, 'PCI e intellettuali a Bologna', Naples, Liguori, forthcoming.

2 See, for example, the discussion in 'Critica del diritto', no.13, January-April 1978.

3 In Giuseppe Vacca, introduction to N.Poulantzas, ed., 'La crisi dello Stato', p.xiv.

4 Ibid., p.xi.

5 See Angelo Bolaffi, Crisi, potere, politica, 'Rinascita', 16 February 1979, and Paolo Franchi, Si può dare 'ordine' alla crisi italiana?, 'Paese Sera', 13 February 1979, on the Convegno 'Politica e potere nella crisi italiana', Bologna, February 1979.

6 M.Cammelli, Politica istituzionale e modello emiliano: ipotesi per una ricerca, 'Il Mulino', no.259, September-October 1978, p.745 (now elaborated in 'Organizzazione amministrativa e amministrazione per collegi').

7 Ibid., p.754.

8 Ibid., passim and pp.765-6. See too the 'Quaderni' of the socialist 'La Squilla', nos 11-12, November-December 1978, on the Emilian model.

9 Umberto Cerroni, Riflessioni sulla nostra strategia, 'Rinascita', 11 July 1975.

10 Francesco Alberoni, quoted and discussed by Franco Cassano, 'Rinascita', 28 November 1975.
11 Pietro Ingrao, 'Crisi e terza via', Rome, Editori Riuniti, 1978, pp.138, 159-60.
12 Ibid., p.155.
13 Giuseppe Di Palma, Risposte parlamentari alla crisi del regime: un problema di istituzionalizzazione, in S.Tarrow and Luigi Graziano, eds, 'La crisi italiana', vol.2, Turin, Einaudi, 1978, pp.370,413.
14 Cited in ibid., p.405.
15 S.Sechi, Non è detto che sia sempre legge truffa, 'L'Espresso', 22 April 1979, against drawing analogies with the 1953 proposal for electoral reform. See too Luigi Berlinguer, I bisogni nuovi della democrazia, 'Rinascita', 6 April 1979.
16 See Sechi, L'austero fascino del centralismo democratico, 'Il Mulino', no.257, May-June 1978.
17 Massimo Cacciari, Trasformazione dello Stato e progetto politico, 'Critica marxista', no.5, 1978, p.31.
18 Ibid., p.47.
19 Ibid., p.56.
20 Ibid., p.61.
21 Luigi Berlinguer, Editoriale: Il problema dello Stato oggi, 'Democrazia e diritto', 18(1), 1978, p.16.
22 Cesare Salvi, Questione dello Stato e progetto di trasformazione, 'Democrazia e diritto', 18(4), 1978, p.511, and the debate, especially Giuliano Amato's contribution Riforma dello Stato e alternative della sinistra, reprinted in Quale riforma dello Stato?, 'Quaderni di Mondoperaio', no.9, 1978.
23 Ibid., p.511.
24 Luigi Berlinguer, contributing to the discussion 'Democrazia autoritaria', sistema delle libertà e trasformazione sociale, 'Democrazia e diritto', 17(3), 1977, p.393.
25 Augusto Barbera, in the discussion Stato, autonomia e sviluppo della democrazia nel Mezzogiorno, 'Democrazia e diritto', 15(2), 1975, p.339.
26 Pietro Barcellona in ibid., p.341.
27 Cf. P.Barcellona, Un nuovo rapporto fra istituzioni e popolo organizzato, 'Democrazia e diritto', 14(4), 1974.
28 Luciano Benadusi, commenting in 'Paese Sera', 22 July 1977, on the timidity of the proposals in the 'Proposta di progetto a medio termine'. See too the 'Quaderni di Mondoperaio', no.9, 1978.
29 For example, Perry Anderson (in 'Passages from Antiquity to Feudalism', London, NLB, 1974, p.204) argues that while productive forces stall and regress in

periods of transition, social relations of production develop. Then, so that new forces of production can develop, the old must be changed. In that sense, relations of production determine forces of production. The forecasting of a more productive mode, with universal, social(ist) relations of production and continuing productiveness, was central to the predictive authority of Marxism. Gouldner, for example, sees transition as essentially the voluntarist (Hegelian) decision of the new class (intellectuals and theorists) to establish control against and amid the old, traditional class. However, the assumptions are large - that the new class represents something beyond itself, is relatively united, rests on (or creates) a new mode of production, devises successful growth politics and is also potentially universal and universally potential. Italy may be an exception, but the future of the new class seems less than assured, less than revolutionary, less than universal and autonomous and, given the subordinate position of the Left's technicians, less than hegemonic. See Alvin W. Gouldner, The New Class Project, 'Theory and Society', 6(2 and 3), September-November 1978, pp.370-1, pt 2.

30 Pietro Barcellona, Non è solo un problema di contropoteri, 'Quaderni di Mondoperaio', no.9, 1978.
31 Massimo Cacciari, Se il socialismo fosse la via per non costruirci più idoli, 'Paese Sera', 12 July 1979.
32 Mario Tronti in 'Paese Sera', 23 March 1979.
33 Napoleone Colajanni, interviewed in 'La Repubblica', 16 February 1979.
34 Gabriele Martignoni and Sergio Morandini, 'Il diritto all'odio - Dentro: fuori: ai bordi dell'area dell'autonomia', Verona, Bertani, 1977, p.18.
35 Ibid.
36 Ibid., p.160.
37 Christian Marazzi, Sulla relativa autonomia dello Stato mondiale, 'Aut Aut', no.164, March-April 1978, p.31; Massimo Cacciari, Classe operaia e bisogni, 'Città futura', 23 November 1977.
38 G.Amato, Riforma dello Stato e alternativa della sinistra, 'Mondoperaio', nos 7-8, July-August 1977, pp.51-2.
39 Pietro Barcellona, 'La Repubblica in trasformazione', pp.28,38.
40 Ibid., pp.205 ff.
41 Marazzi, Sulla relativa autonomia ... .
42 Maria Grazia Meriggi, Classe operaia e società: come si determina un soggetto politico?, 'Aut Aut', no.164, March-April 1978.

43 See Elmar Altvater and Freerk Huisken, 'Lavoro produttivo e improduttivo', Milan, Feltrinelli, 1975, pp.38-40.
44 'Intellettuali e istituzioni dell'Emilia-Romagna per uscire dalla crisi e rinnovare la società', PCI, Emilia-Romagna regional committee, 1977, pp.3-4.
45 Ibid., p.4.
46 Fausto Anderlini, Società, politica, economia, istituzioni nell'esperienza dei comunisti emiliani (I), 'La Società', nos 14-15, July-August 1978, p.20.
47 Cf. the optimistic article by Sandro Magister, 'Non è una legge, è una rivoluzione', 'L'Espresso', 24 July 1977.
48 Ricerca sui delegati PCI: primo rapporto sui risultati, 'Congiuntura sociale', no.6, May 1979.
49 Marzio Barbagli and Piergiorgio Corbetta, Una tattica e due strategie: Inchiesta sulla base del PCI, 'Il Mulino', 27, no.260, November-December 1978, passim and p.961.
50 See Nicola Auciello, Il partito nuovo e la sua capacità intellettuale, 'Rinascita', 20 June 1975, and Luciano Gruppi, ed., 'La politica culturale', Rome, Editori Riuniti, 1974.
51 K.Marx and F.Engels, 'The German Ideology', Moscow, Progress, 1968, p.63.
52 See Domenico Buffarini and Gianfranco Perulli, 'Il cittadino e il potere locale', Venice, Marsilio, 1977; Gian Franci Elia, Silvano D'Alto and Roberto Faenza, 'La partecipazione tradita', Milan, Sugar, 1977; Franco Ferraresi and Pietro Kemeny, 'Classi sociali e politica urbana: Destra e sinistra nelle amministrazioni locali', Rome, Officina, 1977.
53 Nicola Licciardello, Proletarizzazione e utopia, 'Contropiano', no.1, 1968, p.109.
54 A.Asor Rosa, Dalla rivoluzione culturale alla lotta di classe: Note sulla tematica anti-istituzionale del movimento studentesco, 'Contropiano', no.3, 1968; Massimo Cacciari, Sviluppo capitalistico e ciclo delle lotte, in ibid. (part 2 in no.2, 1969). The quotation is from Asor Rosa, Nota sul tema: Lavoro intellettuale, coscienza di classe, partito, 'Contropiano', no.3, September-December 1971, p.474.
55 Cf. Luigi Graziano, A Conceptual Framework for the Study of Clientelistic Behavior, 'European Journal of Political Research', no.4, 1976.
56 Cf. Robert K.Yin and William A.Lucas, Decentralization and Alienation, 'Policy Studies', no.4, 1973; Peter Self, 'Administrative Theories and Politics', University of Toronto Press, 1973, p.22.

57 Self, op.cit., p.151.
58 See Gerald E.Caiden, The Politicization Issue, in his 'The Dynamics of Public Administration: Guidelines to Current Transformations in Theory and Practice', New York, Holt, Rinehart & Winston, 1971.
59 Salvatore Sechi, Il PCI: l'albero, la foresta e la nuova peste, 'Il Mulino', no.250, March-April 1977, p.300.
60 Angelo Bolaffi, Le mitologie sulla germanizzazione, 'Rinascita', 29 July 1977.
61 La nostra assemblea, ed., 'Le radici di una rivolta', Milan, Feltrinelli, 1977, p.61.
62 See Pier Aldo Rovatti's critical analysis of the 'historic compromise' in Intellettuali e compromesso storico, 'Aut Aut', no.147, May-June 1975.
63 Noted in Giuseppe Vacca, PSI, ceti medi e compromesso storico, 'Rinascita', 23 January 1976.
64 Nicos Poulantzas, 'Fascism and Dictatorship: the Third International and the Problem of Fascism', London, NLB, 1974.
65 See the discussion of PCI positions on the crisis, their new Left critics, and Habermas, Offe and O'Connor by Luigi Ferrajoli and Danilo Zolo, 'Democrazia autoritaria e capitalismo maturo', p.17. This is useful on the various currents in the new Left (Stame, Ferrajoli, Melucci), the operaisti, the neo-Gramscians (Vacca, de Giovanni, Ingrao) and the 'Caesarist democracy' of the 'Thomist-Stalinist' Rodano. See too Danilo Zolo's critique of Luigi Berlinguer's Democrazia ed efficienza, unità e autonomia nello sviluppo istituzionale del paese, 'Critica marxista', nos 4-5, July-October 1977, first published as Democrazia corporativa, produzione del consenso, socialismo, 'Problemi del socialismo', 19(9), January-March 1978, now in Ferrajoli and Zolo, op.cit.
66 D.Zolo, 'La teoria comunista dell'estinzione dello Stato', Bari, De Donato, 1974, p.260.
67 D.Zolo, 'Stato socialista e libertà borghesi', Bari, Laterza, 1976, p.97.
68 Ulrich K.Preuss, Tesi sui mutamenti di struttura del dominio politico nello Stato costituzionale borghese, in Lelio Basso, ed., 'Stato e crisi delle istituzioni', Florence, Mazzotta, 1978, pp.18-20.
69 Claus Offe and Volker Ronge, Tesi per una fondazione teoretica della nozione di 'Stato capitalistico' e per una metodologia materialistica della politologia, in ibid., pp.35-8.
70 Michel Foucault, 'Microfisica del potere', Turin, Einaudi, 1977, p.109.

71 Cf. Jean Baudrillard, 'Dimenticare Foucault', Bologna, Cappelli, 1977, p.72.
72 Roberto Ruffilli, Sulla crisi dello Stato nell'età contemporanea, 'Annali dell'Istituto storico italo-germanico in Trento', no.2, 1976, p.536. See too R.Guastini, Teoria e fenomenologia dello stato capitalistico, 'Politica del diritto', 2(6), December 1971.
73 Antonio Negri, 'La forma Stato', Milan, Feltrinelli, 1977, pp.119,120,139,142.
74 Ibid., pp.204-7, 210.
75 Ibid., p.227.
76 Ibid., p.256.
77 A.Negri, Partito operaio contro il lavoro, in S. Bologna, F.Carpignano and A.Negri, 'Crisi e organizzazione operaia', Milan, Feltrinelli, 1974, pp.99-100. See too his 'Dall'operaio massa all'operaio sociale', Milan, Multhipla, 1979, and the review by Francesco Leonetti, Habermas, O'Connor, Negri: non legittimare più, 'Alfabeta', no.2, June 1979.
78 Negri, Partito operaio contro il lavoro, p.119.
79 Ibid., p.128.
80 Ibid., p.131.
81 Ibid., p.136.
82 Negri, 'La forma Stato', p.286.
83 F.Stame, Lo Stato contro i bisogni, 'Aut Aut', no.161, September-October 1977, p.20.
84 Ibid., pp.26-7.
85 Ibid., p.23.
86 F.Stame, Democrazia autoritaria e movimento di libertà, 'Quaderni piacentini', nos 62-3, April 1977, p.4. See also E.Altvater, K.Offe, J.Hirsch and J.Gough, 'Il capitale e lo Stato', Verona, Bertani, 1979.
87 Stame, Democrazia autoritaria, p.7.
88 Ibid., p.9.
89 F.Stame, Le seduzioni della democrazia autoritaria, 'Quaderni piacentini', no.64, July 1977, p.5.
90 Ibid., p.8.
91 F.Stame, Sulla funzione politica della teoria, 'Quaderni piacentini', no.51, January 1974 (now in his 'Società civile e critica delle istituzioni', p.23).
92 F.Stame, Le leggi autoritarie e la nuova sinistra, 'Quaderni piacentini', no.56, spring 1975 (now in 'Società civile', p.59).
93 Ibid.

CONCLUSION

1 See the summary in Aiden Foster-Carter, Can We Articulate Articulation?, in John Clemmer, ed., 'The New Economic Anthropology', London, Macmillan, 1978.
2 Robert Michels, 'Political Parties', p.62. In Italy, we should add, deficiencies in organization lead to the paradoxical equation wherein a weak state represents conflicting and weak (imperfect dominance) social forces and productive forces, but becomes thus, vis-à-vis society, relatively strong.

BIBLIOGRAPHY*

AMENDOLA, GIORGIO, Crisi economica e crisi politica, 'Politica ed economia', no.4, July-August 1971.
AMIN, SAMIR, 'Unequal Development', New York, Monthly Review Press, 1976.
AMIN, SAMIR, 'La crisi dell'imperialismo', Rome, Coines, 1976.
ASOR ROSA, ALBERTO, 'Intellettuali e classe operaia: Saggio sulle forme di uno storico conflitto e di una possibile alleanza', Florence, La Nuova Italia, 1973.
ASOR ROSA, ALBERTO, 'Le due società: Ipotesi sulla crisi italiana', Turin, Einaudi, 1977.
BAGNASCO, A., 'Tre Italie', Bologna, Il Mulino, 1977.
BANCA D'ITALIA annual reports (Assemblea generale ordinaria dei partecipanti).
BARCELLONA, PIETRO, 'La repubblica in trasformazione: Problemi istituzionali del caso italiano', Bari, De Donato, 1978.
BASSI, PAOLO and PILATI, ANTONIO, 'I giovani e la crisi degli anni settanta', Rome, Editori Riuniti, 1978.
BERLINGUER, LUIGI, Democrazia ed efficienza, unità e autonomia nello sviluppo istituzionale del paese, 'Critica marxista', nos 4-5, 1977.
BETTELHEIM, CHARLES, 'The Transition to Socialist Economy', Hassocks, Harvester, 1978 ('La Transition vers l'économie socialiste', Paris, Maspero, 1968).
CACCIARI, MASSIMO, 'Krisis: Saggio sulla crisi del pensiero negativo da Nietzsche a Wittgenstein', Milan, Feltrinelli, 1976.
CAMMELLI, MARCO, 'Organizzazione amministrativa e ammistrazione per collegi', Bologna, Il Mulino, 1979.

* Quotations from these works are wholly or in part translations from the Italian version.

CESPE publications: 'Congiuntura sociale' and 'Politica ed economia'.
CNEL/Censis, annual 'Rapporti sulla situazione del paese'.
D'ANTONIO, MARIO, 'Sviluppo e crisi del capitalismo italiano, 1951-1972', Bari, De Donato, 1972.
DONOLO, CARLO, 'Mutamento o transizione? Politica e società nella crisi italiana', Bologna, Il Mulino, 1977.
DONOLO, CARLO, Struttura sociale, disgregazione e istituzioni nel Mezzogiorno, 'Rassegna sindacale', 71, March-April, 1978.
FERRAJOLI, LUIGI and ZOLO, DANILO, 'Democrazia autoritaria e capitalismo maturo', Milan, Feltrinelli, 1978.
FORCELLINI, PAOLO, 'Rapporto sull'industria italiana', Rome, Editori Riuniti, 1978.
FUA, GIORGIO, 'Occupazione e capacità produttiva: La realtà italiana', Bologna, Il Mulino, 1976.
GALLI, GIORGIO and NANNEI, ALESSANDRA, 'Il capitalismo assistenziale: Ascesa e declino del sistema economico italiano 1960-1975', Milan, Sugar, 1976.
'Gli anni della conflittualità permanente' (Rapporto sulle relazioni industriali in Italia nel 1970-1), Milan, Angeli, 1976.
GORRIERI, ERMANNO, 'La giungla retributtiva', Bologna, Il Mulino, 1972.
GRAMSCI, ANTONIO, 'Quaderni del carcere', 4 vols, Turin, Einaudi, 1975 ('Selections from the Prison Notebooks', ed. and trans. Q.Hoare and G. Nowell Smith, London, Lawrence & Wishart, 1971, 1973).
GRAZIANI, AUGUSTO, ed., 'Crisi e ristrutturazione nell' economia italiana', Turin, Einaudi, 1975.
GRAZIANO, LUIGI and TARROW, SIDNEY, eds, 'La crisi italiana' (2 vols), Turin, Einaudi, 1978.
GROSSMANN, HENRYK, 'Il crollo del capitalismo: La legge dell'accumulazione e del crollo del sistema capitalistico', Milan, Jaca Book, 1977 ('Das Akkumulations- und Zusammenbruchgesetz des kapitalistischen Systems', 1929).
HABERMAS, JÜRGEN, 'Legitimation Crisis', Boston, Beacon Press, 1975.
INGRAO, PIETRO, 'Masse e potere', Rome, Editori Riuniti, 1977.
'L'occupazione occulta', Rome, Censis, 1976.
MARRAMAO, GIACOMO, 'Il politico e le trasformazioni: critica del capitalismo e ideologie della crisi tra anni Venti e anni Trenta', Bari, De Donato, 1979.
MATTICK, P., 'Marx and Keynes: the Limits of the Mixed Economy', Boston, P.Sergeant, 1969.
MICHELS, ROBERT, 'Political Parties: a Sociological Study of the Oligarchic Tendencies of Modern Democracy', New York, Collier, 1962.

MIGLIARO, LUIS RAZETO and MISURACA, PASQUALE, 'Sociologia e marxismo nella critica di Gramsci', Bari, De Donato, 1978.
MOSCA, GAETANO, 'The Ruling Class', New York, McGraw-Hill, 1939 ('Elementi di scienza politica' (Intro. by Benedetto Croce), Bari, Laterza, 1953).*
MUTTI, ANTONIO and SEGATTI, PAOLO, 'La borghesia di Stato', Milan, Mazzotta, 1977.
NAPOLITANO, GIORGIO, A che punto è la crisi, 'Rinascita', 9 May 1975.
NEGRI, ANTONIO, 'La crisi dello Stato-piano: Comunismo e organizzazione rivoluzionaria', Milan, Feltrinelli, 1974 (written 1971).
NEGRI, ANTONIO, 'Il dominio e il sabotaggio: Sul metodo marxista della trasformazione sociale', Milan, Feltrinelli, 1978.
NEGRI, ANTONIO, 'Marx oltre Marx', Milan, Feltrinelli, 1979.
O'CONNOR, JAMES, 'The Fiscal Crisis of the State', New York, St Martin's Press, 1973.
OFFE, KLAUS, 'Strukturprobleme des kapitalistischen Staats', Frankfurt, Suhrkamp, 1972.
PACI, MASSIMO, 'Mercato del lavoro e classi sociali in Italia', Bologna, Il Mulino, 1973.
PARETO, VILFREDO, 'The Mind and Society' (4 vols), New York, Harcourt Brace, 1935 ('Trattato di sociologia generale' (2 vols), Milan, Comunità, 1964).*
POULANTZAS, NICOS, ed., 'La crisi dello Stato', Introduction and ed., G.Vacca, Bari, De Donato, 1979 (Paris, PUF, 1976).
'Proposta di progetto a medio termine', Rome, Editori Riuniti, 1977.
PUGLIESE, ENRICO and MOTTURA, G., 'Agricoltura, Mezzogiorno e mercato di lavoro', Bologna, Il Mulino, 1974.
RIPEPE, EUGENIO, 'Gli elitisti italiani' (2 vols), Pisa, Paccini, 1974.
ROZDOLSKI, ROMAN, 'The Making of Marx's "Capital"', London, Pluto, 1977.
SALVATI, MICHELE, 'Il sistema economico italiano: Analisi di una crisi', Bologna, Il Mulino, 1975.
SARACENO, PASQUALE, Le radici della crisi, 'Il Mulino', 25, no.243, January-February 1976.
SCALFARI, EUGENIO and TURANI, GIUSEPPE, 'Razza padrona: Storia della borghesia di Stato', Milan, Feltrinelli, 1974.
SCALIA, GIANNI, La cosa più importante, in 'Filosofi senza contratto', ed. Davide Bigalli, Bologna, Cappelli, 1978.
SECHI, SALVATORE, Il PCI: L'albero, la foreste e la nuova peste, 'Il Mulino', no.250, March-April 1977.

STAME, FEDERICO, 'Società civile e critica delle istituzioni', Milan, Feltrinelli, 1977.
SWEEZY, PAUL et al., 'The Theory of Capitalist Development', New York, Oxford University Press, 1942.
SYLOS LABINI, PAOLO, 'Saggio sulle classi sociali', Bari, Laterza, 1975.
TELO, MARIO, Strategia consiliare e sviluppo capitalistico in Gramsci, 'Problemi del socialismo', no.2, 1976.
TOGLIATTI, PALMIRO, 'Opere scelte', Rome, Editori Riuniti, 1974.
TRENTIN, BRUNO, 'Da sfruttati a produttori: Lotte operaie e sviluppo capitalistico dal miracolo economico alla crisi', Bari, De Donato, 1977.
TRONTI, MARIO, 'Operai e capitale', Turin, Einaudi, 1966 (1971).
TRONTI, MARIO, 'Sull'autonomia del politico', Milan, Feltrinelli, 1977.
WEBER, MAX, 'Economy and Society' (3 vols), New York, Bedminster Press, 1968 ('Economia e società', Milan, Comunità, 1961, 2 vols).*

INDEX